GARLAND STUDIES IN

THE HISTORY
OF AMERICAN
LABOR

edited by

STUART BRUCHEY

THE NECESSITY OF ORGANIZATION

MARY KENNEY O'SULLIVAN AND TRADE UNIONISM FOR WOMEN, 1892–1912

KATHLEEN BANKS NUTTER

Routledge
Taylor & Francis Group

LONDON AND NEW YORK

First published 2000 by Garland Publishing, Inc.

2 Park Square, Milton Park, Abingdon, Oxfordshire OX14 4RN
52 Vanderbilt Avenue, New York, NY 10017

Routledge is an imprint of the Taylor & Francis Group, an informa business

First issued in paperback 2019

Library of Congress Cataloging-in-Publication Data
Nutter, Kathleen Banks.
   The necessity of organization : Mary Kenney O'Sullivan and trade unionism for women, 1892–1912 / Kathleen Banks Nutter.
      p.   cm.—(Garland studies in the history of American labor)
   Includes bibliographical references and index.
   ISBN 0-8153-3505-9 (alk. paper)
     1. O'Sullivan, Mary Kenney, 1864–1943. 2. Women's Trade Union
League of America—History. 3. Women in trade unions—United States—
History. I. Title. II. Series.
HD6079.2U5N88   2000
331.4'78'0973—dc21   99-35081
                                      CIP

ISBN 13: 978-0-8153-3505-4 (hbk)
ISBN 13: 978-1-138-88342-0 (pbk)

In memory of
Earl Alexander Banks (1916–1979)
Henriette Hodge Banks (1911–1989)
Jason Daniel Peters (1980–1996)

Contents

Acknowledgments

My work on Mary Kenney O'Sullivan began as a dissertation that grew out of my long-held interest in the history of American women and the history of American workers. Given the number of years leading up to the completion of this work, there are many people and institutions that have assisted me along the way. Even before I began graduate school, Mark Aldrich and Dan Horowitz, both of Smith College, encouraged me to become a historian and their continued support is much appreciated.

While a graduate student in the History Department at the University of Massachusetts/Amherst, I was fortunate to work with a faculty of high calibre. In particular, Gerald McFarland was the kind of dissertation chair that all graduate students should have—patient, witty, and knowledgeable. Kevin Boyle was both supportive and intellectually challenging. Kathy Peiss was more than helpful as both Graduate Program Director and reader. Patricia Greenfield took an interest in my work during a busy time in her career and I remain most grateful. Mary Blewett and Jack Tager were a part of this work in its early stages and I am forever indebted to them both. Conference comments from Ava Baron, Ardis Cameron, and Nancy Hewitt caused me to think about my work in important and necessary ways. Dorothy McFarland saved me from many a grammatical slip. My thanks to them all—and to series general editor Stuart Bruchey, University of Maine and assistant editor Richard Koss of Garland Publishing for showing an interest in my work.

During the research and writing of this book in its dissertation phase, I received timely and much appreciated financial assistance from the University of Massachusetts/Amherst History Department through a

Bauer Gordon research grant and from the American Historical Association through an Albert J. Beveridge research grant. Portions of this book appeared in my article, "Organizing Women During the Progressive Era: Mary Kenney O'Sullivan and the Labor Movement," in *Labor's Heritage* Vol. 8:3 (Winter 1997). I thank the journal and especially its managing editor, Bob Reynolds for granting me permission to reprint those portions of the text as well as for their continued support.

My research was made easier by helpful staff at the University of Massachusetts/Amherst W.E.B. DuBois Library Special Collections and Inter-Library Loan Departments, Bryn Mawr College Archives, the Massachusetts Historical Society, the Massachusetts State House Library, the Massachusetts State Archives, Simmons College Archives, the Schlesinger Library at Radcliffe College and Wellesley College Archives. My friends and co-workers at the Sophia Smith Collection/Smith College Archives remain ever supportive, ever interested.

Family and friends have played a major role throughout the many years. I was especially fortunate to be part of a friendly and fun graduate school cohort and am particularly thankful for the continued friendship of Anke and Mark Voss Hubbard. Pat Reeve has read every word of this—I value her commentary almost as much as I treasure her friendship. My scholar-in-training comrade Jane Elkind Bowers is distant only in terms of geography. Deen Leonard, a modern-day Mary Kenney O'-Sullivan, sustains me in the real world as have Jeanne Sisson and Deb Taricano. Jane and Bruce Depper Goldstein blur the lines of friend and family in the best possible way. My children, Alex, Caitlin, and Anna have grown up with this work—I trust they are none the worse for it. I know that my life has been far better (if hectic) because of their presence. They continue to give me immeasurable joy every day. My co-parent, spouse and best friend, Walter, has made it all not only possible but worth while.

List of Figures

Introduction
"The Necessity of Organization"
Gender, Class, and Industrialization
During the Progressive Era

In May, 1893, Mary Kenney O'Sullivan delivered an address at the World's Congress of Representative Women, an auxiliary of the World's Columbia Exposition which had just opened in Chicago.[1] Kenney O'Sullivan spoke of her experiences as an organizer for the American Federation of Labor (AFL) and on her fifteen years as a woman bookbinder. To a primarily middle-class audience, she described her frustration in attempting to organize women workers:

> To say that it is difficult to organize women is not saying the half. There are several reasons which prevent women from wishing to organize. In the first place, they are reared from childhood with one sole object in view . . . that is, marriage. If our mothers would teach us self-reliance and independence, that it is our duty to depend wholly upon ourselves, we should then feel **the necessity of organization** . . .[2]

The reason for her frustration was nineteenth-century gender ideology that revolved around the notion of separate spheres. Men were to work outside the home, earning a family wage while women stayed home, dependent on that wage.[3] Initially a concept of the middle class, the family wage earned by a male head-of-household became the goal of the working class and the AFL as well. Out of economic necessity, however, many working-class women such as Mary Kenney O'Sullivan did work for wages both before and even after marriage.[4] Nonetheless, these women were generally seen as only temporary members of the workforce, earning "pin money" for a brief period before marriage. By urging women to

xiii

look beyond marriage to an independent economic status, Kenney O'-Sullivan was attacking one of the primary justifications for the lower wages earned by working women in the nineteenth century. In her mind, the only way working women could achieve better wages, and thus, "independence," was through organization.[5] As Kenney O'Sullivan knew from her own experience, marriage when and if it did occur did not necessarily ensure a lifetime of economic security—not to mention respectability—for working-class women.

My goal is to add to our discussion of the ways in which class has impacted on gender relations, at the same time acknowledging that the gender ideology of the late nineteenth and early twentieth centuries shaped the very notion of class itself. To do so, I will examine the life and career of Mary Kenney O'Sullivan, her experiences as a working-class woman and as the first woman organizer for the AFL in 1892, and her role in the formation and early years of the Women's Trade Union League (WTUL) from 1903 to 1912.

By the 1890s, the "labor question" had seemingly replaced the "race question." The question of labor, its relation to capital and to the state, to society itself, was as gendered as the sexual division of labor. At the same time, a new identity was being forged for wage-earning women just as the "problem of women workers" was being discussed and investigated. According to the historian Mary Blewett, towards the end of the nineteenth century, women shoeworkers created "a new sense of womanhood" in response to their need to retain their respectability as "ladies" while faced with changes in their work environment.[6] Running parallel to the emerging middle-class identity of "New Woman," for whom this identity represented opportunity and respectability, the "New Industrial Woman" signified instead issues of survival and respectability, as well as confusion.[7] This New Industrial Woman was, in the words of historian Joan Scott, "an anomaly in a world where wage labor and family responsibility had each become full-time and spatially distinct jobs."[8]

The notion and widespread acceptance of the family wage earned by a male worker shaped the discourse regarding the working woman as it impacted on the reality of her experience. Within the rhetoric of the family wage, the "ideal" working-class woman was a wife, a mother, and a consumer. This consumerist role explains, in part, the spread of trade union label leagues as a sort of women's auxiliary for the wives of male trade unionists.[9] In the ideal, working-class women were not seen as producers, certainly not as producers of value, as was seemingly reflected in women's lower wages.[10] Thus, given their status as temporary, unskilled workers earning low wages, women were deemed "unorganizable" by organized—predominately male—labor.[11]

Yet, working-class reality was often far from the middle-class ideal of separate spheres. A working-class woman may have found respectability as a working-class wife but frequently faced issues of economic survival throughout various stages of her life.[12] Economic developments in America towards the end of the nineteenth century only intensified the notion of separate spheres as "a class privilege denied to working men and women."[13] The acceleration of industrial capitalism meant an increase of unskilled/semi-skilled jobs at lower wages, wages generally insufficient for a solitary (male) breadwinner to support a family. In response, the number of women, both single and married, in the industrial workforce grew.[14] The disjunction between the ideal and the reality was reflected in the ambivalant attitude of the AFL regarding the organization of women.[15] Nonetheless, women did organize. They did so despite, and sometimes because of, the attitudes of organized labor.[16] AFL president Samuel Gompers and the rest of the AFL male cadre were very much products of their time and culture regarding the position of women in society as well as within in the labor movement. However, they were sometimes shrewd enough to see the handwriting on the wall, and thus their seemingly conflicting views and actions regarding the organization of women.

The ambiguity of the labor movement regarding women wage-earners created a vacuum into which flowed various strands of the nascent social reform movement known collectively as Progressivism. As much an ideology as a plan of action, Progressivism flourished in America from the 1890s to the 1910s, spreading from the nation's growing cities to the national level.[17] At once a reaction to as well as an acceptance of incredible economic and social change, Progressivism sought to bring forth political reform to meet the new challenges of an increasingly industrialized and non-Anglo-Saxon immigrant America. Steeped simultaneously in the tenets of the Social Gospel and the developing social sciences, Progressivism encompassed a myriad of social reforms touching on almost every aspect of American life.

From public ownership of utilities to the eradication of the near-mythic "white slave trade," Progressive reformers sought to improve the lives of all Americans regardless of their class. Those who had personally benefitted from the economic development of post-Civil War America were most likely those who now sought to seek reforms that would ameliorate the negative effects of unregulated industrial capitalism and unrestricted immigration. White and native-born, of Anglo-Saxon stock, these middle- and upper-class Americans felt at once threatened by change and yet obligated to use their privilege for the betterment of others. At the very heart of Progressivism lay the heightened awareness of class itself in this the supposedly class-less society. Thus, one strand of Progressivism emphasized a particular need to address the conditions of labor as experienced by millions of American men, women and children. Given the Progressive emphasis on political remedies, the passage of labor legislation appealed to many social reformers, either in tandem with but sometimes supplanting labor organization.[18]

This burgeoning social reform movement also facilitated the development of a distinct women's political culture as recently defined by Kathryn Kish Sklar.[19] These women reformers, while carving out an important public role for themselves especially as settlement house workers and residents, seemed particularly suited to address the needs of their wage-earning sisters.[20] But, given the class and ethnic identity of most female social reformers, this potentially empowering women's political culture was severely constricted from the start in terms of class, race, and ethnicity.[21] While the New Middle-Class Woman could find opportunity and respectability within the social reform movement, the New Industrial Woman's concerns often remained unmet.[22] Further, as the historian Jacquelyn Dowd Hall has argued, "the assumption that men and women occupied different political cultures ignores working-class and African American women, who might act on gender consciousness but who could not and did not separate themselves from men."[23]

The development of what has been called "industrial feminism" can be seen as a distinct response to the reality of gendered class relations. In 1915, a University of Chicago graduate student first used the term "industrial feminism" when writing a master's thesis entitled "A History of the Women's Trade Union League of Chicago." More recently, the historian Annelise Orleck has relied upon that concept to differentiate the activism of trade union women from that of their middle- and upper-class female cohorts.[24] Focusing on the lives and careers of Rose Schneiderman, Pauline Newman, and Clara Lemlich, Orleck argues that "[t]heir beliefs were shaped by a deep-seated feminism, though they would never have applied that label to themselves." Orleck continues:

> For they associated feminism with the women of the middle and upper classes, who had the luxury of focusing solely on gender; and they refused to embrace any movement that was blind to class. Their brand of

feminism was deeply imbued with class consciousness and a vivid understanding of the harsh realities of industrial labor.[25]

Those same "harsh realities" shaped the industrial feminism of Mary Kenney O'Sullivan and are the focus of Chapters I and II.

Based upon her personal experiences—as a young single wage-earning woman who was the sole support of an invalid mother, as a semi-skilled worker, as a trade unionist and labor organizer, as a working-class widow with three young children—Kenney O'Sullivan sought a vehicle in which women like herself could achieve respectability and more than mere survival. That vehicle was trade unionism for women. After more than a decade of working for that goal within two communities-in-the-making, organized labor and social reform, and despite her best efforts and personal connections, Kenney O'Sullivan remained outside of both communities. As a co-founder of the Women's Trade Union League (WTUL) in 1903, she sought to institutionalize a coalition of organized labor and social reform for the benefit of wage-earning women. It is the birth of this coalition, known as the WTUL, which I examine in Chapter III.

The WTUL intended that its middle- and upper-class female allies would provide financial support for and actually participate in the effort to secure union representation and protective legislation for working women. The hope was that this collaboration would result in higher wages and better working conditions for women workers and at the same time facilitate improved class relations between women of all classes. The long and close friendship between Irish-American industrial worker and labor leader Kenney O'Sullivan and Boston Brahmin and WTUL ally Elizabeth Glendower Evans was symbolic of the WTUL mission. Examination of the relationship between these two diverse women will add further shape and substance to the significant theoretical arguments in recent work by Ava Baron, Mary Blewett, Ardis Cameron, and Alice Kessler-Harris.[26]

Just as the work of David Roediger and Alexander Saxton has recently shed light on the way in which working-class identity was shaped by a sense of "whiteness," social concepts of gender also played a part in forming working-class identity.[27] As Alice Kessler-Harris has written, "class cannot be conceived, nor class formation analyzed, in the absence of gender as process and as ideology."[28] The notion of gendered class relations is especially critical when looking at the work experiences of Mary Kenney O'Sullivan as a bookbinder and a labor organizer and showing how those experiences led her to be a part of the creation of the WTUL.

When I discuss the formation of the WTUL and its early activities, the gendered structure of union activity will be an important area of my investigation. Also, how did men and women relate on the shop floor itself? On a more personal level, what were the relational dynamics between Mary Kenney O'Sullivan and AFL president Samuel Gompers? Between Kenney O'Sullivan and her labor activist husband? Between Kenney O'Sullivan and WTUL co-founder William English Walling? The experiences of these men and women demonstrate that gender, class, and ethnicity simultaneously shaped their relationships, both personal and professional.

There is a compelling story yet untold in the Boston Women's Trade Union League (BWTUL), its early years and the roles played by Kenney O'Sullivan and others, and it is that which I focus on in Chapter IV. Previous work has focused on either the National WTUL[29] or on two of the other principal branches, Chicago and New York.[30] The Boston League awaits a full treatment. When the BWTUL is mentioned, it is usually in passing and is generally dismissed as the most contentious and/or least successful of all the local branches.[31] Indeed, as will be discussed in Chapter V, the BWTUL, following the lead of the AFL, failed to support the women workers in the critical Lawrence strike of 1912. The BWTUL split over this decision and Mary Kenney O'Sullivan resigned in protest from the organization she had helped create. Also resigning was her good friend Elizabeth Glendower Evans, their vision of the WTUL unrealized.

The history of the WTUL is generally offered as one more failed attempt at achieving, as Annelise Orleck describes it, "the seductive promise of cross-class sisterhood."[32] Yet the complex history of the early years of WTUL, particularly from the standpoint of Kenney O'Sullivan, demands further explanation. The institutionalization of industrial feminism in the formation of the WTUL is best analyzed not in terms of success or failure but rather in terms of the possibilities and limits of coalition building within the gender, class, and ethnic constraints of the day. In this way, at the point of intersection between social and political history, relations of power during the Progressive Era can be seen in sharp detail. At the same time, the implications of this study have current importance as the AFL-CIO continues to seek, albeit at times somewhat tentatively, ways in which to effectively organize women workers.[33] This, after all, is what Mary Kenney O'Sullivan sought to do a century earlier.

In her 1893 speech before the Congress of Representative Women, Kenney O'Sullivan was looking to the future when she concluded by saying:

All the masses need is to be educated to that sense of duty which will demand justice and abolish that system which compels my sex to accept wholesale prostitution, crime, and degradation.[34]

By arguing for the "necessity of organization," she sought justice and dignity as well as respectability and more than mere survival for wage-earning women. Kenney O'Sullivan was far from alone in her efforts to address the inequities of industrial capitalism. A greater understanding of those efforts, in terms of both gender and class, can have meaning for us still.

NOTES

[1]David F. Burg, *Chicago's White City of 1893* (Lexington: University of Kentucky Press, 1976), pp. 239–249; Jeanne Madeline Weimann, *The Fair Women* (Chicago: Academy, 1981), p. 542.

[2]Mary E. Kenney, "Organization of Working Women," *World's Congress of Representative Women* (Chicago, 1893), p. 871, emphasis added.

[3]See: Jean Boydston, *Home and Work: Housework, Wages, and the Ideology of Labor in the Early Republic* (New York: Oxford University Press, 1990). On the judicial reinforcement of separate sphere ideology, see: Sara L. Zeigler, "Wifely Duties: Marriage, Labor, and the Common Law in Nineteenth-Century America," *Social Science History* 20 (Spring 1996): pp. 63–96.

[4]Martha May, "Bread Before Roses: American Workingmen, Labor Unions and the Family Wage," in *Women, Work and Protest: A Century of U.S. Women's Labor History* Ruth Milkman, ed. (New York: Routledge & Kegan Paul, 1985), pp. 1–21. See also: Lawrence Glickman, "Inventing the 'American Standard of Living': Gender, Race and Working-Class Identity, 1880–1925," *Labor History* 34 (Spring/Summer 1993): pp. 221–235; Maurine Weiner Greenwald, "Working-Class Feminism and the Family Wage Ideal: The Seattle Debate on Married Women's Right to Work, 1914–1920," *Journal of American History* 76 (June 1989): pp. 118–149; Alice Kessler-Harris, *A Woman's Wage: Historical Meanings and Social Consequences* (Lexington: University of Kentucky, 1990), esp. Chap. 1; Joanne Meyerwitz, *Women Adrift: Independent Wage Earners in Chicago, 1880–1930* (Chicago: University of Chicago Press, 1988); Carole Turbin, *Working Women of Collar City: Gender, Class, and Community in Troy, New York, 1864–1886* (Urbana: University of Illinois Press, 1992).

[5]Alice Kessler-Harris has argued that notions of woman's "virtue", or what I refer to as respectability, conflicted with the needs of many working-class women to achieve independence. See her essay: "Independence and Virtue in the

Lives of Wage-Earning Women: The United States, 1870–1930" in *Women in Culture and Politics: A Century of Change* Judith Friedlander, Blanche Wiesen Cook, Alice Kessler-Harris, and Carroll Smith-Rosenberg, eds. (Bloomington: Indiana University Press, 1986), pp. 3–17.

[6]Mary H. Blewett, *Men, Women, and Work: Class, Gender, and Protest in the New England Shoe Industry, 1790–1910* (Urbana: University of Illinois Press, 1990), p. 276.

[7]Carroll Smith-Rosenberg perhaps best defines the "New Woman", a term which "originated as a literary phase popularized by Henry James," as "a specific sociological and educational cohort of women born between the late 1850s and 1900" who "were outspoken feminists" while "they continued to accept many of the bourgeois values and genteel habits of [their middle-class] world." See: Smith-Rosenberg, *Disorderly Conduct: Visions of Gender in Victorian America* (New York: Alfred A. Knopf, 1985), pp. 176–177. See also: Patricia Marks, *Bicycles, Bangs, and Bloomers: The New Woman in the Popular Press* (Lexington: University Press of Kentucky, 1990) and Deborah Epstein Nord, *Walking the Victorian Streets: Women, Representation, and the City* (Ithaca, NY: Cornell University Press, 1995). Both Marks and Nord **briefly** reflect upon how the notion of the middle-class New Woman served as a model, shaping social conceptions of the New Industrial Woman.

[8]Joan W. Scott, "The Woman Worker," in *A History of Women in the West* Volume IV Genevieve Fraisse and Michelle Perrot, eds. (Cambridge, MA: Belknap Press, 1993), p. 400. In Great Britain, where the process of industrialization occurred decades before it did in the United States, the "New Industrial Woman" emerged earlier as well. See: Deborah Valenze, *The First Industrial Woman* (New York: Oxford University Press, 1995).

[9]Although she looks at a later time period, I have found Dana Frank, *Purchasing Power: Consumer Organizing, Gender, and the Seattle Labor Movement, 1919–1929* (New York: Cambridge University Press, 1994), esp. Chaps. 8 & 9, to be quite useful.

[10]See: Claudia Golden, *Understanding the Gender Gap: An Economic History of America Women* (New York: Oxford University Press, 1990), esp. Chap. 7; and Sybil Lipschultz, "Hours and Wages: The Gendering of Labor Standards in America," *Journal of Women's History* 8 (Spring 1996): pp. 114–136.

[11]Alice Kessler-Harris, "'Where are the Organized Women Workers?'," *Feminist Studies* 3 (Fall 1975): pp. 92–110. Fifty years earlier, Theresa Wolfson posed the same question in her article "Where Are the Organized Women Workers," *American Federationist* (June 1925): pp. 455–457 which she discussed at length in Wolfson, *The Woman Worker and the Trade Unions* (New York: International Publishers, 1926).

[12]In addition to Meyerwitz, *Women Adrift*, and Turbin, *Working Women of Collar City*, see: Ardis Cameron, *Radicals of the Worst Sort: Laboring Women in Lawrence, Massachusetts, 1860–1912* (Urbana: University of Illinois Press, 1993); Sarah Eisenstein, *Give Us Bread But Give Us Roses: Working Women's Consciousness in the United States, 1890 to the First World War* (Boston: Routledge & Kegan Paul, 1983); and Leslie Woodcock Tentler, *Wage-Earning Women: Industrial Work and Family Life in the United States, 1900–1930* (New York: Oxford University Press, 1979).

[13]Anna Clark, *The Struggle for the Breeches: Gender and the Making of the British Working-Class* (Berkeley: University of California Press, 1995), p. .

[14]Thomas Dublin, *Transforming Women's Work: New England Lives in the Industrial Revolution* (Ithaca, NY: Cornell University Press, 1994), Chapter 7.

[15]As Alice Kessler-Harris wrote in her 1975 article, " 'Where Are the Organized Women Workers?'," in 1925 the AFL, "after nearly forty years of organizing, remained profoundly ambivalent about the fate of nearly eight million wage-earning women." (p. 92)

[16]See for example Alice Kessler-Harris, "Organizing the Unorganizable: Three Jewish Women and Their Union," *Labor History* 17 (1976): pp. 5–23, and Dorothy Sue Cobble, "Rethinking Troubled Relations Between Women and Unions: Craft Unionism and Female Activism," *Feminist Studies* 16 (Fall 1990): pp. 519–548.

[17]The historiography of Progressivism is as vast as the movement itself. Most useful for my understanding of Progressivism are Arthur S. Link and Richard L. McCormack, *Progressivism* (Arlington Heights, IL: Harlan Davidson, Inc., 1983), and Eileen L. McDonagh, "The 'Welfare Rights State' and the 'Civil Rights State': Policy Paradox and State Building in the Progressive Era," *Studies in American Political Development* 7 (Fall 1993): pp. 225–274.

[18]Much like the Progressive reformers themselves, historians have also differed on whether or not labor legislation versus labor organization was the most effective way in which to address the needs of labor. See: Joseph F. Tripp, "Law and Social Control: Historians' Views of Progressive-Era Labor Legislation," *Labor History* 28 (Fall 1987): pp. 447–483. For an intriguing look at how this bifurcated approach carried on into the New Deal era, see Winifred D. Wandersee, " 'I'd Rather Pass a Law Than Organize a Union': Frances Perkins and the Reformist Approach to Organized Labor," *Labor History* 34 (Winter 1993): pp. 5–32.

[19]Kathryn Kish Sklar, *Florence Kelley and the Nation's Work: The Rise of Women's Political Culture, 1830–1900* (New Haven, CT: Yale University Press, 1995).

[20]James J. Kenneally, "Women and the Trade Unions 1870–1920: The Quandary of the Reformer," *Labor History* 14 (1973): pp. 42–55.

[21]Dana Frank's review of Sklar's book, *Florence Kelley and the Nation's Work*, "A Small Circle of Friends," *The Nation* (June 5, 1995): pp. 797–800.

[22]One particularly cogent example would be the issue of protective labor legislation aimed specifically at women. While wage-earning women certainly appreciated the effort to legislate against the worst abuses of industrial labor, those laws which constricted their employment to certain occupations or time of day deemed socially "appropriate" for women had the potential for pecuniary harm as well as perpetuating the notion of women as the "weaker sex". See, for example: Judith A. Baer, *The Chains of Protection: The Judicial Response to Women's Labor Legislation* (Westport, CT: Greenwood Press, 1978); Ava Baron, "Protective Labor Legislation and the Cult of Domesticity," *Journal of Family Issues* 2 (March 1981): pp. 25–38; Jane Jenson, "Paradigms and Political Discourse: Protective Legislation in France and the United States before 1914," *Canadian Journal of Political Science* 22 (June 1989): pp. 235–258; Alice Kessler-Harris, "The Paradox of Motherhood: Night Work Restrictions in the United States," in *Protecting Women: Labor Legislation in Europe, the United States, and Australia, 1880–1920* Ulla Wikander, Alice Kessler-Harris, and Jane Lewis, eds. (Urbana: University of Illinois Press, 1995); Diane Kirkby, " 'The Wage-Earning Woman and the State': The National Women's Trade Union League and Protective Labor Legislation, 1903–1923," *Labor History* 28 (1987): pp. 54–74; and Theda Skocpol, *Protecting Soldiers and Mothers: The Political Origins of Social Policy in the United States* (Cambridge, MA: Belknap Press, 1992).

[23]Jacquelyn Dowd Hall, "O. Delight Smith's Progressive Era: Labor, Feminism, and Reform in the Urban South," in *Visible Women: New Essays on American Activism* Nancy A. Hewitt and Suzanne Lebscock, eds. (Urbana: University of Illinois Press, 1993), pp. 166–198.

[24]Annelise Orleck, *Common Sense and a Little Fire: Women and Working-Class Politics in the Unites States, 1900–1965* (Chapel Hill: University of North Carolina Press, 1995). Orleck cites Mildred Moore's thesis on p. 317, note 6.

[25]Orleck, *Common Sense and A Little Fire*, p. 6.

[26]Ava Baron, "Gender and Labor History: Learning from the Past, Looking to the Future," in *Work Engendered: Toward a New History of American Labor* Ava Baron, ed. (Ithaca: Cornell University Press, 1991); Mary Blewett, *Men, Women, and Work*; Ardis Cameron, *Radicals of the Worst Sort*; Alice Kessler-Harris, "Treating the Male as 'Other': Redefining the Parameters of Labor History," *Labor History* 34 (Spring/Summer 1993): pp. 190–204.

[27]See: David R. Roediger, *The Wages of Whiteness: Race and the Making of the American Working Class* (New York: Verso, 1991) and Alexander Saxton, *The Rise and Fall of the White Republic: Class Politics and Mass Culture in Nineteenth-Century America* (New York: Verso, 1990).

[28]Kessler-Harris, "Treating the Male as 'Other'," p. 193.

[29]Works devoted to the NWTUL include: Susan Amsterdam, "The National Women's Trade Union League," *Social Service Review* (June 1982): pp. 259–272; Gladys Boone, *The Women's Trade Union Leagues in Great Britain and the United States of America* (New York: AMS Press, 1968, orig. pub., 1942); Allen Davis, "The Women's Trade Union League: Origins and Organization," *Labor History* 5 (Winter 1964): pp. 3–17; Robin Miller Jacoby, *The British and American Women's Trade Union Leagues, 1890–1925* (Brooklyn, NY: Carlson Publishers, 1994); Diane Kirkby, "'The Wage Earning Woman and the State': The National Trade Union League and Protective Labor Legislation, 1903–1923," *Labor History* 28 (Winter 1987): pp. 54–74; Elizabeth Anne Payne, *Reform, Labor and Feminism: Margaret Dreier Robins and the Women's Trade Union League* (Urbana: University of Illinois Press, 1988). Substantial treatments of the WTUL, again on the national level, in general works include: Philip S. Foner, *Women and the American Labor Movement: From the First Trade Unions to the Present* (New York: The Free Press, 1982), chaps. 6 & 13; James J. Kenneally, *Women and American Trade Unions* (Montreal: Eden Press Women's Publications, 1981), chaps. 5 & 6; Alice Kessler-Harris, *Out to Work: A History of Wage-Earning Women in the United States* (New York: Oxford University Press, 1982), pp. 137–205 *passim*.

[30]On the Chicago WTUL, see: Sandra Conn, "Three Talents: Robins, Nestor, and Anderson of the Chicago Women's Trade Union League," *Chicago History* 9 (1980–1981): pp. 234–247 and Colette A. Hyman, "Labor Organizing and Female Institution-building: The Chicago Women's Trade Union League, 1904–1924" in *Women, Work, and Protest: A Century of U.S. Women's Labor History* Ruth Milkman, ed. (New York: Routledge & Kegan Paul, 1987). On the New York WTUL, see: Nancy Schrom Dye, *As Equals and As Sisters: Feminism, the Labor Movement, and the Women's Trade Union League of New York* (Columbia: University of Missouri Press, 1980) and Gary E. Endelman, *Solidarity Forever: Rose Schneiderman and the Women's Trade Union League* (Ann Arbor: University Microfilm International, 1979).

[31]In *Labor's Flaming Youth: Telephone Operators and Worker Militancy, 1878–1923* (Urbana: University of Illinois, 1990) Stephen H. Norwood does discuss the BWTUL but primarily after 1913 and only in connection to the telephone operators. Norwood gives a more general overview of the BWTUL in its later years in "Reclaiming Working-Class Activism: The Boston Women's Trade Union League, 1930–1950," *Labor's Heritage* Vol. 10 (Summer 1998): pp. 20–35.

[32] Orleck, *Common Sense and a Little Fire*, p. 34.

[33]As recently as 1996, the AFL-CIO established "for the first time" a Working Women's Department "which will seek to help female workers nationwide."

See: *The New York Times*, Feb. 20, 1996. Even more recently, in January 1997, trade union women in Massachusetts issued a report based on meetings across the state in which the concerns raised differed little from those Kenney O'Sullivan and others faced a century before: sexual harassment in the work place, the need for child care, the need to increase women's membership in unions, as rank-and-file and in leadership, and "Respect for Women and Their Contributions to the Labor Movement." See *Women and the Labor Movement in Massachusetts: Analysis of Issues and Proposed Solutions*, a pamphlet prepared by Cheryl Gooding, Center for Labor Research, College of Public & Community Service, University of Massachusetts-Boston, and Kathleen A. Casavant, Executive Vice-President and Chair, Women's Committee, Massachusetts AFL-CIO. My thanks to Kathy Casavant for giving me a copy of this report and for pointing out the relevance of my work to her own.

[34]Kenney, "Organization of Working Women," p. 874.

"I Must Be That Someone"
Mary Kenney and the Chicago Labor Community

On May Day, 1890, fifteen thousand Chicago working men and women paraded through the city streets. An estimated thirty thousand more Chicagoans watched. The marchers carried banners honoring their trades and reminding the world of their contribution to society and the ideals they stood for. "No Carpenters, No Houses," "Child Labor Should Not Be on the Bench in the Shop but at School," and "Labor and Capital Should Go Hand in Hand for Mutual Benefit" were just a few. Many signs bore mottos demanding the eight-hour day. A coffin labeled "the ten hour day" was carried by eight pallbearers throughout the parade and eventually tossed into Lake Michigan.[1] This show of labor's strength had an immediate impact. On May 6th, the month-long carpenters' strike was won, an eight-hour day secured.

Labor Day, 1890, was an even larger demonstration of labor's might. According to the Chicago *Citizen*, an Irish-American publication, "Fully 30,000 marched to the music of the cause of Labor in Chicago" on the first day of September.[2] The *Citizen* proudly reported that "[a] number of the directors of the World's Fair, the mayor and aldermen, judges and other dignitaries occupied the reviewing stand." Also on the reviewing stand that day as a member of the reception committee was Mary Kenney.[3] As an accepted member of this contentious workers' community, Kenney would use those contacts as she organized women workers in Chicago.

In many ways, Mary Kenney was a typical working-class woman in late-nineteenth century America. Issues of survival and respectability shaped her life as they did the lives of all working-class women. She went to work at an early age and for years she supported herself and her invalid mother. Like many first-generation Irish-American women, Kenney married relatively late, at the age of thirty. After only eight years of marriage, she became a widow with three young children. Among working-class women, her hardships were hardly unique.[4] It would be her efforts to ameliorate at least some of those hardships through trade unionism that set Mary Kenney apart. Kenney had also formed ties with another community, that of middle- and upper-class reformers. Networks of support in both these communities provided critical assistance to Kenney in her efforts to organize working-class women such as herself.[5]

Mary Kenney was born in Hannibal, Missouri on January 8, 1864, the daughter of Michael and Mary Kenney. The Kenneys were Irish immigrants who worked their way west on the railroad, he as a track gang foreman, she as a cook. They settled in Hannibal, where Michael Kenney worked in the railroad yard as a machinist. The youngest of four children, Mary Kenney later remembered a pleasant childhood in this small-town railroad hub.[6] She attended public school, completing the fourth grade at the age of fourteen, "as far as any children of wage earners were expected to go."[7] Growing up in a railroad town, she learned about trade unionism on her front porch, listening to her father and the neighbors discuss the Great Strike of 1877.[8] The following year, in 1878, Kenney's father died and the young girl entered the work force, first as the unpaid apprentice of a local dressmaker. Dissatisfied with this trade, Kenney began work at the Hannibal Printing and Binding Company. By then, both her brothers had left town in search of work and her sister was working in New York as a domestic. By the age of fifteen, Kenney was the sole support of herself and her ailing mother. She entered the work force quite aware of her class and willing to fight for her rights as a wage earner.

As a young woman, Kenney was a devout Catholic, attending Mass every day.[9] Historians of ethnic Catholicism in America have stressed the conservative influence of the Church, especially among the Irish-American working class. According to Eric Hirsh, the Catholic Church emphasized reform over revolution, stressing that "[l]abor politics mobilized through church social networks had to be conscious of the church's antipathy toward any political movement with atheistic or pagan tendencies (such as the anarchist movement and oath-bound societies such as the early Knights of Labor)."[10] For Catholic working-class women, the Church advocated an even more rigid response. Young women should work, rather than marry, only out of dire economic need. Thus, as Paula

Mary Kenney, circa 1885. Schlesinger Library, Radcliffe College.

Kane argues, "wage work legitimized spinsterhood when it was holy and self-denying, like the vocation of being a nun."[11] Within that argument, there could be no room for trade unionism. Yet many Irish-American Catholic women as well as men turned to labor activism as a way of addressing the harsh conditions of work.[12] Mary Kenney, along with other activists such as Mary Harris "Mother" Jones, Leonora O'Reilly, and Elizabeth Gurley Flynn, were part of "a persistent strain of Irish female labor radicalism in America."[13] For Kenney, that radicalism was shaped as much by her ethnic heritage as it was by her experience as a woman worker in the last decades of the nineteenth century.

That work experience, as a bookbinder first in Hannibal, and then in Keokuk, Iowa, and finally in Chicago, was typical of most women bookbinders.[14] While the conditions of labor were harsh for all industrial workers, they were often particularly so for women. In order to earn even half of a man's wage, women were forced to work long hours, jeopardizing their health. According to statistician Carroll Wright, for women bookbinders in Boston it was "not possible to make more than $5 a week on average . . . One girl once made $7.50 a week **but it nearly killed her** . . ."[15]

By the end of the nineteenth century, the notion of a "family wage" earned by a male breadwinner was accepted by the middle and working class alike.[16] Women's lower wages were justified by their temporary status as workers as much as by their unskilled status. But as the historian Alice Kessler-Harris has so cogently argued, women's low wages at the turn of the century "reflected social myth."[17] The reality, however, was far different. Declining real wages meant that a living wage was dependent on the earnings of several family members, both young and old, male and female.[18] The family-based economy was particularly evident in the nation's textile towns. According to Ardis Cameron, the women textile workers who formed the majority of the workforce in the mills of Lawrence, Massachusetts, regarded the idea of the family wage earned by a male bread winner as "something of a strange idea."[19] The reality of these women's lives meant working for low wages, as a daughter, as a wife, as a mother.

Carole Turbin has also demonstrated that working-class women typically lived out their lives in various stages of "dependence, independence, interdependence."[20] Given changing family and marital status, a working-class woman could and did expect to be called upon to earn a wage to support not just herself but dependents as well.[21] But as long as that woman's wage was based upon her gender and its relation to the concept of the family wage and not on the value of her labor, much less her very real needs as a self-supporting woman, often with dependents, that wage never equaled a man's wage.[22]

In 1878, when the fourteen-year-old Mary Kenney found her first job in a bookbindery, she was immediately confronted with the conditions of labor working women faced:

> After many months of caring for the home and nursing Mother, I was able to take a job in the Hannibal [Missouri] Printing and Binding Co. The hours were from 7 A.M. to 6 P.M. and on Saturday until 5 P.M. The wages for all beginners were two dollars a week for the first six months with a fifty cent raise at the end of that time . . . **I was given a chance to learn every branch of the trade done by women** . . . [23]

As in printing and in shoemaking, the gendered division of labor had followed bookbinding out of the artisanal home into the factory. Increased mechanization brought with it a further hardening of that division.[24] As male bookbinders saw their status as craftsmen decline, women such as Mary Kenney were increasingly locked into the unskilled, low-paying facets of book production. Kenney learned her trade, first in Hannibal, and then in Keokuk, Iowa when the firm moved there and she became a forewoman at the age of nineteen. She demanded and won a raise, from $10 to $12 a week.[25] Yet, in 1888, when the bookbindery closed, the twenty-four-year-old Kenney was suddenly unemployed and still caring for her now bedridden mother. Hoping to secure more steady employment, Kenney moved to Chicago. Although she soon found work, she also soon discovered that the gendered division of labor she had experienced in Hannibal and Keokuk was no different in the bookbinderies of Chicago.

The gendered division of labor had the most immediate impact on the lives of women bindery workers on the shop floor. When assigned to take over the work of a man out sick, Kenney happily complied. However, when she asked for the same wage as the man, which was $21 a week in contrast to hers of $7, management refused. As a working woman who supported herself and a sickly mother, Kenney had few options: "I had to take it, because mine was a case of desperate need."[26] Looking for respect as a skilled worker, she was denied even a wage which would guarantee more than mere survival.

The question of respectability for working-class women was also of great importance, not just respectability in a moral sense but in a civic sense as well. Working-class women were generally referred to as "girls," regardless their age, reflecting the societal view that women should only work during that period between childhood and marriage. According to this ideal, marriage to a working-class man who had established his manhood as a worker would transform working girls into working-class women.[27] What was deemed socially and morally respectable for working-class women was made difficult, if not impossible, by low wages. As Mary Kenney told the middle- and upper-class women attending the World's Congress of Representative Women in Chicago in 1893, "In my own trade, bookbinding, the wages paid in Albany are. . . . four dollars and twenty cents a week, and still we are expected to be respectable."[28]

In addition to low wages, seasonal unemployment usually followed by mandatory period of overtime were other negative aspects of bindery work for women, as they were for most industrial workers. Low wages

coupled with periodic unemployment made an already precarious annual
income level worse. For instance, according to Carroll B. Wright, in
Massachusetts bookbinderies during the 1880s "there are two seasons,
September to February, and in July. In this work, the dull season lasts
sometimes for three or four months; the girls during that season are never
certain of the amount of work they can have to do."[29]

Long hours were yet another complicating factor for bookbinders,
both male and female. Slow periods were followed by days that stretched
into the night as rush orders were completed. Kenney remembered one
such job, printing election ballots for the city of Chicago at the J.M.W.
Jones Company:

> Every woman in the bindery worked from Friday morning at seven
> through the night till Saturday afternoon at four . . . [Kenney relates
> several food breaks taken] In spite of the strain, we all worked with a
> good spirit. The job had to be done and we did our best. Many of the
> girls' heads dropped on the table. I held out till about half-past three in
> the morning. Then I sat on the floor, leaned against the wall and gave
> up for about fifteen minutes.[30]

There is, in Kenney's remarks, a sense of pride in a job completed
under tremendous pressure. However, she does not even allude to the
irony of these women working all night to prepare ballots they could not
use.[31] Still, given the low wages and long hours, Kenney was soon
moved by her experiences at the Jones bindery to see the potential benefits of collective action. When she made her decision to organize women
bookbinders, Kenney was at the same time well aware of the antipathy of
employers towards such activity. During the January, 1890 strike of the
pressmen, the president of the J.M.W. Jones Company agreed to the
wage demands of the pressmen. However, Mr. Jones stated:

> There will always be trouble of this kind until the legislature passes a
> law against conspiracies of this kind . . . We had important contracts
> on hand and didn't think the few extra dollars a week should be consid-
> ered. I told the boys, however, I would get even with them. I think girls
> should feed the presses and a few laborers should be employed to bring
> them the stock.[32]

What were a few dollars to Mr. Jones meant the difference between
mere survival and a measure of respectability to the workers. Even more

important, the notion of replacing male workers with compliant women, seen as "girls" by management and male co-workers alike, perpetuated the view of women as strikebreakers who would be willing to work for less pay than a man.[33] For women workers and for those who sought to organize them, this was a dangerous and harmful image, difficult to overcome.

In the 1880s, organized bookbinders were part of the Knights of Labor, usually as members of mixed locals.[34] In 1892, two existing groups, the National Trades Assembly No.230, a Knights of Labor affiliate, and the International Bookbinders Union met in Philadelphia and combined to form the International Brotherhood of Bookbinders (IBB).[35] From its inception, the IBB included women in its ranks. The 1892 preamble of the union constitution claimed that "associated and united effort... [would be] of great benefit to working men and women." Historian Christina Burr argues that inclusion of women in the IBB was a concept inherited from the Knights of Labor.[36]

However, when Mary Kenney organized bookbinders in Chicago in 1890, she followed a different course, seeking women such as herself who had been confined to low-skilled and low-paid positions. She became "convinced that the workers must organize ... Someone must go from shop to shop and find out who the workers were that were willing to work for better living conditions." Recognizing in herself a certain ability, Mary Kenney knew that she "must be that someone."[37]

She entered a volatile labor situation when she decided to organize her fellow women bookbinders in the early 1890s. Strikes among all trades were frequent and bitter. In Chicago, 1890 started with the press-feeders out on strike for higher wages. In April, almost a thousand plumbers struck. In June, railroaders went out, making traveling difficult for commuters.[38] Much of the agitation centered on the continued demand for an eight-hour day. Notably absent from Chicago's eight-hour day movement in 1890 was the violence experienced in 1886.[39] Nonetheless, the Chicago labor community, in which Mary Kenney now played an active role, staged an impressive demonstration of its might, played out over several months. In February, "[a] 'grand eight-hour demonstration and ball' was given ... under the auspices of the Chicago Trade and Labor Assembly." Speakers included Judge John Peter Altgeld (soon to be a progressive Democratic governor) and attorney Clarence Darrow. Another ball was held in April.[40] Also that month, a bitter strike of the city's thousands of carpenters began. By the eve of May Day 1890, rumors that the packinghouse workers would join the carpenters on strike brought fears of a general strike.[41] In an impressive showing of their strength and solidarity, thousands of Chicago's working men and women marched on May Day and Labor Day. During the latter parade, Mary Kenney joined other dignitaries on the reviewing stand.

She appeared on that reviewing stand as a member of the Ladies' Federal Labor Union (LFLU) No. 2703, which another Chicago trade union woman, Elizabeth Morgan, organized in 1888.[42] The LFLU was affiliated with the Chicago Trade and Labor Assembly and the American Federation of Labor (AFL).[43] Upon joining the LFLU, Kenney "was immediately elected [as its] delegate" to the Chicago Assembly.[44] As part of this organized labor community, she had a useful support system when she set out to organize the women bookbinders of Chicago. Her fellow delegates in the Assembly helped Kenney secure a hall for an initial meeting. Thus "[t]he Women's Bookbinding [sometimes Bindery] Union No. 1 was born."[45]

In an effort to reach the 450 women bookbinders working in Chicago in 1890, Kenney became a roving or "tramp" bookbinder. She went from shop to shop, references in hand, staying only a week or two. She stayed long enough to inform her fellow workers of her efforts to establish a union and to report to the Chicago Board of Health the unsafe and unsanitary working conditions she frequently found.[46] Kenney also organized a ball which raised $600 for the sick benefits fund of the Women's Bindery Union No. 1. In these efforts, she had the continued support of the Trade and Labor Assembly.

For Mary Kenney, the solution to women's low wages and uncertain employment was trade unionism. Yet, the organized labor community was dominated by white, skilled men. By organizing women, Kenney was seeking not only to join a male community, she was challenging its exclusive power.[47] The objective of a family wage for skilled male workers was a principal tenet of the recently formed AFL. Although the reality was usually far from the myth, the myth sustained the notion of women as temporary workers. This temporary status justified their lower wages and their exclusion from trade unions. It also sustained working-class men's "masculine identity as the working sex."[48] Within this male community, women workers often felt out of place. When Mary Kenney organized Women's Bindery Union No. 1 in Chicago in 1890, the only place the fledgling local could afford to meet was a "dirty and noisy" room above a neighborhood saloon, a typical meeting place for male trade unionists but one completely inappropriate for respectable working women.[49]

While organizing bookbinders and looking for an affordable place to meet, Kenney accepted Jane Addams' invitation to dinner at Hull House.[50] She was initially skeptical about any involvement with someone like Addams. The middle-class, college-educated Addams represented everything Kenney was not except for her womanhood. As Kenney would later explain, "Small wages and the meagre [sic] way Mother and I had been living had made me grow more and more class conscious."[51] Still, Hull House could provide Kenney's union with an aura of middle-class respectability as well as with much-needed financial help. Before Kenney's first visit was over, Addams volunteered to pay for and pass out pamphlets about the union, which was now to meet at Hull House.[52]

Such willingness on the part of a middle-class woman to work for the cause of labor in a tangible way demonstrated to Kenney the potential efficacy of cross-class alliances based on gender. "When I saw there was someone who cared enough to help us and to help in our way, it was like having a new world opened up."[53] Kenney and her mother soon moved into Hull House and the young labor organizer took advantage of the social and educational amenities offered there. She later remembered the impact this association had on her, claiming her "whole attitude toward life changed."

In *Twenty Years at Hull House*, Jane Addams recalled her first meeting with the young activist bookbinder. "She came in rather a recalcitrant mood, expecting to be patronized and so suspicious of our motives." According to Addams, only after several weeks of residence at Hull House did Kenney become "convinced of our sincerity and of the ability of 'outsiders' to be of any service to working women."[54] Kenney was keenly aware of what working women such as herself needed— a steady wage and affordable housing. She was able to describe the harsh realities of working-class life to Jane Addams, who listened and learned from the young organizer. According to one biographer of Addams, "Mary Kenn[e]y, perhaps more than anyone, except Florence Kelley, broadened Jane Addams' perspective and made her sympathetic to organized labor, and helped her to move from a position of wanting to comfort the poor to one of a determination to eliminate poverty."[55]

Unlike the male-dominated trade union movement, the world of the settlement house in the 1890s was fundamentally a feminine one.[56] As part of what historian Kathryn Kish Sklar has called "women's political [or public] culture," the settlement house movement embodied a powerful opportunity for achieving social change and not just for the middle- and upper-class women who flocked to settlements at the end of the nineteenth century. Sklar argues that "[a]t its moments of greatest power, women's public culture fostered coalitions among diverse social identities, especially diverse class identities."[57] Mary Kenney's experience, however, was somewhat different. When working-class women entered into the arena of women's political culture, the resulting cross-class coalitions were frequently fraught with tension.[58]

Class concerns remained a potential stumbling block, but the social reform community in Chicago offered Kenney a base of support she did not find among that city's labor community. Nevertheless, her goal remained the same: she sought to bring women wage-earners into the trade union movement, not the social reform movement. For Kenney, the social reform community could serve as a conduit to the community of organized labor. This tactic was evident when Kenney organized the Chicago cloakmakers, a group of women workers also plagued by low wages, long hours, and regular seasons of unemployment. In a pamphlet announcing a "Musical Entertainment with Addresses" to be held at Hull House, she explained what women workers would gain as union members:

> The objects of our Union are to . . . make each individual feel that she is not alone in her daily efforts to make a respectable livelihood; to make her look upon herself as a part of that entire body of workers who form an important element in the commercial interests of a great community.[59]

In spite of the location of the meeting at Hull House, a center of women's political culture, Kenney believed that trade unionism would bring women workers into "that entire body of workers," both male and female.

But the Chicago labor community was ambivalent about her efforts to organize women workers because this challenged their position as primary wage earners on which their identity as men was based. Still, Kenney and women like her were very much a part of that community. Working-class women lived with and worked in factories with men of their own class every day.[60] While gender may have divided them by skill and wages, class concerns were shared, sustaining for women like Kenney what historians have called "industrial feminism."[61] Industrial feminism embodies a consciousness of both gender and class and recognizes that for women of the working class the notion of separate spheres becomes problematic when applied to their experiences as women and workers.[62]

As part of the Hull House circle, Kenney's activism was shaped by what could now be termed "industrial feminism" as she expanded her organizing efforts to women in other trades, especially among garment workers. In organizing women shirtmakers, she also managed to get herself involved in the growing factionalism within the Chicago Trade and Labor Assembly. According to the local labor press, the Assembly was "on the eve of destruction."[63] During this difficult time, Kenney took aim at Elizabeth Morgan, the organizer of the LFLU, claiming that Morgan was trying to undermine Kenney's newly formed shirtmakers' local. The dispute was actually between Morgan's husband Thomas, a Socialist labor organizer, and William Pomeroy, a Democratic party activist and head of the local Waiters' Union.[64] Pomeroy infuriated both the Morgans with his threat to take over the Trade and Labor Assembly, causing Elizabeth Morgan to challenge Kenney's new local because the shirtmakers were " 'Pomeroy girls'."[65] Brought in to mediate, AFL president Samuel Gompers was impressed with Kenney's verve and in 1892 chose the twenty-eight-year-old bookbinder as the Federation's first woman organizer.[66] In his autobiography, Gompers recalled meeting Kenney in 1891 and said he "found [her] to be an intelligent union woman with much to learn of the labor movement but anxious to learn and anxious to be of service."[67] Perhaps what this union woman learned from her dispute with the Morgans was that the internal politics of the local central labor union could at times impede her primary goal of organizing women workers.

In 1891, the AFL annual convention established a committee to investigate the issue of organizing women.[68] By April of 1892, with Gompers' approval, the AFL hired Kenney and she left Chicago for New York. Although her job lasted less than six months, she managed to contact collar makers in Troy, New York, shirt makers in Albany, New York and shoe workers in Middleboro and Haverhill, Massachusetts.[69] She spoke to scores of other working women—bindery workers like herself, printers, and textile workers—throughout New York and Massachusetts, often assisted by Leonora O'Reilly, an organizer for the United Garment Workers.[70] The official newspaper of Boston's AFL-affiliated Central Labor Union (BCLU) reported on Kenney's activities in New York:

> Miss Kenney's method is to get together perhaps a dozen or twenty girls of a trade. She then talks to them in her sweet, enthusiastic way of the real objects of womanhood, and points out the necessity of their being independent and industrious.[71]

Within her remarks there appears an inherent contradiction. In the late nineteenth century, independence was not considered an object of womanhood. Yet in urging working-class women to join trade unions, Kenney often reminded women of the dependence that low wages entailed. As she soon realized, hers was not an easy task.[72] In September, 1892 she wrote Gompers as follows: "I don't believe organization of women can be accomplished as readily as men. To me it seems slow, and if I had my choice of either, I would take the men every time—it would make a better showing. I believe though much can be done for the women and I also do the best I can."[73]

Much of this difficulty stemmed from the ambivalent attitude of organized labor towards the employment of women, especially if married.[74] Throughout the 1890s and into the twentieth century, the AFL convention delegates annually endorsed the organization of women. However, such organization was seen as a necessary evil as long as the inequities of capitalism forced women to be wage earners. The ultimate goal of the AFL, and the Knights of Labor before them, was that male workers should earn the family wage.[75] As Samuel Gompers reported to the AFL convention in 1901:

> It is a sad commentary upon our industrial system that the tendency is ever to take the woman and child from the home and immure them within the factory's walls. For the protection of the woman we concur in the suggestion that to them to be further extended the benefits of organization.[76]

Many women within the AFL agreed with Gompers that woman's proper place was within the home. In 1900, Eva MacDonald Valesh, an AFL organizer and assistant editor of the *American Federationist*,

> addressed the convention on the benefits of organization, and made an eloquent appeal for the organization of the women into trade unions, so that in time, they might, through organization, emancipate themselves from the industrial field back into the home, and the man would take up her place in the factory and store as breadwinner.[77]

Like the Knights of Labor, the AFL saw the organization of women workers mainly as a device for improving the conditions of male labor, which was the ultimate goal. If women organized, their wages might increase to the point at which they would no longer be seen as a cheaper source of labor.[78] Also, employers might not view trade union women as a more compliant, and therefore exploitable, substitute for men. The final result would be improved working conditions for men and the exclusion of married women from employment. Kenney had quite a different goal in taking on the position of AFL women's organizer. She did not see marriage to a "breadwinner" as the working-class woman's salvation:

> Women make the great mistake of sitting down, or practically that, and waiting for someone to come along who will support them, and meantime they lose all the benefit that they might have if they would interest themselves in their work enough to become highly skilled workwomen.[79]

Mary Kenney had acted on her own advice. She took pride in her years as a woman bookbinder and demanded fair treatment from her employers and from organized labor as a skilled worker. She knew that higher wages could mean more than just survival but a measure of respectability as well. As an AFL organizer, she sought to secure these benefits for all working women. After less than six months on the job, however, she was dismissed by the AFL executive council which claimed that the Federation could ill afford to pay an organizer who had produced so few results.[80] Never truly committed to organizing women, the AFL could easily dismiss Kenney's preliminary efforts. Their ambivalent, even contradictory attitude regarding women workers would hamper the AFL's organization of women for years to come.[81]

However frustrating her short stint as AFL organizer, during the time she held the position Kenney met several people from the Boston area who would become an important part of her life in the years to come. Hannah Parker Kimball, a well-to-do Boston woman interested in the plight of working women, contacted Kenney, urging her to come to Boston. After spending several weeks organizing in and around New York City, Kenney finally arrived in Boston in late June. Once there, Kimball introduced Kenney to several other prominent Boston women interested in reform, among them Kimball's sister, Mary Morton Kehew.

A wealthy and active reformer, Kehew had just become president of the Boston Women's Educational and Industrial Union (WEIU), an office she would hold for the next twenty-one years. Founded in 1877 by several Boston elite women, the WEIU was intended as a "class-bridging" organization which would give greater meaning to the lives of middle- and upper-class women as they sought to address the perceived needs of working-class women.[82] Through their mutual acquaintance Jane Addams, Kenney met Vida Scudder and Helena Dudley, two women she would later come to know well through their shared association with Denison House in Boston.[83] Through Samuel Gompers she met her future husband. Gompers wrote to local AFL general organizer and labor editor for the *Boston Globe*, John F. O'Sullivan, to inform him of the twenty-eight-year-old woman organizer's impending arrival, telling him, "She's a great girl."[84]

Born in Charlestown, Massachusetts in 1857, John O'Sullivan had been active in Boston labor circles since the early 1880s.[85] He served as an organizer first for the Knights of Labor and then later for the AFL, holding a variety of union offices on the local and state level. In 1889, as secretary of the organizing committee of the Boston Central Labor Union (BCLU), O'Sullivan took over the almost defunct Seaman's Union local and turned that organization around. He was also a newspaper man, writing on labor issues for the BCLU weekly newspaper, *Labor Leader*, as well as for the Boston dailies, the *Herald* and the *Globe*, where he was appointed labor editor in 1891. Good-looking and possessing an engaging personality with a great sense of humor, the man known as Jack O'Sullivan was a leader of the Boston labor community. When Mary Kenney arrived in Boston in 1892, it would be love at first sight for both O'Sullivan and the labor community.[86]

Only a few weeks after Mary Kenney's arrival in Boston, the *Labor Leader*'s editor, veteran trade unionist Frank Foster, raved about her as a woman and as an organizer:

> She has fine physical proportions, a rich, sweet voice, a fascinating smile and a good command of language, besides a practical knowledge of the working girl and her needs, all of which fit her for reaching the confidence of the girls and drawing them into her organization.[87]

The daily press agreed. A woman reporter for the *Boston Globe* described Kenney as "a rather pretty young woman, with bright sympathetic eyes and an engaging smile."[88] Focusing on her physical attractiveness may have been an attempt to blunt Kenney's potentially radical message. In bringing "working girls" into "her organization," she hoped to turn those "girls" into "independent and industrious" women, and she was thereby challenging the male dominance of the trade union movement. While the AFL recognized the need to organize women workers, the threat to their power, not to speak of their very identity as workers and as men, was clear. The result was the continued ambivalence of the AFL and Kenney's continuing difficulties while AFL woman organizer.

After her dismissal in September, 1892, Kenney returned to Chicago, where her mother had remained as a resident of Hull House. Despite her engagement to a Boston labor leader, Kenney had been unable to make much headway in the organization of working women during her months on the East Coast and perhaps needed to return to the city where she had been more successful. Working again out of Hull House, she immediately joined a garment workers' strike and served on a committee involved with the Women's Pavilion at the 1893 Chicago World's Fair.[89] Collaborating with Florence Kelley, Kenney spent several months lobbying the Illinois state legislature for the passage of labor laws designed to protect sweatshop workers.

In February 1893, she was one of the main speakers, along with Kelley and Chicago reformer Henry Demarest Lloyd, at a large rally sponsored by Hull House and the Chicago Trades and Labor Assembly.[90] About one thousand people filled Chicago's Central Music Hall to hear about the horrors of sweated labor and the dire need for state inspection. After months of intense lobbying, the Illinois legislature finally acted. On July 1, 1893 Governor John Peter Altgeld signed into law the State Factory Inspection Act. The efforts of Florence Kelley on behalf of this legislation were recognized by Gov. Altgeld when he appointed her chief factory inspector. In turn, Kelley recognized the assistance of Kenney who was promptly appointed a deputy inspector.[91]

While organizing the bookbinderies of Chicago during the early 1890s, Mary Kenney had not hesitated to anonymously report those shops in violation of city health codes. Yet in turning to the state to control the conditions of labor, Kenney was reflecting the political interests of social reformers rather than of trade unionists. Some historians have seen reformers' efforts to obtain labor legislation as an attempt to undercut the power of the labor movement.[92] For these historians, Progressive Era social reforms were really directed at the perceived need for social control rather than seen as attempts to improve society.[93] More recently, the historian Kathryn Kish Sklar sees in Progressive Era labor legislation the formal emergence of women's political culture.[94]

Regarding Florence Kelley's campaign to establish state factory inspection in Illinois, Sklar admits that "[t]he Chicago Trades and Labor Assembly would never have recommended such an active role for the state, but Kelley viewed 'the law officer' at the door as salutary—partly because she saw herself in that role."[95] However, the efforts of women social reformers were not entirely self-serving. Positive change did eventually occur in the conditions of labor experienced by American industrial workers—conditions which were often dangerous and frequently exploitative, particularly for women and child workers.[96]

In turning to state intervention, Mary Kenney was not turning her back on the trade union movement. For her, it was not an "either/or" choice. Rather, Kenney was remaining true to her fundamental goal to improve work conditions for women such as herself and ultimately for all workers, male and female. For women workers especially, such a flexible policy, relying on both organization and legislation was critical. Separately, each had its limitations in assuring women workers a decent wage and safe work conditions.

Organization of women would often prove difficult as long as women were perceived as temporary workers. Legislation could be and was ineffective through lack of enforcement.[97] It could also handicap women workers by placing restrictions on their labor, making them less competitive with their male counterparts.[98] As a labor organizer and in her association with the middle- and upper-middle-class women reformers of Hull House, Kenney came to understand both sides of the protective legislation versus trade union position. By 1894, she knew all too well the necessity of organization in spite of the gendered position of the AFL. She had also seen first hand the political efficacy of middle-class social reform despite the class-driven interests of many social reformers. It would be a much-more experienced trade unionist who returned to Boston in 1894 to marry the man she loved.

NOTES

[1]*Chicago Times*, May 2, 1890.

[2]*Chicago Citizen*, Sept. 5, 1890.

[3]*Chicago Daily News*, Sept. 2, 1890.

[4]On self-supporting women of the working class, see Joanne J. Meyerowitz, *Women Adrift: Independent Wage Earners in Chicago, 1880–1930* (Chicago: University of Chicago Press, 1988). On Irish-American women, the standard remains Hasia R. Diner's *Erin's Daughters in America: Irish Immigrant Women in the Nineteenth Century* (Baltimore: John Hopkins University Press, 1983). For an examination of working-class women at work and in their communities during the late nineteenth century, see especially Mary H. Blewett, *Men, Women, and Work: Class, Gender, and Protest in the New England Shoe Industry, 1780–1910* (Urbana: University of Illinois Press, 1988), chaps. 8 and 9; Ardis

Cameron, *Radicals of the Worst Sort: Laboring Women in Lawrence, Massachusetts, 1860–1912* (Urbana: University of Illinois Press, 1993); Thomas Dublin, *Transforming Women's Work: New England Lives in the Industrial Revolution* (Ithaca, NY: Cornell University Press, 1994); and Carole Turbin, *Working Women of Collar City: Gender, Class, and Community in Troy, New York, 1864–1886* (Urbana: University of Illinois Press, 1992).

[5]While studies of specific labor communities abound, most helpful in framing my approach have been Lizabeth Cohen, *Making a New Deal: Industrial Workers in Chicago, 1919–1939* (New York: Cambridge University Press, 1990); Dana Frank, *Purchasing Power: Consumer Organizing, Gender, and the Seattle Labor Movement, 1919–1929* (New York: Cambridge University Press, 1994); Michael Kazin, *Barons of Labor: The San Francisco Building Trade and Union Power in the Progressive Era* (Urbana: University of Illinois Press, 1987); Roy Rosenzweig, *Eight Hours For What We Will: Workers and Leisure in an Industrial City, 1870–1920* (New York: Cambridge University Press, 1983). Of the various works focusing on the settlement house movement in general, most useful to me have been Mina Carson, *Settlement Folk: Social Thought and the American Settlement Movement, 1885–1930* (Chicago: University of Chicago, 1990); Allen F. Davis, *Spearheads for Reform: The Social Settlements and the Progressive Movement, 1890–1914* (New York: Oxford University Press, 1967); and Judith Ann Trolander, *Professional and Social Change: From the Settlement House Movement to Neighborhood Centers, 1886 to the Present* (New York: Columbia University, 1987).

[6]Mary Kenney O'Sullivan, unpublished autobiography, n.d., ca. 1920s, Schlesinger Library, Radcliffe College, Cambridge, Mass., microfilm edition, the Papers of the National Women's Trade Union League and Its Principal Leaders, Smaller Collections reel, p. 1; hereafter, Kenney O'Sullivan, autobio.,. On railroads, see Walter Licht, *Working for the Railroads: The Organization of Work in the Nineteenth Century* (Princeton: Princeton University Press, 1983).

[7]Kenney O'Sullivan, autobio., p. 6.

[8]On the Great Strike of 1877, see: Jeremy Brecher, *Strike!* (Boston: South End Press, 1972), Chap. 1; Robert V. Bruce, *1877: Year of Violence* (New York: Bobbs-Merrill, 1959).

[9]Kenney O'Sullivan, autobio., p. 25.

[10]Eric L. Hirsh, *Urban Revolt: Ethnic Politics in the Nineteenth-Century Chicago Labor Movement* (Berkeley: University of California Press, 1990), p. 142. See also: Kerby Miller, *Emigrants and Exiles* (New York: Oxford University Press, 1985).

[11]Paula Kane, *Separatism and Subculture: Boston Catholicism, 1900–1920* (Chapel Hill: University of North Carolina Press, 1994), p. 246.

[12]As Carole Turbin writes in *Working Women of Collar City*, "The influence of religion on Irish-American trade unionism is ambiguous." n. 39, p. 131; see also: n. 41, p. 132, as well as pp. 188–120. According to David Montgomery, "By the late sixties increasing numbers of Catholics were emerging from behind the psychological walls of the ghetto to join, at times even to lead, labor organization." in *Beyond Equality: Labor and the Radical Republicans, 1862–1872* (Urbana: University of Illinois Press, 1981), p. 126. The Church, however, did not approve of the more radical labor movements such as the Molly Maguires. See: Kevin Kenney, "Molly Maguires and the Catholic Church," *Labor History* (Summer 1995): pp. 345–376. By 1893, after Pope Leo XIII issued his socially reform-minded encyclical, *Rerum Novarum*, the Catholic clergy in America and Europe, were freed to speak out in support of trade unionism—as long it was not associated with Socialism. See: Neil Betten, *Catholic Activism and the Industrial Worker* (Gainesville: University Presses of Florida, 1976), pp. 10–11.

[13]Kane, *Separatism and Subculture*, p. 247. See also: Diner, *Erin's Daughters* and Turbin, *Working Women of Collar City*, passim.

[14]Mary Van Kleeck, *Women in the Bookbinding Trade* (New York: Survey Associates, 1913).

[15]Carroll D. Wright, *The Working Girls of Boston* (New York: Arno & The New York Times, 1969, orig. pub., 1884), p. 97, emphasis added. When he conducted his survey of Boston's working women in the 1880s, Wright was more concerned with the issue of morality than physical health. Seeking to find an answer to why working-class women turned to prostitution, Wright gathered information on women working in a variety of industrial occupations. According to Wright, women bookbinders had no monopoly on low wages. Women boot and shoe workers in Boston made on average $5.48 a week when employed. Paper box makers made $5.16 a week and women retail clerks earned a weekly wage of $6.20. Women employed in the manufacture of men's garments could make between $4.93 and $7.74 per week. The average weekly wage for the working women of Boston in 1884 was $6.47 per week. Wright found that the average expenses of the women he interviewed were $261.30 per year while their yearly income was $269.07, "leaving a margin for everything outside of the absolute necessaries of life of $7.77." Wright, *The Working Girls of Boston*, p. 83, p. 109.

[16]On the growing acceptance of the family wage among skilled male workers, see Martha May, "Bread Before Roses: American Workingmen, Labor Unions and the Family Wage," in Ruth Milkman, ed., *Women, Work and Protest: A Century of U.S. Women's Labor History* (New York: Routledge & Kegan Paul, 1985), pp. 1–21; on the acceptance among unskilled immigrant men, see Ron Rothbart, " 'Homes Are What Any Strike Is About': Immigrant Labor and the Family Wage," *Journal of Social History* 23 (1989): pp. 267–284. See also Maurine

Weiner Greenwald, "Working-Class Feminism and the Family Wage Ideal: The Seattle Debate on Married Women's Right to Work, 1914–1920," *Journal of American History* 76 (1989): pp. 118–149.

[17]Alice Kessler-Harris, *A Woman's Wage: Historical Meanings and Social Consequences* (Lexington: University of Kentucky Press, 1990), p. 11.

[18]Dublin, *Transforming Women's Work*, p. 255.

[19]Cameron, *Radicals of the Worst Sort*, p.41.

[20]Turbin, *Working Women of Collar City*, see esp. pp. 72–76. On the potential divisiveness of differences in age or marital status among women seeking to organize, see: Blewett, *Men. Women, and Work*, pp. 322–323.

[21]Meyerowitz, *Women Adrift*.

[22]Kessler-Harris, *A Woman's Wage*, p. 17.

[23]Kenney O'Sullivan, autobio., p. 16, emphasis added.

[24]A similar process occurred in several fields during the nineteenth century. On bookbinding, see: Felicity Hunt, "The London Trade in the Printing and Binding of Books: An Experience in Exclusion, Dilution and De-Skilling for Women Workers," *Women's Studies International Forum* 6 (1983): pp. 517–524 and Felicity Hunt, "Opportunities Lost and Gained: Mechanization and Women's Work in the London Bookbinding and Printing Trade," in *Unequal Opportunities: Women's Employment in England, 1800–1918* Angela V. John, ed. (Oxford: Basil Blackwell, 1986), pp. 71–93; in the printing trade, see Ava Baron, "Contested Terrain Revisited: Technology and Gender Definitions of Work in the Printing Industry, 1850–1920," in *Women, Work and Technology: Transformations* Barbara Drygulski Wright et al., eds. (Ann Arbor: University Of Michigan Press, 1987), pp. 58–83; in the shoe industry, see Mary H. Blewett, "The Sexual Division of Labor and the Artisan Tradition in Early Industrial Capitalism: The Case of New England Shoemaking, 1780–1860," in *'To Toil the Livelong Day': America's Women at Work, 1780–1980* Carol Groneman and Mary Beth Norton, eds. (Ithaca: Cornell University Press, 1987), pp. 35–46; in textiles, see Sonya O. Rose, "Gender Segregation in the Transition to the Factory: The English Hosiery Industry, 1850–1910," *Feminist Studies* 13 (Spring 1987): pp. 163–184.

[25]Kenney O'Sullivan, autobio., p. 18.

[26]*Boston Globe*, July 7, 1892.

[27]Sarah Eisenstein, *Give Us Bread But Give Us Roses: Working Women's Consciousness in the US, 1890–the First World War* (Boston: Routledge & Kegan Paul, 1983), p. 137.

[28]Mary E. Kenney, "Organization of Working Women," *World's Congress of Representative Women* (Chicago, n.p., 1893), p. 873. Sometimes, women workers could turn the notion of respectability to their advantage. Maintaining their dignity as "lady stitchers," women shoemakers could elicit much-needed community

support during strikes. Yet, according to Mary Blewett, the respectable woman role could also stymie union organization as women worried about their reputations hesitated to take a public, much less active role, in trade unionism. See: Blewett, *Men, Women, and Work*, p. 236, p. 276.

[29]Wright, *The Working Girls of Boston*, p. 101.

[30]Kenney O'Sullivan, autobio., p. 33.

[31]I thank Sandra Christoforidis for pointing this out to me.

[32]*Chicago Times*, Jan. 1, 1890.

[33]For an interesting discussion of the gendered division of labor in the knitting industry and the contrasts therein between English and Canadian factories, see: Joy Parr, *The Gender of Breadwinners: Women, Men, and Change in Two Industrial Towns, 1880–1950* (Toronto: University of Toronto Press, 1990), Chap. 3.

[34]Christina Burr, "Defending the 'Art Preservative': Class and Gender Relations in the Printing Trades Unions, 1850–1920," *Labour/Le Travail* 31 (Spring 1993): p. 68. In the 1830s, a period of much labor unrest in New York, women bookbinders there formed a union and struck for higher wages. According to historian Sean Wilentz, the "Journeymen's Revolt" of the mid-1830s was due as much to changing economic conditions as to the social impact of the nascent industrial revolution. Wilentz, *Chants Democratic: New York City and the Rise of the American Working Class, 1788–1850* (New York: Oxford University Press, 1984), pp. 219–220. In their own quest for recognition, the journeymen bookbinders supported the striking women in 1835. The men pledged to "'use all honorable means to sustain them [women bookbinders] in their difficulties' and expressing their 'utter contempt' for the employers who worked the women at starvation wages while 'fattening on the sweat of their brow.'" Quoted in Christine Stansell, *City of Women: Sex and Class in New York, 1789–1860* (Urbana: University of Illinois Press, 1987), pp. 141–142.

[35]*The International Bookbinder* 6 (June 1905): p. 170.

[36]Burr, "Defending 'The Art Preservative'," p. 69. Preamble as quoted in Burr, p. 68. See also: Blewett, *Men, Women, and Work*, Chap. 8; Susan Levine, *Labor's True Woman: Carpet Weavers, Industrialization, and Labor Reform in the Gilded Age* (Philadelphia: Temple University Press, 1984; and on the Knights in general, see: Leon Fink, *Workingmen's Democracy: The Knights of Labor and American Politics* (Urbana: University of Illinois Press, 1983); Kim Voss, *The Making of American Exceptionalism: The Knights of Labor and Class Formation in the Nineteenth Century* (Ithaca: Cornell University Press, 1993); Norman J. Ware, *The Labor Movement in the United States, 1860–1895: A Study in Democracy* (New York: D. Appleton & Company, 1929).

[37]Kenney O'Sullivan, autobio., p. 34.

[38]*Chicago Daily News* and *Chicago Times*, Jan. 1, 1890; *Chicago Citizen*, Apr. 5, 1890 and June 28, 1890.

[39]The movement for an eight-hour day, demanded by organized labor since the 1850s, reached frequently violent proportions in 1886, most notably in Chicago during the Haymarket Riot on May 4, 1886. On the eight-hour movement and the strikes associated with that movement, especially in 1886, see: Paul Avrich, *The Haymarket Tragedy* (Princeton, NJ: Princeton University Press, 1984); Brecher, *Strike!*, chap. 2; Fink, *Workingmen's Democracy*, pp.190–195; Jama Lazerow, "'The Workingman's Hour': The 1886 Labor Uprising in Boston," *Labor History* 21 (1980): pp. 200–220; David Montgomery, *The fall of the house of labor: The workplace, the state, and American labor activism, 1865–1925* (New York: Cambridge University Press, 1987), pp. 193–196.

[40]*Chicago Daily News*, Feb. 24, 1890 & Mar. 3, 1890.

[41]*Chicago Daily News*, Apr. 14, Apr. 18, Apr. 24–26, 1890; *Chicago Times*, Apr. 30, 1890. See also: James R. Barrett, *Work and Community in the Jungle: Chicago's Packinghouse Workers, 1894–1922* (Urbana: University of Illinois Press, 1987).

[42]Ralph Scharnau, "Elizabeth Morgan, Crusader for Labor Reform," *Labor History* 14 (1973): p. 341.

[43]On the Chicago Trade and Labor Assembly during the early 1890s, see: Eugene Stanley, *History of the Illinois State Federation of Labor* (Chicago: University of Chicago, 1930), Chaps. 5 & 6. On the Chicago labor scene more generally, see: Richard Schneirov, "Rethinking the Relation of Labor to the Politics of Urban Social Reform in Late Nineteenth-Century America: The Case of Chicago," *International Labor and Working-Class History* 46 (1994): pp. 93–108.

[44]Kenney O'Sullivan, autobio., p. 33a.

[45]Kenney O'Sullivan, autobio., p. 44.

[46]See: Tax, *The Rising of the Women*, Chapter 3.

[47]In their dealings with management, trade unions in the 1890s may not have wielded as much power as they would have liked; but within the labor community itself, they often did. Alice Kessler-Harris has argued that "Formal labor institutions and informal associations of working people can be seen as outgrowths of male efforts to develop strategies for accessing economic power or to construct defenses against change." Kessler-Harris, "Treating the Male as 'Other': Redefining the Parameters of Labor History," *Labor History* 34 (1993): pp. 198–199. Even more to the point, John Tosh states that "All-male associations sustained gender privilege, while at the same time imposing a discipline on individuals in the interests of patriarchal stability." Tosh, "What Should Historians Do With Masculinity? Reflections on Nineteenth-century Britain," *History Workshop Journal* 38 (1994): p. 187.

[48]Tosh, "What Should Historians do with Masculinity?," p. 186.

[49]Kenney O'Sullivan, autobio., p. 64. Roderick N. Ryon discusses the gender dynamics of "segregated" meeting space and its effects on the organization of

women in "Craftsmen's Union Halls, Male Bonding, and Female Industrial Labor: The Case of Baltimore, 1880–1917," *Labor History* 36 (Spring 1995): pp. 211–231.

[50]Kenney O'Sullivan, autobio., pp. 63–65; Jane Addams, *Twenty Years at Hull House* (New York: MacMillan Co., 1910), p. 212; Allen F. Davis, *American Heroine: The Life and Legend of Jane Addams* (New York: Oxford University Press, 1973), pp. 78–79; Kathryn Kish Sklar, "Hull House in the 1890s: A Community of Women Reformers," *Signs* 10 (Summer 1985): pp.658–677. See also Sklar's more recent work, which while a comprehensive biography of the reformer Florence Kelley, has much to say about the Hull House community of the 1890s in Part III of *Florence Kelley and the Nation's Work: The Rise of Women's Political Culture, 1830–1900* (New Haven: Yale University Press, 1995).

[51]Kenney O'Sullivan, autobio., pp. 63–64; also quoted in Meredith Tax, *The Rising of the Women: Feminist Solidarity and Class Conflict, 1880–1917* (New York: Monthly Review Press, 1980), p. 60.

[52]Kenney O'Sullivan, autobio., p. 65.

[53]Kenney O'Sullivan, autobio., pp. 64–65; also quoted in Tax, *The Rising of the Women*, p. 60.

[54]Addams, *Twenty Years at Hull House*, p. 212.

[55]Davis, *American Heroine*, p. 79. Not only did Addams provide a home for the women's bookbinders union. She also assisted Kenney in setting up a cooperative living space for working women known as the Jane Club. See: Dolores Hayden, *The Grand Domestic Revolution: A History of Feminist Designs for American Homes, Neighborhoods and Cities* (Cambridge: MIT Press, 1981), pp. 167–169.

[56]According to Robin Muncy, the "numbers only began to suggest the degree of female superiority in the settlements; women also dominated by strength of character." Muncy, *Creating a Female Dominion in American Reform, 1890–1935* (New York: Oxford University Press, 1991), p. 10. On the settlement house movement in general see: Mina Carson, *Settlement Folk: Social Thought and the American Settlement Movement, 1885–1930* (Chicago: University of Chicago Press, 1990) and Allen F. Davis, *Spearheads for Reform: The Social Settlements and the Progressive Movement, 1890–1914* (New York: Oxford University Press, 1967).

[57]Sklar, *Florence Kelley and the Nation's Work*, p. xiii.

[58]Ellen Carol Dubois, "Working Women, Class Relations, and Suffrage Militance: Harriot Stanton Blatch and the New York Woman Suffrage Movement, 1894–1909," *Journal of American History* 74 (1987): pp. 34–58 and Lori Ginzberg, *Women and the Work of Benevolence: Morality, Politics and Class in the Nineteenth-Century United States* (New Haven: Yale University Press, 1990).

[59]Cloakmakers Announcement, March 19, 1892, The Jane Addams Papers, microfilm edition, reel 52, frames 531–532.

[60]Jacqueline Dowd Hall, "O. Delight Smith's Progressive Era: Labor, Feminism, and Reform in the Urban South," in *Visible Women: New Essays on American Activism* Nancy A. Hewitt and Suzanne Lebscock, eds. (Urbana: University Of Illinois Press, 1993), p.168.

[61]Annelise Orleck, *Common Sense and a Little Fire: Women and Working-Class Politics in the United States, 1900–1965* (Chapel Hill: University of North Carolina Press, 1995), p. 6. See also: Diane Kirkby, *Alice Henry: The Power of Pen and Voice: The Life of an Australian-American Labor Reformer* (New York: Cambridge University Press, 1991) and Kirkby, "The Wage-Earning Woman and the State: The National Women's Trade Union League and Protective Labor Legislation, 1903–1923," *Labor History* 28 (1987): pp. 54–74.

[62]Historian who have discussed the inadequacies of the notion of separate spheres when applied to working-class women include: Blewett, *Men, Women and Work*; Cameron, *Radicals of the Worst Sort*; Turbin, *Working Women of Collar City*; Nancy A. Hewitt, " 'The Voice of Virile Labor': Labor Militancy, Community Solidarity, and Gender Identity among Tampa's Latin Workers, 1880–1921," in *Work Engendered: Toward a New History of American Labor* Ava Baron, ed. (Ithaca: Cornell University Press, 1991), pp. 142–167. See also: Hewitt, "Beyond the search for sisterhood: American women's history in the 1980s," *Social History* 10 (1985): pp. 299–321 in which she argues that "The sisterly bonds that bolstered working-class communities. . . . were forged from material necessity, and were employed in the interests of men as well as women," p. 309. See also: Anna Clark, *The Struggle for the Breeches: Gender and the Making of the British Working Class* (Berkeley: University of California Press, 1995), p. 2.

[63]Quoted in Stanley, *History of the Illinois State Federation of Labor*, note 2, p. 88.

[64]In his history of the Illinois State Federation of Labor, Eugene Stanley, who had the pleasure of interviewing him late in life, characterized William Pomeroy as "a scheming, joking genius." As for Morgan, although a socialist, he was at least "honest," a trait not usually associated with the more shifty Pomeroy, as according to Stanley, *History of the Illinois State Federation of Labor*, pp. 87–97.

[65]Cited in Sklar, *Florence Kelley*, p. 215.

[66]Philip S. Foner, *Women and the American Labor Movement: From the First Trade Unions to the Present* (New York: The Free Press, 1982), pp. 111–115, and Foner, *Women and the American Labor Movement: From Colonial Times to the Eve of World War I* (New York: The Free Press, 1979), pp. 226– 230; See also: Tax, *The Rising of the Women*, pp. 61–63.

[67]Samuel Gompers, *Seventy Years of Life and Labor: An Autobiography* Nick Salvatore, ed. (Ithaca: ILR Press, 1984, orig. pub., 1925), pp. 127–128.

[68]*Proceedings of the American Federation of Labor*, Eleventh Annual Convention, 1891, p. 16.

[69]Kenney O'Sullivan, autobio., pp. 84–86; *Boston Globe*, July 7, 1892; *Labor Leader*, June 18, 1892, July 9, 1892, Aug. 13, 1892. See also: Blewett, *Men, Women and Work*, p. 275.

[70]O'Reilly, like Kenney, was a working-class woman, the daughter of Irish immigrants. She would go on to be a leader of the WTUL in New York. See: Mary J. Bularzik, "The Bonds of Belonging: Leonora O'Reilly and Social Reform," *Labor History* 24 (1984): pp. 60–83; Tax, *The Rising of the Women*, pp. 95–124.

[71]*Labor Leader* June 18, 1892.

[72]Leonora Barry, a hosiery worker turned organizer for the Knights of Labor during the 1880s had similar problems organizing women. See: Blewett, *Men, Women, and Work*, pp. 248–251; James J. Kenneally, "Women and Trade Unions 1870–1920: The Quandary of the Reformer," *Labor History* 14 (1973): pp. 43–44; Susan Levine, *Labor's True Woman: Carpet Weavers, Industrialization, and Labor Reform in the Gilded Age* (Philadelphia: Temple University Press, 1984), esp. pp. 105, 111, 113–114, 117.

[73]Foner, *Women and the American Labor Movement* (1982), p.114.

[74]Alice Kessler-Harris, "'Where are the Organized Women Workers?'" *Feminist Studies* 3 (Fall 1975): pp. 92–110.

[75]Levine, *Labor's True Woman*, Chap. 6.

[76]*Proceedings of the American Federation of Labor*, Twenty-First Annual Convention, 1901, p. 187.

[77]*Proceedings of the American Federation of Labor*, Twentieth Annual Convention, 1900, p. 85. See also the article by Valesh in the AFL's monthly journal, the *American Federationist*, entitled "Woman and Labor," Feb. 1896, pp. 221–223.

[78]Edward O'Donnell, "Women as Bread Winners—The Error of the Age," *American Federationist* 4 (Oct. 1897): pp. 186–187.

[79]"Woman's Champion," an interview with Mary Kenney, Boston *Globe*, July 7, 1892. On the positive relationship to family and marriage for working-class women, see: Sarah Eisenstein, *Give Us Bread But Give Us Roses: Working Women's Consciousness in the United States, 1890 to the First World War* (Boston: Routledge & Kegan Paul, 1983), esp. chap. 5; for a more negative analysis, see: Leslie Woodcock Tentler, *Wage-earning Women: Industrial Work and Family Life, 1900–1930* (New York: Oxford University Press, 1979), esp. Part II.

[80]Foner, *Women and the American Labor Movement* (1982), p. 114.

[81]Kessler-Harris, "'Where Are the Organized Women Workers?'" p. 92.

[82]On the WEIU, see: Barbara J. Balliet, "'What Shall We Do With Our Daughters?': Middle-Class Women's Ideas about Work, 1840–1920" (Ph.D.

diss., New York University, 1988); Karen J. Blair, *The Clubwoman as Feminist: True Womanhood Redefined, 1868–1914* (New York: Holmes and Meier Publications, Inc., 1980); Sarah Deutsch, "Learning to Talk More Like a Man: Boston Women's Class-Bridging Organizations, 1870–1940," *American Historical Review* 97 (1992): pp. 379–404 and "Reconceiving the City: Women, Space and Power in Boston, 1870–1910," *Gender & History* 6 (Aug. 1994): pp. 202–223; Robert B. Jennings, "A History of the Educational Activities of the Women's Educational and Industrial Union from 1877–1927" (Ph.D. diss., Boston College, 1978); Judith Becker Ranlett, "Sorority and Community: Women's Answer to A Changing Massachusetts, 1865–1895" (Ph.D. diss., Brandeis University, 1974).

[83]On Denison House, see: Deutsch, "Learning to Talk More Like a Man . . ."; Deutsch, "Reconceiving the City . . ."; Susan Traverso, " 'The Road Going Down to Jericho': The Early History of Denison House, 1887–1912," (B.A. Honors thesis, Simmons College, 1983). The Denison House papers are held by the Schlesinger Library, Radcliffe College, Cambridge, Mass.

[84]Kenney O'Sullivan, autobio., p. 85. On John O'Sullivan's career as labor editor, see: Louis M. Lyons, *Newspaper Story: One Hundred Years of the Boston Globe* (Cambridge: Belknap Press of Harvard University Press, 1971), p. 82.

[85]No biography of John O'Sullivan exists. The following account relies on his obituary in the *Boston Globe*, September 23, 1902 as well as those which appeared in *The Pilot*, Sept. 27, 1902 and the *American Federationist*, Nov. 1902.

[86]Kenney O'Sullivan, autobio., p. 124.

[87]*Labor Leader*, Aug. 13, 1892. On Frank Foster, see: Arthur Mann, *Yankee Reformers in the Urban Age* (Cambridge: The Belknap Press of Harvard University Press, 1954), pp. 188–200 and Joseph DePlasco, "The University of Labor vs. the University of Letters in 1904: Frank K. Foster Confronts Harvard University President Charles W. Eliot," *Labor's Heritage* 1 (April 1989): pp. 52–65.

[88]July 7, 1892.

[89]On the participation of Hull House residents in the Chicago World's Columbian Exposition, see: Lana Ruegamer, " 'The Paradise of Exceptional Women': Chicago Women Reformers, 1863–1893," (Ph.D. diss., Indiana University, 1982), Chap. 6. See also: Jeanne Madeline Weimann, *The Fair Women: The Story of the Woman's Building, World's Columbian Exposition, Chicago, 1893* (Chicago: Chicago Academy, 1981).

[90]Joan Waugh, "Florence Kelley and the Anti-Sweatshop Campaign of 1892–1893," *UCLA Historical Journal* 3 (1982): p. 31. According to Chester McArthur Destler, Kenney was part of prominent reformer Henry Demarest Lloyds' social reform circle. See: Destler, *Henry Demarest Lloyd and the Empire of Reform* (Philadelphia: University of Pennsylvania Press, 1963), p. 219.

[91]Waugh, "Florence Kelley," p. 33; Sklar, *Florence Kelley*, pp. 237–239.

[92]Rivka Shpak Lissak, *Pluralism and Progressives: Hull House and the New Immigrants, 1890–1919* (Chicago: University of Chicago Press, 1989), p. 23; Waugh, "Florence Kelley," p. 33.

[93]The classic condemnation of Progressivism as social control rather than social justice remains Paul Boyer, *Urban Masses and Moral Order in America, 1820–1920* (Cambridge: Harvard University Press, 1978), Part IV. For a succinct and relatively balanced discussion of the social control versus social justice question see: Arthur S. Link and Robert L. McCormick, *Progressivism* (Arlington Heights, IL: Harlan Davidson, Inc., 1983), Chap. 3.

[94]Sklar, "The Historical Foundations of Women's Power in the Creation of the American Welfare State," in *Mothers of a New World: Maternalist Politics and the Origins of Welfare States* Seth Koven and Sonya Michel, eds. (New York: Routledge, 1993), pp. 43–93. See also: Paula Baker, "The Domestication of Politics: Women and American Political Society," *American Historical Review* 89 (1984): pp. 620–649; Theda Skocpol, *Protecting Soldiers and Mothers: The Politics of Social Provision in the United States, 1870s-1920s* (Cambridge: Harvard University Press, 1992).

[95]Sklar, *Florence Kelley*, p. 233.

[96]Alice Kessler-Harris, *Out to Work: A History of Wage-Earning Women in the United States* (New York: Oxford University Press, 1982), Chap. 7.

[97]Clara M. Beyer, *History of Labor Legislation for Women in Three States* Women's Bureau Bulletin No. 66 (Washington, DC: Government Printing Office, 1929), pp. 24–26.

[98]See: Susan Lehrer, *Origins of Protective Labor Legislation for Women, 1905–1925* (Albany: State University of New York Press, 1987).

CHAPTER 2

"A Noble Young Woman on Fire for Her Cause"
Mary Kenney O'Sullivan and the Boston Labor Community

As she had in Chicago, in Boston, Mary Kenney found support for her efforts among both the male-dominated trade union movement and the female-based social reform organizations. Both communities, as well as the women Kenney tried to reach, were touched by the severe economic downturn which began in 1893. In Boston alone, unemployment rose into the tens of thousands while union membership dropped.[1] In response, Frank Foster, editor of the *Labor Leader*, suspended subscription payments for a time.[2] As Helena Stuart Dudley, head resident of the Boston settlement, Denison House, later recalled:

> My first year [1893] in Boston was marked by a financial crisis and memorable unemployment: not less than 40,000 were out of work from three to eight months. Savings disappeared, furniture and clothes were pawned, charity organizations were snowed under. We listened day after day to tales of misery.[3]

This misery spurred potentially violent protest. On February 20, 1894, Socialist Morrison I. Swift led a demonstration of thousands of Boston's unemployed to the steps of the statehouse, demanding work or relief. A month later, at a rally at Faneuil Hall, Swift announced, "We propose to take away the property of the rich—by law."[4] The trade union leaders who spoke that day, including Frank Foster and Boston carpenter Harry Lloyd as well as AFL president Samuel Gompers, delivered a much less radical message, arguing that simple trade unionism would alleviate most economic woes. As Foster editorialized a few days after the rally,

Samuel Gompers, 1890s. The George Meany Memorial Archives.

"The trade union movement cannot possibly favor the undefinable, un-limited policy of state socialism; the experiment is too dangerous."[5] However much the trade unionists sought to distance themselves from radicals like Swift, the discontent over periodic and often devastating un-employment remained widespread, creating a danger of its own. Accord-ing to historian Arthur Mann, "The bitter winter of 1893–94 in Boston, as elsewhere, impressed many social reformers as being the beginnings of those hard times preceding a secular day of judgement."[6]

The city of Boston attempted to respond to its residents' needs before that day of judgement occurred. Mayor Nathan Matthews established a Citizen's Relief Committee which, in cooperation with the Wells Memorial Institute and Denison House, set up a work program for the wives of unemployed male workers. Three hundred and twenty-four women sewed hospital garments for seventy-five cents a day. Even in the midst of the depression, much of the relief effort was shaped by concerns over who was and who was not deserving of which sort of relief. In keeping with the notion of a family wage **earned** by a man, a "make work" program for women was established. Perhaps this was conceived as less threatening to the givers as well as the receivers. In any case, as Helena Dudley later remembered, "It was but a drop in the bucket, as we had applications from 500 a day." According to the Denison House head resident, "No one who has not lived through such a period among working people can fully realize how cruel and inhuman our industrial system seems . . ."[7]

When Mary Kenney arrived in depression-bound Boston in the spring of 1894, the former Hull House resident gravitated to the female community of Denison House. There, in Dudley and several other residents, Kenney found willing partners in her efforts to organize working women.[8] Opened in 1892, Denison House was one of three settlement houses sponsored by the College Settlement Association (CSA). The CSA was organized in 1890 by several recent graduates of elite women's colleges, including Vida Dutton Scudder.[9] Scudder, a daughter of one of Boston's socially prominent families and a graduate of Smith College in 1884, joined the Wellesley College faculty as an English professor in 1887.[10] She would remain at Wellesley for more than forty years, a beloved teacher and a respected scholar. At the same time, Scudder was perhaps one of the most active participants in the myriad of Progressive causes which made Wellesley, in particular, "a hothouse of reform."[11]

Scudder saw the college woman—of Wellesley, Radcliffe, Smith, Vassar, and Bryn Mawr—as ideally suited to the settlement house movement. These educated women of some means held "an immediate position between the two great orders of the rich and the poor." There, between "the pinched face of the sewing-woman" and "the *ennui* of restless luxury that besets the rich lady," stood the woman college graduate. The application of her "womanly qualities" combined with her education could bring "the re-adjustment of elements [that] would go far towards the creation of a new harmony."[12] Scudder emphasized that, despite her education, the college woman remained "womanly." Her female role as nurturer could be extended out of the home and into the community at large, as part of what some historians have referred to as "social housekeeping," at the same time answering the query, "After College, What?"[13] The settlement house was also uniquely suited for those young college women who sought not just to establish themselves as useful to society but to create a community of women somewhat like the one they had experienced during their college years.[14] Denison House head resident Helena Dudley stressed this aspect of settlement house life when she wrote: "The residents in a Settlement have quite as much to learn from the community about them as they have to give it."[15] As a member of the Denison House community, veteran labor organizer and former bookbinder Mary Kenney would serve as an ideal teacher.

Located on Tyler Street in Boston's South End, Denison House sought to bring "social democracy" rather than charity to the residents of the city's largest working-class neighborhood.[16] In the early years of the settlement, the neighborhood was comprised of "industrious working people, mainly Irish American," many of whom were skilled workers, a generation or two removed from the dire poverty which had prompted their immigration to America.[17] Yet just as Denison House opened its doors, the neighborhood known as the South End was beginning to experience a change in its ethnic composition. Reporting on its first year of operation for the CSA annual report, the Denison House executive committee noted that "[t]he Jews are coming in, while Italians, Germans, Hungarians, Poles and Armenians are [also] to be found."[18]

Like most settlements, Denison House offered children's activities, cooking classes, and lectures on literature. At the same time, the early residents of Denison House such as Dudley, Scudder, and Emily Greene Balch, a classmate of Dudley's at Bryn Mawr who would soon join Scudder on the faculty at Wellesley, became intensely interested in labor organizing as a way of addressing the needs of their neighbors.[19] The great depression beginning in 1893 made clear to the residents of Denison House the direct link between unemployment, under-employment, and the poverty they saw around them. In describing their neighborhood for the CSA annual report, the Denison House executive committee recognized that "[t]here is much destitution, especially this autumn [of 1893], since employment has failed so many bread-winners." Seeking to foster an "awakening of the social conscience" which would lead to "social betterment," Helena Dudley opened up Denison House to the organized labor community of Boston, particularly to veteran AFL organizer John O'Sullivan.[20]

John F. O'Sullivan, 1895. The George Meany Memorial Archives.

O'Sullivan provided Denison House with a direct link to the trade union movement in Boston and on the state level. The Boston Central Labor Union (BCLU), founded in 1878, represented for the most part skilled, white, native-born male workers, many of Irish-American descent.[21] Delegates from the various trade unions in Boston and surrounding cities met every other week for "the promotion of trade unionism and the furtherance of any movement which in its opinion is beneficial to the working classes."[22] Initially associated with the Knights of Labor, within

three years of its founding the BCLU began to break with the Knights.[23]
In 1881, the BCLU was one of several central labor organizations which
participated in the formation of the Federation of Organized Trades and
Labor Unions.

That Federation, after only five years of continued strife with the
Knights of Labor, evolved into the AFL in 1886.[24] By then, the BCLU
break with the Knights was about complete. The Chicago Haymarket riot
of 1886 caused many in organized labor to distance themselves from the
Knights or any hint of radicalism.[25] In that spirit, the Massachusetts State
Federation of Labor (also known as the Massachusetts State Branch of the
AFL) was formed at a convention of the state's trade union representatives held in Boston in 1887.[26] AFL president Samuel Gompers was in
attendance as were most of the delegates to the BCLU, including Frank
Foster. Jack O'Sullivan was also active in the BCLU and the Massachusetts State Federation as both organizations went through their formative years.

As a respected representative of organized labor, O'Sullivan offered
the Denison House residents an opportunity to cooperate with trade
unionists even before Mary Kenney moved to Boston. In a March 1894
meeting at the settlement, he organized Federal Labor Union No. 5915,
made up of "wage earners and professional people."[27] Federal labor
unions were an attempt by the AFL to allow those organized workers
who did not have sufficient numbers within their respective crafts to sustain their own local to form one nonetheless. Such non-craft organizations, generally composed of the unskilled, especially women, were
particularly beneficial to those seeking to organize but frequently unwelcome in the male-dominated trade unions.[28] The open membership of the
Federal Labor Unions also allowed women reformers to join the labor
movement in an official capacity, thus forging an alliance with the community they sought to assist. Helena Dudley, writing for the Denison
House executive committee report to the CSA for 1894, was probably re-
ferring to Jack O'Sullivan when she wrote:

> [N]or is it without value that the far-sighted men who have influence in
> the councils of labor should be ever eagerly ready to share their best
> wisdom with us and should seem to think that we may in time be of
> service to women wage-earners. . . . [29]

In the eyes of Helena Dudley, and many other social reformers like
her, women workers were especially at risk. Physical degeneration and

moral depravity were seen as the logical, if tragic, outcome of the low wages and long work hours that most working-class women endured. The long-term goal of reformer and trade unionist alike was generally an improvement of the wages earned by male heads of families, thus ending the need for the women to work at all. But there was a recognition that something had to be done in the short-term. Helena Dudley shared Mary Kenney's belief that trade unionism for women was the answer, serving not just the interests of the women but of society as a whole. However, Dudley knew that

> [t]he organization of women-workers is beset by difficulties which at present seem insuperable. But the mere knowledge which we are gaining, and which we in turn may hope to share with many, will assuredly help to that awakening of the social conscience which must precede all social betterment.[30]

Like the residents of Denison House, and unlike many male trade unionists, Jack O'Sullivan felt that the organization of women was as critical as that of men. Perhaps Mary Kenney had impressed the labor leader professionally as well as personally during her visit to Boston in the summer of 1892. When she returned to Boston two years later, Kenney immediately went to work organizing women like herself, using Denison House as her base of operations. According to the historian Susan Traverso, "Much of the labor activism at Denison House can be attributed to the influence of the young labor organizer Mary Kenney."[31] Kenney, who had forged a similar relationship with Jane Addams at Hull House, would play much the same role in the early years of Denison House.[32]

Jack O'Sullivan may have had "influence in the councils of labor," and, in his willingness to reach out to the residents of Denison House, he provided an important link between the two communities. But it was Mary Kenney, as a working-class woman and experienced labor organizer who had learned the usefulness of cooperation with female social reformers during her days at Hull House, who cemented the bond. At the same time, Kenney and O'Sullivan were more than a convenient link to Boston's labor community. As Vida Scudder later remembered, "Jack O'Sullivan was our romance; he married Mary Kenney, a noble young woman on fire for her cause."[33]

Mary Kenney moved to Boston in the spring of 1894 and immediately joined Jack O'Sullivan in support of striking silk weavers in nearby Newton Upper Falls. There, 150 workers, two-thirds of whom were described as "young girls," walked out over a reduction in wages.[34] Prompted by the severe economic depression which began a year earlier, the factory owner had reduced the women's wages from $5 a week to $3.10 by cutting their hours from fifty-eight to forty hours. According to the *Boston Globe*, men's wages were between $6 and $10 a week, "married and single men alike." As the historian Alice Kessler-Harris has argued, "If a woman lived independently, her wage was normally not sufficient to support her."[35] Such was the case for the women silk mill strikers, most of whom boarded in company-owned housing at $3 a week and then had to survive on the remaining ten cents. Facing imminent eviction or submission, the strikers chose to "fight this thing out."[36]

They did so out of desperation but also because they had the support of organized labor. Early in the strike, Mary Kenney:

> promised the strikers the hearty support of the labor unions. . . . and claimed that through the power of united labor the firm would be compelled to pay living wages to the men **and** women at the silk mill.[37]

She and Jack O'Sullivan organized the striking workers, both men and women, into separate locals and the strike was won after only two weeks. In a region where 60,000 women workers were unemployed, such a victory was amazing. As the pro-labor *Boston Globe* pointed out, the silk weavers could thank Mary Kenney for "organizing a new union of women workers and winning a strike and restoration of a wage reduction during the depths of a depression."[38] The great depression of the 1890s only further convinced Kenney of the necessity of organization.[39] The organization of wage-earning women even provided a measure of social respectability, briefly turning striking "girls" into "women workers" by virtue of their union status.

Committed to each other and to the labor movement, Kenney and O'Sullivan continued to organize women workers as the city struggled through the second difficult summer of depression. As the depression dragged on into 1894, millions of workers across the country suffered. Upwards of twenty percent of the American industrial workforce was unemployed.[40] Those lucky enough to still have a job saw their wages slashed. As the silk workers in Newton Upper Falls were striking over their wage cuts, railroad car workers in the company-owned village of Pullman, Illinois went out on strike on similar grounds, protesting wage cuts while rents remained the same.[41] The silk workers' strike was far less violent and ultimately more successful. That strike over, Kenney and O'Sullivan later turned their attention to the city's women garment workers.

By the end of August 1894, just as Boston's garment industry entered its busy season, the city's manufacturers slashed their workers' already low wages by almost 20 percent.[42] As a member of Federal Labor Union No. 5915, Mary Kenney spoke with one Boston shirt manufacturer about his recent "cut in wages of girls." Previously paid 48 cents for every dozen shirts made, the women were now to be paid 39 cents per dozen. Such a reduction was intolerable, as the "best girls had made $5 a week [and] could not make it on reduced wages."[43] The women, referred to as girls even by Helena Dudley, had formed a union and gone out on strike, joining hundreds of other garment workers, both male and female. By mid-September, the strike had spread to several small shops, but Jack O'Sullivan worried that if the strike dragged on past the busy season (usually the end of October), the strikers would lose what leverage they had.[44] On September 26th, Dudley and Kenney attended a meeting of the striking garment workers, both men and women. According to Dudley, many employers were ready to meet the strikers' demands, and the "same terms are being made for women and men, only women must be members of unions in order to get terms."[45]

The male-dominated garment workers' locals in Boston had shown little interest in organizing women workers, fearing that bringing the lower-paid women into the union would drive the men's wages down too. As the *Boston Globe* put it, "A strong feeling has heretofore existed between the men and women, the latter making bitter complaints that the men were driving them out of the business." In seeing women garment makers as competitors, not allies, these men were perpetuating the sanctity of the family wage earned by a man and preserving their sense of masculine identity. However, the *Globe* also reported that "[t]his feeling seems to be gradually passing away since the men, without consulting the women, have demanded equal pay for equal work regardless of sex."[46] On the surface, the efforts of the male garment workers to secure "equal pay for equal work" may appear as a gesture of solidarity with their women co-workers. But such a demand was more likely to have been the usual ploy of turning the problem of women in the trade over to the employer. If forced to hire men and women at the same rate of pay, the employer would most likely choose the men. Given a working woman's perceived temporary status, a male worker was seen as a better "investment for the future."[47] To compound the difficulty for working women, the garment workers stipulated that in order to qualify for equal wages, a worker had to be a member of the union. Yet the garment workers entered the strike of 1894 knowing full well that most women in the trade remained unorganized, mostly as a result of union indifference.

While the existing locals would not organize female garment makers and the BCLU would do nothing, Mary Kenney had yet another resource. With the backing of the Denison House residents, she organized Garment Workers Local No. 37 which initially had fifty women members. Kenney was elected president and Helena Dudley served as the local's first treasurer. The strike was soon favorably settled and the women's local grew in numbers and strength.[48] Kenney and Dudley eventually stepped down and the women garment makers then ran their own local. Meeting weekly at Denison House, Local No. 37 had over 800 women members one year later and was in a much better position to negotiate that season's contract.[49] Mary Kenney continued to find *more* support for the organization of women workers within the social reform community.

Kenney was beginning to realize that reliance on the AFL, nationally or on the local level, could not solve the problems women workers faced. The unwillingness of the BCLU to assist in organizing Boston's women garment makers could only have reminded Kenney of the refusal of the AFL to renew her appointment as woman organizer two years earlier. The timing of the garment workers' strike might have also been a factor. During the summer of 1894, the BCLU was much more concerned about internal divisions caused not by the organization of women but by the growing ethnic diversity of Boston's workers, exacerbated by the severe economic depression.

On August 13th, the *Boston Globe* reported that "a race war" between "the sons of the Emerald Isle" and "the children of Italy" had erupted during construction of the West End Street Railway.[50] The following Sunday, the BCLU discussed the matter at their regular weekly meeting. While the BCLU did not wish to appear to question the nationality of the workers involved, they also could not allow "non-union foreign born" laborers to undercut wages. According to the *Boston Globe*, "This matter caused considerable discussion, it being the opinion of some of the delegates [to the BCLU] that the work should be given exclusively to citizens."[51] Yet a majority of those present felt otherwise—the issue should be the use of union versus non-union workers, not the nationality of those workers. However, as long as Italian laborers were unwelcome, and thus seemingly not interested, in the Irish-dominated construction unions, non-union status could be and was easily conflated with "foreigners."[52] As a public gesture of tolerance, the BCLU closed this meeting by electing its "only colored delegate," James Taylor, president of the Street Laborers Local No. 6164, as commander of the BCLU Labor Day parade delegation.[53]

For the BCLU, as for much of organized labor, the conflicts over the organization of women frequently paled in the face of the often violent ethnic conflict within the working class.[54] As the voice of the BCLU, *Labor Leader* editor Frank Foster wrote in his semi-autobiographical novel, *The Evolution of a Trade Unionist* (1901), "The problem of immigration is a vexed one."[55] Yet there were many similar concerns regarding African Americans and the employment of women and their relation to organized labor. All three tended to be outside of the union fold, seen as "unorganizable" as well as undesirable.[56] Women, African Americans, and recent immigrants were frequently used as strikebreakers or were castigated by organized labor for accepting lower wages, thus potentially decreasing the wages of all workers. The inclusion of either African Americans, women, or recent immigrants in the workplace, much less in the union, could be viewed as undermining the white, male, native-born or naturalized union worker's very identity as a man, thus diluting what little power he had within the industrial system.[57] Also at stake was the concept of worker as citizen, a status denied to all women and recent immigrants lacking the vote entirely and severely limited for African American men.[58]

Equally divisive was the split within the BCLU between Socialists and more conservative trade unionists, a reflection of the same factionalism on the national level within the AFL. Thomas Morgan of Chicago, with whom, as noted earlier, Mary Kenney had crossed swords shortly before her move to Boston, led the Socialist charge at the 1894 AFL convention. In Boston, Henry Abrahams, the BCLU delegate from the Cigarmakers Union local and a perennial thorn in the side of the more conservative Frank Foster, represented the Socialists within the BCLU.[59] Through he agitated for several months, Abrahams was unable to get a majority of the BCLU to vote in favor of so-called Plank 10, which advocated collective ownership of the means of production. For Massachusetts trade unionists, the debate came to a head at the annual convention of the Massachusetts State Branch of the AFL. Held in Boston in early August, 1894, John O'Sullivan and Mary Kenney led the effort to defeat Plank 10.

On August 6, the convention opened with a report from the legislation committee, of which O'Sullivan was a member. The committee's report regarding Plank 10 set the tenor of the debate. According to the report, organized labor in Massachusetts needed "[t]o avoid on one hand a timid and halting policy, and on the other a rashness which will alienate the support of our constituents and thus defeat the purpose at which we aim. . . . We meet in stirring times."[60] That purpose was AFL trade unionism and how that effort might or might not be advanced through politics, conventional or socialist, was of constant concern during this period.[61] Therefore, the committee went on to recommend that a special committee of seven be established to look into, "with careful considera-tion. . . . the subject of independent political action." Mary Kenney and Frank Foster were among those elected to that special committee.[62]

Debate on Plank 10 consumed much of the second day of the con-vention. The majority report of the special committee of seven recom-mended that the state convention not endorse Plank 10, urging instead endorsement of the more moderate platform of the Massachusetts Work-ingmen's Political League.[63] Debate then opened on the floor of the con-vention. Supporters urged that Plank 10 be adopted because "only through the collective ownership of production and distribution could the wage earner ever secure industrial emancipation."[64] Jack O'Sullivan op-posed Plank 10 because he saw socialism as a potential violation of the "political and religious freedom" which the AFL guaranteed all its mem-bers. After an attempt to end debate was blocked by Foster, the Boston *Globe* reported that

> Delegate Mary E. Kennedy [sic] then took the floor, and in a convinc-ing manner expressed it as her belief that the industrial organization of women would be retarded by the adoption of socialist ideas. She stated that for the past two years she had favored the 10th plank, but time and experience had convinced her that it would be unwise for this conven-tion to adopt it.[65]

In fact, Kenney had had more than two years to reflect upon her experi-ences in Chicago where political differences within that city's Trade and Labor Assembly had threatened to undermine her organizational efforts among the women cloakmakers. Now she appealed to the Massachusetts state convention of the AFL to reject socialism for the much more press-ing issue of the "industrial organization of women."[66]

Such a request was not unreasonable, given that earlier that day the delegates had voted favorably on the following resolution introduced by Jack O'Sullivan:

> Whereas the working women of Massachusetts are almost wholly un-organized; and whereas, such lack of organization is an injury to them-selves as well as to all wage-earners. . . . this organization endorses

any movement looking to the organization of working women on trade union lines, and we call upon all trade unions to assist in the organization of women by forwarding names of working women to Mary E. Kenney.[67]

Such resolutions had been made before and would be made again.[68] Yet all the resolutions in the world could not change the reality that women remained under-represented and unwelcome in trade unions. Not only were women workers seen as economic competitors. Their very presence on the shop floor, if in any other than an unskilled and presumably temporary position, was threatening to the concepts of white male working-class identity and the family wage. However, the Massachusetts Branch of the AFL did make its position regarding Plank 10 clear. On the third and final day of the convention, delegates voted 23 to 10 against adoption.[69] A few months later, Plank 10 also failed to get the support of the national AFL convention delegates, pleasing self-defined "collective individualists" such as Frank Foster.[70]

While the Socialists may have lost Plank 10, they did manage to get some revenge in voting Samuel Gompers out of the national AFL presidency for one year.[71] The BCLU, for its part, continued the debate into 1895 and the majority soon made its wishes evident once again. On February 3, Samuel Gompers' good friend and ally, Jack O'Sullivan was elected president of the BCLU.[72] Although he frequently served on the legislative committees of both the BCLU and the Massachusetts State Branch of the AFL, O'Sullivan represented the AFL position that any direct involvement in politics, such as a third party effort, would do more harm than good for labor's cause. His election as president of the BCLU in 1895 was therefore a repudiation by that group of any drift towards third party politics.[73]

Mary Kenney shared O'Sullivan's views, on this and most other public issues. The two must have made a stunning couple, both handsome and well-spoken, "on fire for [their] cause." Finally the two found some time to make legal their commitment to each other. On October 10, 1894, with the garment strike just successfully settled, Mary Kenney and John O'Sullivan were married in New York City, where Kenney's sister then lived. The woman who had been a daily communicant when she first came to Chicago in 1890 was married in a civil ceremony at City Hall with Samuel Gompers as a witness.[74] Her shifting views on religious faith remain unclear but implicit in her choice of a civil ceremony seems a growing willingness to turn her back on the dictates of her religion both personally and professionally.[75]

A week after their marriage, the O'Sullivans were the guests of honor at a dinner held at Denison House. Those in attendance at the festive occasion represented the two communities that the newly-married labor organizers passed through in their daily work. In addition to the settlement house workers, such as Helena Dudley, were veteran Boston labor leader George McNeill and up-and-coming trade union leader Harry Lloyd. Also in attendance was Robert Woods from the South End Settlement House and Cornelia Warren, a wealthy benefactor of the CSA and of Denison House in particular. Later in the evening, Frank Foster, Emily Greene Balch, and the Unitarian minister and social reformer John Graham Brooks joined the party. Between toasts to the bride and groom, Brooks proposed that those involved in the trade union movement should join the Twentieth Century Club. According to Helena Dudley, the "[i]dea was very well received by those present."[76]

The Twentieth Century Club had began in 1893, meeting at a fashionable address on Boston's Beacon Hill.[77] In a parody of that club, Frank Foster describes the class divide that workers often faced when they associated with "intellectual and educated people who felt compelled to unite for social and civic progress." Although Foster wrote that labor leaders were supposed to be part of what he called the "New Era Club," they were actually "conspicuous in their absence."[78] In describing one occasion in which several semi-fictional Boston labor leaders attended a meeting of the New Era Club, Foster provides the reader with a fictionalized conversation between two working women. Lizzie Bolton's comments to her friend Vera, while waiting for the program to begin, indicate the enormous gulf between the labor community and the social reformers.[79] Lizzie, a typographer, says to Vera:

> This is out of my line. . . . but I don't mind rubbering on these guys who wear good clothes and talk with a Lunnon [sic] accent, don't you know. . . . there must be a great moral consolation in a tailor-made gown and a diamond ring such as my lady over there has on. I know one working-girl who would like to be 'helped' to a few of those.

Vera admonishes Lizzie to be quiet, saying, "They're good-hearted folk, no doubt. They are not at fault for dressing well." Lizzie responds:

> Sure not!. . . . I only wish I could do the same. But how do you suppose that elegant dame would like to stick type for nine hours per diem, day in and day out, never minding such things as headaches and colds and

aching bones! It must be a soft snap to wrestle with the question from the outside. . . . [80]

Certainly, working-class women such as Mary Kenney O'Sullivan knew that the support they received from middle- and upper-class women would not translate into diamonds, but gems symbolized money and power. Support led to more tangible assistance in the organization of working women, such as the money to print pamphlets announcing a union meeting or providing a respectable place for a women's union to meet. Kenney O'Sullivan had received this sort of vital aid as part of her association with settlement house workers in both Chicago and Boston. But as she moved out of the settlement house and into the wider social reform community, the frequent inability of middle- and upper-class women to "wrestle with the [labor] question from the outside" became clearer.

In the fall of 1894, Kenney O'Sullivan organized the Women's Industrial Education Association under the auspices of the Women's Educational and Industrial Union (WEIU).[81] WEIU president Mary Morton Kehew had first met Kenney O'Sullivan in 1892. The two women met again two years later, probably at Denison House which both women frequented. As part of her efforts to attract working-class women to this "class-bridging" organization, Kehew secured the use of the WEIU lecture hall for what was sometimes referred to as "Mary Kenney's Club."[82] Upwards of sixty women workers and a sprinkling of social reformers gathered every other week for various talks followed by games, dancing, and refreshments. The subjects of the talks, always followed by "informal discussion," ranged from the efforts of the Massachusetts Consumers' League on behalf of the union label to why working-class women avoided domestic service.[83] Utilizing her personal contacts, Kenney arranged for Wellesley professor Emily Greene Balch to speak, as well as Samuel Gompers.[84]

While the WEIU considered Kenney O'Sullivan's group "a kindred society" worthy of free meeting space, their initial generosity had its limitations.[85] As she later remembered:

> The directors of the WEIU were conservative. . . . They let us use their building, but the sign with gold letters of the Union for Industrial Progress must be put up at the back door on Providence Street and all literature intended for the mills and factories must have the Providence Street address. That [back] door must also be our entrance.[86]

While such class bias was frustrating, Kenney O'Sullivan did not give up. Nor, in remembering the incident years later, was she bitter. Making reference to the nickname of her home state, Kenney O'Sullivan wrote that "though, I was the only one born in Missouri, they [the WEIU directors] had to be shown."[87]

And show them she did. Over the next several months, Kenney O'Sullivan arranged to have several prominent, middle-class social reformers speak at the WEIU "with a message for a hope of a better world." She personally advertised the meetings by handing out flyers outside various workplaces in the area. Thus, as she later wrote, "in less than a year the front entrance on Boylston Street was opened to us. . . . The Women's Educational and Industrial Union had grown and we workers had grown, too."[88]

By the time the front door of the WEIU was opened, the Women's Industrial Education Association had changed its name to Union for Industrial Progress."[89] The choice of the word "union" was significant. Throughout the 1890s, Kenney O'Sullivan would use the Union for Industrial Progress (UIP) as a vehicle for the union organization of women, about which the reform-minded WEIU, with its emphasis on education not organization, continued to be ambivalent. They had equally mixed feelings about asking Mary Kenney O'Sullivan to join the WEIU Board of Directors.

The heated discussion over inviting Kenney O'Sullivan to become a board member reveals the frequent tension that most cross-class alliances experienced.[90] On February 5, 1895 the WEIU Board of Directors recording secretary took the following minutes:

> The wisdom of inviting Mrs. Kenney O'Sullivan to become a member
> of this Board was again discussed at considerable length, she seeming
> on many accounts a very desirable member as a connecting link with
> the wage earning women of our community who we wish to draw to
> the [WEI] Union.

WEIU president Mary Morton Kehew probably sponsored the addition of her friend Kenney O'Sullivan to the Board. Despite Kehew's influence, there was still disagreement. The February 5th meeting was not the first time the Board had debated the advisability of inviting this working-class woman to join them, as at least some of them "feared that she [Kenney O'Sullivan] might represent to the community the **element of violence or extreme radicalism** with which we should not willingly or wisely ally ourselves."[91]

Mary Kenney O'Sullivan had never engaged in any acts of violence. Nor did she represent a radical faction of the labor community. She consistently supported the conservative AFL and its local affiliate, the BCLU, which had done its best during the previous year to disassociate itself from any of the depression-related worker violence or radical politics. Ironically, the WEIU's concerns about what Kenney O'Sullivan might represent were based upon her association with the male-dominated trade union movement, a movement which had never wholeheartedly welcomed her. Moreover, what "community" were the middle- and upper-class WEIU Board members worried about? They seemed not to be concerned about those women they sought to serve. The working-class women of Boston would very likely be pleased to see one of their own, so to speak, on the WEIU Board.

The WEIU recognized the credibility that Kenney O'Sullivan's appointment would bring to the organization as it attempted to attract working-class women to its reading rooms, employment bureau, and lunchroom. But some Board members resisted the efforts of President Kehew to actively involve working-class women in the programs offered by the WEIU. Sharing power is never easy, nor was it the intent of most of the middle- and upper-class women who organized and led cross-class alliances.[92] However, after further and, unfortunately, unrecorded discussion, "it was finally voted to invite Mrs. O'Sullivan to become a member of the Board." Although she served on the WEIU Board for only two years, Kenney O'Sullivan maintained her association with that organization for several more years as she continued to organize the working women of Boston.

Kenney O'Sullivan was hardly alone in her efforts to organize working women. Nor was she the only organizer to make the most of what trade unionists and the reform-minded wealthy could do when they joined forces. Mary Nason, a Haverhill shoeworker and head of the stitchers' union, used such a combination in assisting striking women shoe workers in early 1895. Possibly through introductions provided by Kenney O'Sullivan, Nason was able to bring her cause into the meeting halls and parlors of Boston's elite, raising funds and support for the strike.[93] Nason also appeared at a bi-weekly meeting of the BCLU on January 20, 1895. Noting that the Haverhill shoe workers were "engaged in a **manly** contest against the unjust methods of their employers," the BCLU recording secretary went on to "commend those **heroines**, the working women of Haverhill, who are foremost in resisting injustice."[94] Nason was sent home with those ringing words and $47 for the strike fund.

In the eyes of organized labor, women who engaged in strike activities both entered into a man's world and ennobled themselves in the process. Trade unionism itself could give both working men and women qualities generally associated with the middle class. Speaking before Boston's Massachusetts Reform Club in early March, 1895, Samuel Gompers told his middle-class audience that "[t]he organized labor movement is the natural heir of all the struggles of by-gone ages—for justice and humanity; for a nobler manhood and a more beautiful womanhood."[95] Speaking to reformers, Gompers painted a picture of labor's struggle as a historic effort carried out by noble men and beautiful women. For Kenney O'Sullivan, trade unions for women remained a simple necessity. This was soon underscored by the strike of the Hyde Park rubber workers during the spring of 1895.

On March 23rd, 200 women and almost 100 men walked out of the Boston Gossamer Rubber Company, protesting a severe forty percent wage cut.[96] The factory, located in the Boston neighborhood of Hyde Park, was experiencing no decline in production of rubberized apparel. Thus, "the news was a disagreeable surprise to the employees," who immediately sent a committee to speak with the factory manager and owner's son, Henry Klous.[97] Klous said only that the reduction in wages would bring the workers more in line with those working in other, similar concerns and refused to discuss the matter any further. Hearing that, the workers walked out, including those who had other grievances, such as the policy of forcing sewers to pay for their own needles and thread. Within a few days, only about 100 of the factory's 500 workers remained on the job.[98]

Kenney O'Sullivan read about the strike in a Boston newspaper and, as she later wrote, "went to Hyde Park to see if I could be of any use to them."[99] In short order, she organized the workers into a union and assisted in the formation of a strike committee of five women from the factory who, as representatives of the majority of the strikers, visited several other unions in the city. The BCLU voted to assist the strikers financially and a week later admitted a delegate from the rubber workers' union.[100] The residents at Denison House, many of whom were members of Federal Labor Union No. 5915, also followed the Hyde Park strike. The Denison House daybook entry for April 13, 1895 noted:

> Strike on for two weeks . . . Women who could by piece-work earn
> ten dollars each week now get but $6.50. The women, in addition, have
> to buy their own thread and needles . . . He[factory owner] refuses to

submit the prices to state board arbitration and does not deny his violation of fifty-eight hour law . . . Almost all women in both rooms now out . . . Mrs. O'Sullivan chairman of all meetings. Strikers are excellent women. Very intelligent—but little money to carry on the fight.[101]

On April 11th, Bernard G. Supple of the State Board of Arbitration met with the strike committee. The strikers told Supple that the company owner was "not willing to concede anything. Organizers for labor unions had come from Boston and called upon him when the strike began and suggested a reference to the State Board [of Arbitration], but he was not willing to defer the dispute."[102] According to the *Labor Leader*, the unwillingness of the Klous family to speak with either the strikers or the State Board of Arbitration proved that the company was "not sure of the justice of its position" regarding its workers. But editor Foster warned: "[o]rganized labor can make the company sorry for its course."[103] They would do so, in large part, by trying to activate the existing state mechanisms to address labor disputes.

A week later, the Hyde Park strike committee reported to the BCLU that there had been no progress. The following day, John O'Sullivan appealed to the State Board of Arbitration for mediation. At the first meeting, on April 24th, while the Board easily located the strikers, finding the factory owner or superintendent proved much more difficult. Finally, the owner's son, Henry Klous, called to say "that there was nothing to arbitrate, and that, having had one talk with their employees since the strike, they had no desire for another."[104] Despite state policy regarding the resolution of labor disputes as embodied in the voluntary workings of the State Board of Arbitration, the power of the state seemed no match for the power of capital. Nor could the state even enforce the Fifty-eight Hour law.[105] As Frank Foster later commented, "The cause of the Hyde Park strikers was just, but Klous appears to have the heaviest artillery."[106]

Regardless of its ineffectiveness, the state commission continued its efforts at mediation, holding a series of meetings as the strike continued into May. Jack and Mary Kenney O'Sullivan usually accompanied the strikers, who, according to the labor press, "were making a splendid fight for victory."[107] According to Kenney O'Sullivan, the strikers said that "their courage was better when I was with them. So I went with them day and night."[108] Such a commitment was crucial but exhausting for Kenney O'Sullivan as she was now six months pregnant with her first child. Still, Kenney O'Sullivan continued to attend all strike meetings, including an

outdoor meeting in Hyde Park at which her old Chicago friend Ellen
Gates Starr spoke.[109]

Kenney O'Sullivan called upon her WEIU associates to assist in the
Hyde Park rubber workers' strike. On May 20th, the WEIU meeting
room, Perkins Hall, was the site of a public meeting at which two women
strikers spoke. Kenney O'Sullivan also spoke, as did South End Settlement House founder Robert Woods, and Jack O'Sullivan "asked questions."[110] In June, Kenney O'Sullivan approached Mary Morton Kehew
about holding a mass meeting at Fanueil Hall. Perhaps because the strike
had dragged on for more than two months, Kehew was not immediately
sure that a mass meeting was "the right thing to do."[111] But, putting more
trust in her working-class friend than many of her WEIU associates
might have, Kehew soon told Kenney O'Sullivan to make the necessary
arrangements and to send her the bill. Kenney O'Sullivan later remembered the meeting as "a roaring success" and that "the strike was soon
settled, thanks to Mrs. Kehew's faith." However, other reports of the
strike differ from that happy ending.

Despite Kehew's somewhat qualified faith and timely financial assistance, as well as support from the settlement house community and
the contributions of various unions from the Boston area, the rubber
workers' strike fizzled out by the end of June. The demands of the
women workers remained unmet.[112] The State Board of Arbitration had
failed to mediate a settlement, primarily because the company repeatedly
refused to take part in any meetings, public or private, with the strikers.
The only response from the owner had been to hire strikebreakers and
open another factory, elsewhere in Boston.[113] The lingering economic
depression, a totally recalcitrant owner, and the limits of the state commission's power to arbitrate combined to defeat the Hyde Park rubber
workers' strike.

On June 22nd, the BCLU newspaper the *Labor Leader* editorialized
that "[t]he Hyde Park strike is ended and the old and obvious moral is
that the time to strike is after, not before, organizing. No pluckier lot of
girls, however, ever resisted oppression."[114] Was Mary Kenney O'Sullivan being chided for her organizational tactics? Perhaps. But, given the
gender dynamics of trade unionism in this period, when women workers
were routinely referred to as girls, even if "plucky," and unions refused to
organize them, Kenney O'Sullivan did what she could, when she could.
She repeatedly found that the organization of women was more likely to
be achieved in that moment when the workers themselves had finally decided to strike, thus drawing the attention of organizers such as herself

and the support of the labor and social reform communities.[115] Such had been the case in the garment workers strike during August, 1894. That strike, unlike that of the rubber workers a few months later, had been a successful one. In its wake, the women's local continued to function. Yet conflicts between the men and women garment workers were not resolved through the organization of the women in the trade.

During the rubber workers' strike, the AFL's second national vice-president, James Duncan, visited Boston. Duncan was in town, not for the rubber workers, but to assess the on-going New England-wide strike of male granite cutters, for whose union he served as general secretary. Nonetheless, Duncan said a few words regarding "the necessity of organization among women wage workers and complimented the BCLU for its work in that direction."[116] Despite official AFL policy, which recognized the necessity of organization for women workers, the continued complaints of women garment makers regarding their relationship with their male co-trade unionists illustrated the limits of that policy.

In January, 1895, Jack O'Sullivan and Harry Lloyd had met at Denison House with some of the women from Local No.37 to discuss "their treatment from the men of the union."[117] Although Lloyd promised to report the matter to the BCLU, nothing seemed to come of the women's complaint, which remained unspecified. On March 18th, at their regular meeting, the women of Local No. 37 again complained, this time claiming that a member of the male pressmen's local No. 25 had verbally insulted the woman president of Local No. 37.[118] Again, nothing more was said or done regarding the alleged ill-treatment of the women garment makers by their trade union brothers. At work, away from familial protection, harassment of women on the shop floor was hardly uncommon. Nor should we see such harassment as simple lechery; it was an expression of male power. As historian Kathy Peiss has pointed out, "Then, as now, sexual harassment limited women's position in the workforce and maintained male privilege and control."[119] It often spilled over into the union hall, with the same result.

As already noted, women garment workers on strike in the fall of 1894 had publicly charged their male counterparts with attempting to block the organization of women in the trade. In response, Mary Kenney O'Sullivan, with the help of Denison House head resident Helena Dudley, had formed an all women's local, No. 37, in response.[120] The local had survived the strike intact and had grown to over 800 members a year later. Despite continued verbal bickering, which probably occurred at the periodic meetings of all Boston garment locals, the women's local entered the brief strike of 1895 as a strong and unified force.

On August 21, 1895, both male and female garment workers agreed to strike over wages as well as a nine-hour day.[121] Kenney O'Sullivan, however, "was bitterly disappointed" at the timing of the strike. Any day, she "expected to go to the hospital for the birth of [her] first child."[122] The birth of a son, however, did not keep Mary Kenney O'Sullivan out of the fight for long. "Committee after [strike] committee came to the hospital" and all were referred to the attending physician, who acted as an intermediary between the strikers and the new mother. The constant coming-and-going of the strikers caused a fair amount of commotion within the hospital. In an era when women labor leaders were few in number, even more rare was it that a woman who had just given birth would lead a strike from her hospital bed. Yet Kenney O'Sullivan saw herself as needed and the strikers agreed, flocking to the hospital. As she would later write in her autobiography, "One day she[the doctor] said, 'Mrs. O'Sullivan, since you came here I've had more worry on your account than from the entire hospital, and I don't know who I'm hurting most, the strike or you.'"[123]

Despite the doctor's concerns, Kenney O'Sullivan quickly recovered and just as quickly, the strike was over. After only three days, the workers' demands were all met.[124] The strength of the garment workers' union, including women's Local No. 37, played a large part in forcing the 120 clothing manufacturers of Boston to accept the demands of their 4000 or so union workers, forty percent of whom were women.[125]

Towards the end of the strike, the *Globe* reported,

> Every attempt to criticize either sex is promptly resented by the other, and while the men are not invited to attend the women's gatherings, yet when they do present themselves on a mission relating to the affairs of the organization, or to bring in the news of another victory, they are treated with a dignified courtesy.[126]

Apparently, there was still much tension between the men and women's locals. Not surprisingly given the past abuse, the women's meetings were closed to the male strikers. Yet the women were able to rise above the pattern of male harassment, treating the male strikers with "dignified courtesy" when necessary. The need for unity explains the women's willingness to be civil despite the strained relations. This unity, however, was not to last.

On May 3, 1896, a letter from the women of Local No. 37 was read into the official record of the BCLU. The women garment makers charged that they had been treated in an "unjust manner . . . by the delegates of [United Garment Workers of America] District Council No.2 from Local Unions No. 1 [tailors] and 25 [pressmen]." Local No. 37 appealed to the BCLU in the hopes that "some steps could be taken to secure to us the rights that properley[sic] belong to us." The letter went on to say:

> Because of insulting and abusive treatment our delegates have refused to attend any more of the meetings of District Council No. 2. We are called insulting names and the worst kind of language is used towards our delegates. We believe than an attempt is made to break up the womens [sic] union, and to deprive us of the means of earning our living in the clothing trade.[127]

Much as we might like to, we will never know just what those insulting names were. Presumably they were so offensive that the women were unable to print them. But, more important, the women of Local No. 37 were not complaining about anything new. As unspecific as the charges may have been, we do know that the women garment makers had been harassed at union meetings since at least January, 1895. Even before they organized, the women had been made to feel unwelcome in the trade, much less in the union. Now, rather than rely on supposedly supportive male trade unionists, such as Jack O'Sullivan and Harry Lloyd, to relay their concerns to the BCLU, the women spoke for themselves, forcing a discussion.

After first debating whether or not this was an internal union problem, and thus outside the realm of a Central Labor Union, the BCLU decided that they could intercede. A special committee of three was appointed to investigate and report at the next regular meeting. However, no record later appears of that committee's report.[128] The minutes for May 3rd did not include any specific reference to the previous complaints lodged by the women or any comments regarding the men's position, much less any clarification of the letter being discussed. However, the minutes do state that "[d]uring the discussion, it was intimated that this was a movement to prevent Christians from being in the trade."[129]

A lack of extant union membership lists for the Boston men's Locals No. 1 and 25 prevents a full assessment of this apparently anti-Semitic remark. However, when the women's Local No. 37 presented their credentials to the BCLU in 1895, those few names listed appear (with one exception) to be English or Irish surnames, thus presumably "Christian."[130] It may have been easier for the BCLU delegates to regard conflict between two locals of the same trade in terms of religious or even ethnic conflict rather than harassment of women. In spite of their frequent public pronouncements supporting the organization of women, the BCLU turned any discussion away from gender conflict to religious differences as a way of maintaining their progressive image regarding women. The "insulting names" were not recorded. Thus whether this was indeed a religious, ethnic, or gender dispute remains unclear. What is certain is that a women's local was under attack by a men's local in the same trade.

Mary Kenney O'Sullivan's role in all this is also unclear. She sought to organize women to improve their conditions of labor, not to subject them to harassment from their fellow trade unionists. Kenney O'Sullivan must have been aware of the charges against the male garment workers. She knew the women involved and it was her husband the women had first turned to a year and a half earlier. Although there is no record of her response, one can imagine her indignation as well as her frustration with yet another example of the limitations she and all women faced within organized labor.

Nonetheless, she remained active both within the BCLU and the WEIU, serving on various committees for both organizations. It seemed that neither the WEIU or the BCLU could fully meet the needs of working-class women, especially the need for organization. Kenney O'Sullivan learned that lesson time and time again during the 1890s. Even that seemingly endless source of support, Denison House, gradually turned away from labor organizing after 1897. One historian of the settlement claims that this was due to a fear of lost contributions. I would argue that the new-found discretion of Denison House residents was more related to the change in ethnicity in the neighborhood as the Irish American population was increasingly replaced by Italians, Syrians, and Armenians. Formerly well-meaning reformers became less inclined to support the labor activities of the "newer races," who showed the potential and/or had a history of radicalism.[131] Kenney O'Sullivan, however, continued to do so, even as her family grew and despite her great personal losses as the century came to a close.

In 1897, the O'Sullivans' first child, a son named John Kenney, died of diphtheria before his second birthday. The death of Kenney O'Sullivan's mother and a fire which destroyed their first home, on Boston's Carver Street, also occurred around the same time.[132] Yet, within a year, the first of three more children was born even as Kenney O'Sullivan and her husband continued to be actively engaged in organizing. Before the fire, their home on Carver Street had been a meeting place for trade unionists and reformers alike. According to Kenney O'Sullivan, "Our Carver Street home was like the cradle of a newborn movement."[133] The Welsh Socialist and Parliament member Keir Hardie stayed with the O'Sullivans when he came to town. Boston settlement house leader Robert Woods was a frequent dinner guest who was especially fond of Kenney O'Sullivan's mashed potatoes.[134]

Kenney O'Sullivan shared this busy life with her husband, Jack, who fully supported his wife's involvement in the labor cause. More important perhaps, Jack agreed to share the household duties with his wife who was frequently out at meetings.[135] Yet even this rather exceptional man had his limits. During the 1898–1899 shoeworkers strike in Marlboro, Massachusetts, O'Sullivan objected to his once-again pregnant wife's plan to attend a strike meeting in the midst of a New England blizzard. Much like during the garment workers' strike of 1895, Kenney O'Sullivan, however, felt her involvement was critical to the strike, regardless of her condition or the weather. The train from Boston could only travel as far as Framingham and she was forced to go the last several miles in an open sleigh. As she later recalled, "In that storm my hat was a negligible quantity." But her presence was all that mattered, as it "worked up great enthusiasm. Later a settlement was made and living conditions were kept from going below the margin of subsistence."[136]

Even with the support of her husband, balancing the needs of her young family with her career as labor organizer must have been difficult. Unlike her middle- and upper-class allies, Kenney O'Sullivan could not afford the hired help that would free her from domestic duties. Sometimes these family chores threatened to take precedence over her work, which ironically included an active role in the formation of the WEIU's Domestic Reform Committee. Founded in 1896, the Domestic Reform Committee sought to "increase the supply of workers in domestic service by suggesting housework to the industrial wage-earner who is commonly conceded to be in an over-crowded occupation."[137] The "domestic problem," that is, the seemingly constant shortage of competent servants, was of great concern to the middle- and upper-class women who ran the WEIU and depended on the labor of others to free them from their household responsibilities.[138] As a member of the Domestic Reform Committee, Kenney O'Sullivan was a critical link to the industrial workers the committee wanted to convert into servants. At the same time, as a working-class woman with young children and a constant stream of guests, she could well understand the drudgery of housework. Apparently, Kenney O'Sullivan never suggested the unionization of domestic workers, but perhaps some employers were educated about the unappealing aspects of domestic work. Her membership on the committee also brought Kenney O'Sullivan into contact with the wealthy social reformer, Elizabeth Glendower Evans, who soon became her closest, lifelong friend.

Born in 1856 in New Rochelle, New York, Glendower Evans was connected, by blood and marriage, to several prominent Boston families. When Glendower Evans' father died in 1859, her mother moved the young family into the Boston home of her father-in-law, William Howard Gardiner. There, Glendower Evans grew up, attending the best private schools with her wealthy cousins, yet often feeling like a poor relation.[139] Despite the fact that at the age of twenty-six she inherited a sizable fortune from her grandfather, Glendower Evans retained a sensitivity to issues of class and the power of money the rest of her life. Although she never formally attended college, Glendower Evans was nonetheless in the cohort of that first generation of women college graduates who, denied access to most occupations, turned instead to social reform.

An extraordinary woman and the quintessential Progressive, Glendower Evans devoted her life and her considerable fortune to numerous social reform movements after her young husband suddenly died in 1886.[140] As a State Reform school trustee, she was a leading advocate for the case-work approach and vocational training for juveniles in need.[141] During the 1890s, Glendower Evans had become an active member of the Women's Educational and Industrial Union in Boston as well as the Massachusetts Consumers League. She was also a woman with important connections, willing to introduce her friend to those who could help Kenney O'Sullivan in her work. Furthermore, Glendower Evans was willing in even more concrete ways to make sure that Kenney O'Sullivan could meet those people.

One evening in the late 1890s, Glendower Evans arrived in her carriage to take the O'Sullivans to dinner at the home of her good friends, Louis and Alice Brandeis. But Kenney O'Sullivan still had much ironing to do and felt they should decline the invitation. Glendower Evans insisted on helping with the ironing. As Kenney O'Sullivan later remembered, "Here was a new experience in my life. A woman of wealth did my ironing!"[142] Women of wealth and power such as Glendower Evans proved useful to working-class organizers such as Kenney O'Sullivan in several ways. Their financial contributions were often the key ingredient needed to keep a strike going.[143] Their social connections were just as useful. Brandeis' dinner conversations with labor leaders such as the O'Sullivans were part of his transformation to activist attorney.[144]

Glendower Evans' connections were of use in tragic times as well. In September, 1902, Jack O'Sullivan stepped off the wrong side of a streetcar in Lynn and was instantly killed. He was survived by his wife of eight years and three children ranging in age from four years to seven months.[145] Kenney O'Sullivan must have been paralyzed with shock but was fortunately surrounded by caring friends. The crowd at the funeral was so large that a stranger passing by asked who it was that had died. One of the mourners replied, "He was a big and great man."[146] The day after the funeral, one of Glendower Evans' wealthy and well-meaning cousins offered Mary Kenney O'Sullivan a job. Philip Cabot, treasurer of the Lawrence Minot Real Estate Company, hired her as an agent for rental properties in Roxbury.[147] There was an outpouring of support from the organized labor community as well. Meeting shortly after his death, the Massachusetts State Branch of the AFL ended their 1902 convention with a half hour culogy for Jack O'Sullivan, "paying high tribute to his energy, generosity and self-sacrificing spirit."[148] Those present were urged to contribute to a memorial fund, and a year later Kenney O'Sulli-van was presented with $5200. The generosity of the AFL allowed the widow to eventually purchase an old farmhouse in West Medford, just outside of Boston. There she raised her children but was still faced with the realities of working-class widowhood.

As the mother of three children under the age of four, Kenney O'Sullivan was once again the sole support of dependents. She supple-mented her work as realty agent with writing assignments for the *Boston Globe*. Despite the terrible loss of her husband's financial and emotional support, Kenney O'Sullivan carried on as a labor organizer. Unlike many working-class women, she was part of two dynamic communities, both of which could be at times very supportive. During the 1890s, Kenney O'Sullivan had helped to organize women rubber workers and book-binders, laundry workers and shoe workers, achieving the best results within the immediate Boston area where her connections to the women's reform and organized labor communities were strongest. It was no coin-cidence that most of her organizing was done outside the single industry towns and cities of Massachusetts. In the Commonwealth, those indus-tries made textiles and shoes and their economic and political power re-mained formidable well into the twentieth century.[149]

Still, in the small shops and factories of Boston, Kenney O'Sullivan sought to gain for women workers that which she herself sought as a bookbinder—conditions and wages which meant not just survival but re-spectability. The continued ambivalence of the male trade union commu-nity and the limitations of the women's social reform community would frustrate her efforts throughout the 1890s. That frustration was due, in part, to her position as perpetual outsider in those two communities. In 1903, when Kenney O'Sullivan joined fellow trade unionists and social reformers in the founding of the Women's Trade Union League, she sought to shape an organization which would rise above the divisive gender and class conflicts she constantly faced. She also attempted to create an organization in which she would be a powerful insider from the very beginning.

NOTES

[1]Alexander Keyssar, *Out of Work: The First Century of Unemployment in Massachusetts* (New York: Cambridge University Press, 1986), pp. 50–52.

[2]*Labor Leader*, Dec. 30, 1893–Mar. 10, 1894; see also: Arthur Mann, *Yankee Reformers in the Urban Age* (Cambridge: Belknap Press, 1954), p. 194; Geoffrey Blodgett, *The Gentle Reformers: Massachusetts Democrats in the Cleveland Era* (Cambridge: Harvard University Press, 1966), pp. 161–162. The *Labor Leader* was the official weekly newspaper of the Massachusetts State Branch of the AFL, the Maine Federation of Labor, the Web Weavers Union, and the Shoeworkers International Association.

[3]Helena Stuart Dudley, Twentieth-fifth Reunion statement, c. 1914, Bryn Mawr College Archives, p. 1. Also quoted in Susan Traverso, " 'The Road Going Down to Jericho': The Early History of Denison House, 1887–1912," (BA honors thesis, Simmons College, 1983), p. 39.

[4]*Labor Leader*, Feb. 24, 1894; *Boston Globe*, Feb. 21, 1894; see also: Mann, *Yankee Reformers*, p. 194 & Blodgett, *Gentle Reformers*, p. 164.

[5]*Labor Leader*, Mar. 24, 1894; the rally was covered by the Boston *Globe* on Mar. 21, 1894. According to Keyssar, in *Out of Work*, while Swift's demands would go long unmet, his "rallies in 1894 spurred the labor movement into action." p. 248.

[6]Mann, *Yankee Reformers*, p. 194; also quoted in James R. Green and Hugh Carter Donahue, *Boston's Workers: A Labor History* (Boston: Trustees of the Public Library of the City of Boston, 1979), p. 75.

[7]Dudley, Reunion statement, p. 1; see also Traverso, " 'The Road Going Down to Jericho'," p. 40; Blodgett, *Gentle Reformers*, p. 163.

[8]Mary Kenney O'Sullivan Autobiography, Schlesinger Library, Radcliffe College; hereafter: Kenney O'Sullivan, autobio., pp. 87–88.

[9]College Settlement Association, Second Annual Report (1892), p. 7, the College Settlement Association papers, Sophia Smith Collection, Smith College, Northampton, Mass. On the CSA, see John P. Rousmaniere, "Cultural Hybrid in

the Slums: The College Woman and the Settlement House, 1889–1894," *American Quarterly* 22 (Spring 1970): pp. 45–66; according to Rousmaniere, "Three-fifths of all settlement house residents between 1889 and 1914 were women and, of these, almost nine-tenths had been to college." p. 46.

[10]On Scudder, see: Sister Catherine Theresa Corcoran, *Vida Dutton Scudder: The Progressive Years* (Ann Arbor: UMI, 1974); on Scudder and her cohort, Hull House co-founder Ellen Gates Starr, see: Elizabeth P.H. Carrell, *Reflections in a Mirror: The Progressive Woman and the Settlement Experience* (Ph.D diss, UMI edition, 1981); Peter J. Frederick, "Vida Dutton Scudder: The Professor as Social Activist," *New England Quarterly* 43 (Sept. 1970): pp. 407–433, examines the theoretical influences on Scudder, especially those of John Ruskin yet makes no mention of her role in the formation of the CSA, of Denison House or of Scudder's later involvement in the WTUL; in *Yankee Reformers in the Urban Age*, Arthur Mann discusses Scudder at some length (pp. 217–226), citing her as an example of "this newer kind of emancipated woman." (p. 217). See also: Mina Carson, *Settlement Folk: Social Thought and the American Settlement Movement, 1885–1930* (Chicago: University of Chicago Press, 1990) and Allen F. Davis, *Spearheads for Reform: The Social Settlements and the Progressive Movement, 1890–1914* (New York: Oxford University Press, 1967), both passim. See also: Scudder's autobiography, *On Journey* (New York: E.P. Dutton, 1937) and her semi-autobiographical novel, *A Listener in Babel* (Boston: Houghton, Mifflin & Co., 1903). Scudder's papers, though sparse, are held by the Sophia Smith Collection, Smith College, the Wellesley College Archives, and Companions of the Holy Cross Archives, So. Byfield, Mass.

[11]Patricia A. Palmieri, "Here Was Fellowship: A Social Portrait of Academic Women at Wellesley College, 1895–1920," *History of Education Quarterly* 23 (Summer 1983): p. 206; see also: Florence Converse, *The Story of Wellesley College* (Boston: Little, Brown & Co., 1915), pp. 190–193.

[12]Vida D. Scudder, "The Relation of College Women to Need," a paper presented to the Association of Collegiate Alumnae, Oct. 24, 1890, p. 4, copy in the Vida Dutton Scudder papers, Sophia Smith Collection. Scudder's colleague at Wellesley, Katherine Coman, a professor of History and Political Economy, and an early and active participant in the CSA, agreed. Coman claimed that "To fit women for active service. . . . this is the end and aim of preparation for citizenship at Wellesley College." See Coman, "Preparation for Citizenship at Wellesley College," *Education* 10 (Feb. 1890): pp. 341–347, quote p. 347.

[13]Regarding "social housekeeping," see: Cameron, *Radicals of the Worst Sort*, p. 69; Paula Baker, "The Domestication of Politics: Women and American Political Society, 1780–1920," *American Historical Review* 89 (June 1984): pp. 620–647; Barbara Epstein, *The Politics of Domesticity: Women, Evangelism,*

and Temperance in Nineteenth-Century America (Middletown, Conn.: Wesleyan University Press, 1981. Vida Scudder's former student and lifelong companion, Florence Converse, emphasized the impact college women could have on society as a whole through the social settlement: "They have exerted an influence upon social thought and conscience exceeded, in this period, by few other agencies. . . ." *The Story of Wellesley College* (Boston: Little, Brown & Co., 1915), p. 193. In a period when women had little influence of any kind, especially in the political or economic realms, acting as social housekeepers could be an opening wedge—for middle- and upper-class women. Such is Kathryn Kish Sklar's argument, as pointed out in Chap. 1. For Sklar's discussion of the potential benefits of settlement life for its non-working-class residents, see *Florence Kelley and the Nation's Work*, Chap. 8. For a balanced and succinct account of the Progressive era, see Eileen L. McDonagh, "The 'Welfare Rights State' and the 'Civil Rights State': Policy Paradox and State Building in the Progressive Era," *Studies in American Political Development* 7 (Fall 1993): pp. 225–274. Rather than emphasize the gains made by some, McDonagh sees "a disjunctive pattern characterized by support for positive welfare rights on the one hand and negative civil rights on the other, " p. 229. My thanks to Pat Reeve for pointing this article out to me.

[14]Barbara Miller Solomon, *In the Company of Educated Women: A History of Women in Higher Education in America* (New Haven: Yale University Press, 1985), p. 109; see also Helen Lefkowitz Horowitz, *Alma Mater: Design and Experience in the Women's Colleges from Their Nineteenth-Century Beginnings to the 1930s* 2nd edition (Amherst: University of Massachusetts Press, 1993), Chap. 9.

[15]Helena S. Dudley, "Women's Work in Boston Settlements," *Municipal Affairs* 2 (1898): p. 495.

[16]Traverso, " 'The Road Going Down to Jericho'," pp. 33–34.

[17]Dudley, Reunion statement, p. 1. On the Irish in Boston around the end of the century, see: Thomas H. O'Connor, *The Boston Irish: A Political History* (Boston: Northeastern University Press, 1995), esp. chaps. 5–6; O'Connor, somewhat surprisingly, does not discuss the Irish dominance of Boston's trade union community; in *Beyond the Ballot Box: A Social History of the Boston Irish, 1845–1917* (Amherst: University Of Massachusetts Press, 1989), Dennis P. Ryan does refer briefly to the BCLU as an "Irish-led organization," p. 142; James R. Green and Hugh Carter Donahue put forward an interesting argument in chap. 5 of their *Boston's Workers: A History*, paralleling the rise of the Irish ward boss with the emergence of the Irish union business agent. According to John F. Stack, Jr., *International Conflict in an American City: Boston's Irish, Italians, and Jews, 1935–1944* (Westport, CT: Greenwood Press, 1979), the Irish continued to

dominate Boston trade unions well into the twentieth century (p. 29). Nor was Irish domination limited to Boston. See Warren R. Van Tine, *The Making of the Labor Bureaucrat: Union Leadership in the United States, 1870–1920* (Amherst: University of Massachusetts Press, 1973), p. 9.

[18]College Settlement Association, Fourth Annual Report (1894), p. 41. In 1898, using 1895 census figures and personal observation, South End settlement house worker Frederick A. Bushee noted that "[T]he Irish. . . . will not long maintain their familiar predominance in the South End," p. 57 in his chapter "Population," pp. 33–57 in *The City Wilderness: A Settlement Study by the Residents and Associates of the South End House* Robert A. Woods, ed. (New York: Garrett Press, 1970, orig. pub 1898).

[19]Balch, another daughter of an old and prominent Boston family, graduated from Bryn Mawr College in 1889. One of the founders of the CSA, she served as the temporary head resident when Denison House first opened until her classmate Helena Dudley could relieve her. Balch did graduate work at the Universities of Chicago and Berlin before joining the Wellesley economics department in 1896 where she went on to become a specialist in Slavic studies. She served on innumerable state commissions and was active in the Boston Women's Trade Union League. However, it is for her work as a peace activist for which she is remembered today and for which she was fired from Wellesley in 1919. A co-founder of the Women's International League for Peace and Freedom, Balch was the second American woman, after Jane Addams in 1931, to receive the Nobel Peace Prize in 1946. Most biographical sources concentrate on Balch's peace work. See: Harriet Hyman Alonso, "Nobel Peace Laureates, Jane Addams and Emily Greene Balch: Two Women of the Women's International League for Peace and Freedom," *Journal of Women's History* 7 (Summer 1995): pp. 6–26; Mercedes M. Randall, *Beyond Nationalism: The Social Thought of Emily Greene Balch* (New York: Twayne Publishers, 1972) and *Improper Bostonian: Emily Greene Balch* (New York: Twayne Publishers, 1964); Sam Bass Warner, Jr., "Emily Greene Balch," in *Province of Reason* (Cambridge: Harvard University Press, 1984), pp. 90–115, notes pp. 271–274. Balch's extensive papers are held by the Swarthmore College Peace Collection, Swarthmore, Pennsylvania.

[20]CSA, Fourth Annual Report (1894), p. 41, p. 43.

[21]The most recent and thorough discussion of the BCLU can be found in Stephen H. Norwood, *Labor's Flaming Youth: Telephone Operators and Worker Militancy, 1878–1923* (Urbana: University Of Illinois Press, 1990), esp. Chap. 3; see also: Green, *Boston's Workers*, Chap. 5; Mann, *Yankee Reformers*, Chap. 8. Discussion of other city-wide labor organizations include Dana Frank, *Purchasing Power: Consumer Organizing, Gender, and the Seattle Labor Movement, 1919–1929* (New York: Cambridge University Press, 1994) and Michael Kazin,

Barons of Labor: The San Francisco Building Trades and Union Power in the Progressive Era (Urbana: University of Illinois Press, 1987).

[22]The constitution of the Workingmen's Central Union [original name of the BCLU] as quoted in Ethel M. Johnson, "Labor Progress in Boston," in *Fifty Years of Boston* Elisabeth M. Herlihy, ed. (Boston: Tercentenary Committee, 1932), p. 217. The minutes of the BCLU are held by the Massachusetts Historical Society, Boston.

[23]In his article on the Boston labor scene in the 1880s, with a particular emphasis on the Knights of Labor, Jama Lazerow argues that the Knights and the BCLU were "ideologically similar" as late as 1886. However, within the year, leaders of the BCLU, such as Frank Foster and Jack O'Sullivan, both of whom started out as Knights, renounced that order and participated in the formation of the Massachusetts State Branch of the newly formed AFL. See Lazerow, " 'The Workingman's Hour': The 1886 Labor Uprising in Boston," *Labor History* 21 (1980): pp. 200–220, esp. pp.206– 208. Also on the Knights, see Leon Fink, *Workingmen's Democracy: The Knights of Labor and American Politics* (Urbana: University of Illinois Press, 1983); Susan Levine, *Labor's True Woman: Carpet Weavers, Industrialization, and Labor Reform in the Gilded Age* (Philadelphia: Temple University Press, 1984); Kim Voss, *The Making of American Exceptionalism: The Knights of Labor and Class Formation in the Nineteenth Century* (Ithaca: Cornell University Press, 1993).

[24]Bruce Laurie, *Workers into Artisans: Labor in Nineteenth-Century America* (New York: The Noonday Press, 1989), p. 176. For a discussion of the formation of the AFL from the standpoint of women, see: Foner, *Women and the American Labor Movement* (1979), Chap. 12; William E. Forbath, *Law and the Shaping of the American Labor Movement* (Cambridge: Harvard University Press, 1991) emphasizes the role that a conservative judiciary played in shaping the "voluntarism" of the early AFL.

[25]On the riot and its consequences, see: Paul Avrich, *The Haymarket Tragedy* (Princeton: Princeton University Press, 1984).

[26]Albert M. Heintz and John R. Whitney, *History of the Massachusetts State Federation of Labor, 1887–1935* (Boston: n.p., n.d.), p. 14. Although the Federation organized, in part, to seek favorable legislation, it also stressed "the need for united action in organizing new unions, and strengthening new ones." Heintz and Whitney, *History*, p. 16. Gary M. Fink, *Labor's Search for Political Order: The Political Behavior of the Missouri Labor Movement, 1890–1940* (Columbia: University Of Missouri Press, 1973) and Philip Taft, *Labor Politics American Style: The California State Federation of Labor* (Cambridge: Harvard University Press, 1968) both argue that it was in the political realm that state federations were most effective during this period.

[27]CSA, Fifth Annual Report (1894), p. 43.

[28]Meredith Tax, *The Rising of the Women: Feminist Solidarity and Class Conflict, 1880–1917* (New York: Monthly Review Press, 1980), pp. 54–55.

[29]CSA, Fourth Annual Report (1894), p. 44.

[30]CSA, Fourth Annual Report (1894), p. 44.

[31]Traverso, " 'The Road Going Down to Jericho'," p. 44.

[32]Jane Addams came to see a similar need for the cooperation between settlement house and trade unions, especially for women, at Hull House, crediting Mary Kenney for the " 'good and regular' " relations between the two. See: Jane Addams, "The Settlement as a Factor in the Labor Movement," in *Hull-House Maps and Papers* (New York: Arno Press, 1970, orig. pub. 1895), pp. 183–204, quote in Appendix, p. 214.

[33]Vida Dutton Scudder, *On Journey* (New York: E.P. Dutton & Co., 1937), p. 155. Scudder goes on to relate a visit, at her request, that O'Sullivan made to Wellesley around this time. Speaking there to some junior faculty, the veteran trade unionist attempted to organize them. According to Scudder, "My colleagues were outraged, and never wanted to hear that dangerous man again." (p. 156)

[34]John F. O'Sullivan to Samuel Gompers, May 24, 1894, AFL Correspondence, quoted in Philip S. Foner, *Women and the American Labor Movement: From Colonial Times to the Eve of World War I* (New York: The Free Press, 1979), p. 236.

[35]*Boston Globe*, May 27, 1894; Alice Kessler-Harris, *A Woman's Wage: Historical Meanings and Social Consequences* (Lexington: University of Kentucky Press, 1990), p. 9.

[36]O'Sullivan to Gompers, May 24, 1894. See also: the *Boston Globe*, May 27, 1894.

[37]*Boston Globe*, May 27, 1894, emphasis added. For a discussion of the "living wage" as a gendered concept, see: Kessler-Harris, *A Woman's Wage*, Chap. 1.

[38]*Boston Globe*, June 6, 1894; also quoted in Foner, *Women and the American Labor Movement* (1979), p. 237. See also: *Labor Leader*, June 9, 1894.

[39]In his recent survey, *Industrializing America*, Walter Licht states that economic developments, such as the depression of 1893, "played a role in the labor unrest of the late nineteenth century. But it was not a matter of material hardship per se. . . . It was critically a matter of economic security. The upheavals, however, were also about power, at a time of the rise of the corporation. . . ." Licht, *Industrializing America* (Baltimore: John Hopkins Press, 1995), p. 186. On the rise of the modern American corporation and its hegemonic qualities which came to redefine the relationship between industry and labor, see: Sarah Lyons Watts,

Order Against Chaos: Business Culture and Labor Ideology in America, 1880–1915 (Westport, CT: Greenwood Press, 1991). For Alexander Keyssar, *Out of Work: The First Century of Unemployment in Massachusetts* (New York: Cambridge University Press, 1986), it was "the era of uncertainty," p. 39.

[40]Nell Irvin Painter, *Standing at Armageddon, The United States, 1877–1919* (New York: W.W. Norton & Co., 1987), p. 116.

[41]For a general discussion of the connection between economic cycles and labor unrest see: Licht, *Industrializing America*, pp. 181–186; specifically on the Pullman strike, see: Stanley Buder, *Pullman: An Experiment in Industrial Order and Community Planning, 1880–1930* (New York: Oxford University Press, 1967), esp. Chap.4.

[42]Boston's garment industry never reached the level of output found in New York City and the histories of the garment trade reflect that. See: Joan Jensen and Sue Davidson, eds., *A Needle, A Bobbin, A Strike! Women Needleworkers in America* (Philadelphia: Temple University Press, 1984) and Carolyn Daniel Mc-Creesh, *Women in the Campaign to Organize Garment Workers, 1880–1917* (New York: Garland Press, 1985).

[43]Denison House daybooks, 1894–1897, Vol. 2, p. 117, Schlesinger Library, Radcliffe College, Cambridge, MA.

[44]Denison House Daybooks, Vol. 2, p. 133.

[45]Denison House daybooks, Vol. 2, p. 135. See also: the *Boston Globe*, Sept. 27, 1894.

[46]*Boston Globe*, Sept. 27, 1894.

[47]Kessler-Harris, *A Woman's Wage*, p. 21.

[48]*Boston Globe*, Sept. 28 & 29, 1894.

[49]CSA Sixth Annual Report (1895), p. 37.

[50]*Boston Globe*, Aug. 13, 1894. The conflict began when a crew of Irish laborers refused to work on a Sunday unless they received an extra fifty cents for that day's labor. The company responded by bringing in a crew of Italian workers and fighting between the two groups broke out. Such conflicts were all too familiar in Boston and other major cities where the "newer" immigrants were frequently used as strikebreakers by employers who played off the antagonism between the "older" immigrants, i.e., the Irish who in many cases were union members, and more recent arrivals such as Italians who were not welcome in the Irish-run locals. According to Dennis P. Ryan, in *Beyond the Ballot Box*, not until 1904 did Italians in Boston organize their own Laborers' Union which remained unaffiliated with the BCLU for several more years. (p. 142) For a discussion of similar conflict in another American city, see: Richard Jules Oestreicher, *Solidarity and Fragmentation: Working People and Class Consciousness in Detroit, 1875–1900* (Urbana: University of Illinois Press, 1986).

[51]*Boston Globe*, Aug. 20, 1894.

[52]Ryan, *Beyond the Ballot Box*, p. 142. See also: Edwin Fenton, "Immigrants and Unions, A Case Study: Italians and American Labor, 1870–1920" (Ph.D. diss., Harvard Univ., 1957), pp. 142–145. According to Fenton, not until 1903 did serious efforts to organize Italian laborers begin in Boston; see: pp. 219–231.

[53]For a report of the parade, see: *Boston Globe*, Sept. 4, 1894.

[54]After the July 4, 1895 anti-Catholic riot, sparked by a parade organized by the American Protective Association, in which one man died, Foster editorialized that the riot was evidence of "the existence of an element dangerous above most else to the solidarity of the labor movement, i.e., race and religious prejudice." *Labor Leader*, July 13, 1895. On the A.P.A. riot, see: Blodgett, *The Gentle Reformers*, p. 151; O'Connor, *The Boston Irish*, pp. 154–156; and Barbara Miller Solomon, *Ancestors and Immigrants: A Changing New England Tradition* (Cambridge: Harvard University Press, 1956), p. 105.

[55]Frank Foster, *The Evolution of a Trade Unionist* (Boston: n.p., 1901), p. 77; also see: James R. Barrett, "Americanization from the Bottom Up: Immigration and the Remaking of the Working Class in the United States, 1880–1920," *Journal of America History* 79 (Dec. 1992): pp. 996– 1020; David R. Roediger, *Towards the Abolition of Whiteness: Essays on Race, Politics, and Working Class History* (New York: Verso, 1994), Chap. 11.

[56]Alice Kessler-Harris, "Organizing the Unorganizable: Three Jewish Women and Their Union," *Labor History* 17 (1976): pp. 5–23; in Vida Scudder's semi-autobiographical novel depicting a Boston settlement house in the 1890s, a resident asks "Do you think it is really wise to attempt to build up this laundry union out of all the different nationalities? If the girls were all of one race, it might be done. . . ." Scudder, *A Listener in Babel* (Boston: Houghton, Mifflin & Co., 1903), p. 97. Dolores Janiewski, "Southern Honor, Southern Dishonor: Managerial Ideology and the Construction of Gender, Race, and Class Relations in Southern Industry," in *Work Engendered: Toward a New History of American Labor* Ava Baron, ed. (Ithaca: Cornell University Press, 1991), pp. 70–91, succinctly illustrates how racial and gender categories were used to maintain class divisions.

[57]According to David Montgomery, in *The Fall of the House of Labor: The Workplace, The State, and American Labor Activism, 1865–1925* (New York: Cambridge University Press, 1989), p. 25: "The craftsmen's definition of who could live up to their code of 'manly' behavior was usually cast in ethnic and racial terms." See also: David R. Roediger, *The Wages of Whiteness: Race and the Making of the American Working Class* (New York: Verso Press, 1991), p. 179, who makes a similar point. A working man's identity as a "manly"

worker was hardly trivial. As John Tosh has argued, "[F]or the majority of men who wielded comparatively little social and economic power, loss of masculine self-respect was as much an occupational hazard as loss of income." See: Tosh, "What Should Historians do with Masculinity? Reflections on Nineteenth-century Britain," *History Workshop Journal* 38 (1994): p. 193. Thus, we should see the worker identity as one which is shaped by race, ethnicity, and gender, as well as by class and not necessarily simultaneously. See: Roediger, *Towards the Abolition of Whiteness:*, p. 76.

[58]David Montgomery, *The Fall of the House of Labor*, p. 167; Kessler-Harris, *A Woman's Wage*, p. 31.

[59]On the national scene, see: Laurie, *Artisans Into Workers*, pp. 189–190; on Boston, see: Green and Donahue, *Boston's Workers*, p. 75 and Mann, *Yankee Reformers*, p. 195. In his novel, *The Evolution of a Trade Unionist*, Frank Foster calls the character Dave Bernstein, presumably based on Henry Abrahams, "something of a bore" who represented a "militant minority" within the BCLU. (p. 56)

[60]Report as reprinted in the *Labor Leader*, Aug. 11, 1894.

[61]Melvyn Dubofsky, *The State and Labor in Modern America* (Chapel Hill: University of North Carolina Press, 1994), esp. Chap. 2; Leon Fink, "Labor, Liberty and the Law: Trade Unionism and the Problem of the American Constitutional Order," *Journal of American History* 74 (Dec. 1987): pp. 904–925. William E. Forbath, in *Law and the Shaping of the American Labor Movement* (Cambridge: Harvard University Press, 1991), argues that the conservative reaction of American courts to labor law enacted on the state and national level played a critical part in shaping the "voluntarism" of the AFL during the Gompers period. While I do not wish to negate this assertion, I would emphasize again the role that popular fears of radical politics played in the desire of the AFL to distance itself from that radicalism in its attempt to legitimize and solidify their position.

[62]*Boston Globe*, Aug. 8, 1894; *Labor Leader*, Aug. 11, 1894.

[63]For a brief discussion of the League, see: Mann, *Yankee Reformers*, p. 197. For the most part, the League encouraged workers as individuals to support (usually) Democratic candidates who supported the interests of labor. See: *Labor Leader*, Aug. 1, 1895.

[64]*Boston Globe*, Aug. 8, 1894.

[65]*Boston Globe*, Aug. 8, 1894.

[66]Sklar, *Florence Kelley*, p. 215.

[67]*Boston Globe*, Aug. 8, 1894; *Labor Leader*, Aug. 11, 1894.

[68]At its founding convention in 1887, the Massachusetts State Federation had passed a resolution in favor of equal pay for equal work, regardless of sex, as well as a resolution endorsing the organization of working women. See: Heintz and Whitney, *History*, p. 16 and p. 19.

[69]*Labor Leader,* Aug. 11, 1894.

[70]Foster defined "collectivism-individualism" as a philosophy "defending democratic institutions on the one hand and establishing concerted action for industrial justice on the other. . . ." in *The Evolution of A Trade Unionist,* p. 118.

[71]Laurie, *Artisans into Workers,* p. 190. Gompers would return to the AFL presidency the following year, remaining in office until his death in 1924.

[72]According to the minutes of the BCLU, O'Sullivan received 103 votes while Abrahams received 44; carriage maker Edward Brennan received 52 votes. Minutes of the BCLU, Massachusetts Historical Society, Boston, Mass., Vol. IV, Feb. 3, 1895.

[73]*Labor Leader,* Feb. 2, 1895. O'Sullivan would maintain this stance the following year when Populism, not socialism, offered itself as an alternative to the two-party system. According to O'Sullivan, "The Trade unionist [is] distinctly an independent voter. . . . He is a practical man rather than a theorist, and he knows enough to keep the skirts of his organization above the mud of a political campaign, because he realizes that he will need his trade union long after the questions involved in this or any campaign have become dead issues." *Boston Globe,* July 19, 1896.

[74]Eleanor Flexner and Janet Wilson James, "Mary Kenney O'Sullivan," *Notable American Women 1607–1950* Vol. II (Cambridge: Harvard University Press, 1971), p. 656, citing marriage record at the New York City Dept. of Health. In the unabridged version of his autobiography can be found Samuel Gompers' account of the wedding, which he claims he made the arrangements for after facetiously telling O'Sullivan that "before two organizers of the A. F. of L. marry they should ask for a 'special dispensation' from the president of the A. F. of L." Samuel Gompers, *Seventy Years of Life and Labor: An Autobiography* Vol. I (New York: E.P. Dutton, 1925), pp. 484–485.

[75]In his unabridged autobiography, Gompers later recalled that on the way to the restaurant after the ceremony O'Sullivan, also born a Catholic and a member of the Ancient Order of the Hiberians, said, "Do you know why Mary married me? Her name was Mary Kenney and now her name is either Mrs. John F. O'Sullivan or Mary O'Sullivan and there is no question about her nationality or her religion." Gompers, *Seventy Years of Life and Labor,* p. 486.

[76]Denison House Daybooks, Vol. II, p. 146.

[77]Herlihy, *Fifty Years of Boston,* pp. 37–38 and p. 723.

[78]Foster, *Evolution of a Trade Unionist,* p. 137.

[79]Carole Turbin, *Working Women of Collar City: Gender, Class, and Community in Troy, New York, 1864–1886* (Urbana: University of Illinois Press, 1992) points out that "Scholars of women's cross-class alliances do not systematically analyze the role that working-class women's backgrounds and ideologies play in relationships between women of different classes." p. 218. In part, this omission

may stem from a lack of extant sources. While Foster's *Evolution of a Trade Unionist* may be a work of fiction and written by a man, it is nonetheless useful for gaining some understanding of how the working class, male or female, viewed reformers.

[80]Foster, *Evolution of a Trade Unionist*, p. 138.

[81]On the WEIU, see: Barbara J. Balliet, "'What Shall we Do With Our Daughters?' Middle-Class Women's Ideas About Work, 1840–1920," (Ph.D. dissertation, New York University, 1988); Karen J. Blair, *The Clubwoman as Feminist: True Womanhood Redefined, 1868–1914* (New York: Holmes & Meier Publishers, 1980), chap.5; Mary H. Blewett, *Men, Women, and Work: Class, Gender, and Protest in the New England Shoe Industry, 1780–1910* (University of Illinois Press, 1988), pp. 293–296; Sarah Deutsch, "Learning to Talk More Like a Man: Boston Women's Class-Bridging Organizations, 1870–1940," *American Historical Review* (April 1992): pp. 379–404 and "Reconceiving the City: Women, Space and Power in Boston, 1870–1910," *Gender & History* 6 (Aug. 1994): pp. 202–223; Robert B. Jennings, "A History of the Educational Activities of the Women's Educational and Industrial Union from 1877–1927" (Ph.D. diss., Boston College, 1978); Judith Becker Ranlett, "Sorority and Community: Women's Answer to a Changing Massachusetts, 1865–1895" (Ph.D. diss., Brandeis University, 1974).

[82]Denison House Daybooks, Vol. 2, p. 172.

[83]*Labor Leader*, Nov. 24, 1894; Dec. 8, 1894; Jan. 19, 1895. On domestic workers, see: Faye E. Dudden, *Serving Women: Household Service in Nineteenth-Century America* (Middletown, Conn.: Wesleyan University Press, 1983) and David M. Katzman, *Seven Days A Week: Women and Domestic Service in Industrializing America* (New York: Oxford University Press, 1978). On the union label leagues, see: Blewett, *Men, Women, and Work*, Chap. 9 and Frank, *Purchasing Power*, Chaps. 8 & 9.

[84]While Gompers was in Boston to speak to Kenney O'Sullivan's group, the recently, and temporarily, ousted AFL president was also honored with a lunch, presided over by George McNeill. Presumably, Gompers' good friends the O'Sullivans were also on hand. Frank Foster, with no irony intended, "presented [Gompers] with a fifteen volume set of the works of Herbert Spencer." See: the *Labor Leader*, Jan. 12, 1895 and the *Boston Globe*, Jan. 9, 1895. On the perhaps surprising influence of Spencer on Gompers, see his unabridged autobiography, *Seventy Years of Life and Labor* Vol. I, p. 362; for Spencer's influence on Foster, see Mann, *Yankee Reformers*, p. 186.

[85]WEIU Annual Report for 1895, p. 15.

[86]Kenney O'Sullivan, autobio., pp. 125–126; also quoted in Deutsch, "Reconceiving the City," p. 211.

[87]Kenney O'Sullivan, autobio., p. 125. Missouri is known as the "Show Me State."

[88]Kenney O'Sullivan, autobio., p. 125.

[89]WEIU Annual Report for 1896, p. 16. Kenney O'Sullivan does not discuss the reasons for the name change in her autobiography but the WEIU's 1896 Annual Report "happily" noted the name change given the similarity between Women's Industrial Educational Association and Women's Educational and Industrial Union. The front door may have been opened to Kenney O'Sullivan's group but a distance was still to be maintained.

[90]Discussions of such seemingly inherent tensions within cross-class alliances include Ellen Carol DuBois, "Working Women, Class Relations, and Suffrage Militance: Harriet Stanton Blatch and the New York Woman Suffrage Movement, 1894–1909," *Journal of American History* 74 (June 1987): pp. 34–58 and Meredith Tax, *The Rising of the Women: Feminist Solidarity and Class Conflict, 1880–1917* (New York: Monthly Review Press, 1980), esp. Part I.

[91]WEIU Board of Governors Minutes, Volume 6, Feb. 5, 1895, Carton 2, WEIU Collection, Schlesinger Library, Radcliffe College, Cambridge, MA. Emphasis added.

[92]According to Betty G. Farrell in *Elite Families: Class and Power in Nineteenth-Century Boston* (Albany: State University of New York Press, 1993), "Although a detailed analysis of the charitable and political activities of the women of the Boston elite [such as the WEIU] has yet to be done, historical and contemporary studies from other cities suggest that [such activities] were significant ways in which elite women entered the public arena while helping to preserve their family's class power." (p. 79). See also: Deutsch, "Learning to Talk More Like a Man."

[93]Blewett, *Men, Women, and Work*, pp. 279–280.

[94]BCLU minutes, Vol. IV, Jan. 20, 1895.

[95]*Boston Globe*, Mar. 5, 1895.

[96]Less than six months earlier, thirty "mackintosh makers" went out on strike at the same company, protesting a wage reduction. According to the *Boston Globe*, Oct. 11, 1894, the striking workers had a union, "which they let go to pieces."

[97]Massachusetts State Board of Arbitration, Tenth Annual Report (1896), p. 82.

[98]*Boston Globe*, Apr. 2, 1895.

[99]Kenney O'Sullivan, autobio., p. 137.

[100]*Boston Globe*, Apr. 2 and 8, 1895.

[101]Denison House Daybook, Vol. 1, p. 219.

[102]Massachusetts State Board of Arbitration, Daily Log of Hearings, 1886–1923 (LA4, 535x) Vol. 1, p. 35, Massachusetts State Archives, Boston, MA.

[103]*Labor Leader*, Apr. 13, 1895.

[104]Board of Arbitration, Daily Log, p. 41.

[105]Labor laws are only as good as their enforcement and generally were not systematically enforced in Massachusetts until after the 1913 creation of the State Board of Labor and Industry. Until then, as Mary Blewett has pointed out, "State policy made no real difference inside the mills," in "Deference and Defiance: Labor Politics and the Meanings of Masculinity in the Mid-Nineteenth-Century New England Textile Industry," *Gender & History* 5 (Autumn 1993): p. 402. See also: Clara M. Beyer, *History of Labor Legislation for Women in Three States* Women's Bureau Bulletin No. 66 (Washington: GPO, 1929), pp.24–25; Blodgett, *Gentle Reformers*, p. 128. On the efforts to create the State Board of Labor and Industry, see my article "Female Reformers and the Limitations of Labor Politics in Progressive Era Massachusetts," in *Massachusetts Politics: Selected Historical Essays*, Jack Tager, Michael Konig and Martin Kaufman, eds. (Westfield: Westfield State College, 1998).

[106]*Labor Leader*, May 25, 1895.

[107]*Labor Leader*, May 4, 1895.

[108]Kenney O'Sullivan, autobio., p. 138.

[109]*Boston Globe*, May 7, 1895.

[110]Denison House daybooks, Vol 2., p. 228.

[111]Kenney O'Sullivan, autobio., p. 138.

[112]For the support of Boston's organized labor community, see: the *Boston Globe*, May 10 and May 13, 1895.

[113]Board of Arbitration, Tenth Annual Report (1896), p. 84. See also: *Labor Leader*, May 18, 1895 which reported that police protection was necessary to keep the relocated factory open.

[114]*Labor Leader*, June 22, 1895.

[115]Writing in 1911, John Andrews partially supported Kenney O'Sullivan's organizational tactics, claiming that women's unions "have usually been organized in time of strikes," but he goes on to say that "frequently they have disappeared upon the settlement of the industrial disputes which called them into being." in Andrews and W.D.P. Bliss, *Woman and Child Wage-Earners in the United States*, Vol. X: "History of Women in Trade Unions," (Washington: GPO, 1911), p. 17.

[116]*Boston Globe*, May 20, 1895. In a show of support for O'Sullivan, Duncan also reminded the BCLU of the AFL position "regarding political action," saying that "he did not think the trade union was its proper place."

[117]Denison House Daybooks, Vol. II, p. 190.

[118]Denison House Daybooks, Vol. II, p. 212.

[119]Kathy Peiss, *Cheap Amusements: Working Women and Leisure in Turn-of-the-Century New York* (Philadelphia: Temple University Press, 1986), p. 51.

From retail stores to textile mills, women workers were at risk of mistreatment, which could range from verbal insults to inappropriate physical contact, sometimes even rape. Domestic workers, isolated within their employers' home, were especially vulnerable. See: Dudden, *Serving Women*, p. 215; Katzman, *Seven Days a Week*, p. 216. See also: Cameron, *Radicals of the Worst Sort*, p. 50; Regina G. Kunzel, *Fallen Women, Problem Girls: Unmarried Mothers and the Professionalization of Social Work, 1890–1945* (New Haven: Yale University Press, 1993), p. 34 and pp. 59–60.

[120]The formation of an all women's local was hardly unique to garment makers. It was quite common among shoeworkers as well as bookbinders. On shoeworkers, see: Blewett, *Men, Women, and Work*, Chaps. 6–9; on bookbinders, see: Christina Burr, "Defending 'The Art Preservative': Class and Gender Relations in the Printing Trades Unions, 1850–1914," *Labour/Le Travail* 31 (Spring 1993): pp. 47–73.

[121]*Boston Globe*, Aug. 20, 1895.

[122]Kenney O'Sullivan, autobio., p. 160.

[123]Kenney O'Sullivan, autobio., p. 162.

[124]*Boston Globe*, Aug. 21–24, 1895.

[125]Within Boston, there were four locals representing garment makers, all part of the United Garment Workers of America, District Council No. 2: Local No. 1 represented tailors and operatives; pressmen were part of Local No. 25; Local No. 37 was the all-women local; Local No. 43 was made up of Lithuanian garment workers. *Boston Globe*, Aug. 21, 1895.

[126]*Boston Globe*, Aug. 23, 1895.

[127]BCLU Minutes, Vol. IV, May 3, 1896. Letter signed by Sarah Pearlstein, dated Apr. 27, 1896.

[128]After the May 3rd meeting the next mention of the garment makers' union is July 19, 1896 when the minutes state that "Garment workers report trade stagnant and repudiated the current rumor that the organization had dismantled." BCLU minutes, Vol. IV. There is also no mention of the discussion in the May 4th *Boston Globe* account of the May 3rd meeting.

[129]BCLU minutes, Vol. IV, May 3, 1896.

[130]According to the BCLU minutes for Feb. 3, 1895, other than the three Denison House residents listed, those presenting the credentials of Local No. 37 were: Maria Meade, Gussie Rosenthal, Mary Donovan, Annie Collins, Jennie Cross, and Katie O'Rourke. The letterhead on which the complaint letter of April 27, 1896 was written, also within the BCLU minute book, lists Rose E. Angell as Corresponding and Financial Secretary for Local No. 37 but the letter was signed by Sarah Pearlstein.

[131]Susan Traverso argues that a fear of lost contributions caused Denison House residents to become more "discreet in their labor activities," " 'The Road

Going Down to Jericho'," pp. 46–47. Traverso also points out, on p. 44, that the Social Science Club at Denison House suspended its public lecture series in 1897, "for certain reasons connected to political and industrial disturbances." See: Solomon, *Ancestors and Immigrants*, p.199 and Cameron, *Radicals of the Worst Sort*, pp. 171–176, for a discussion of the impact of the "new immigration" and reformers' support of labor organizing, especially after the 1912 Lawrence strike.

[132]Kenney O'Sullivan, autobio., pp. 167–168.

[133]Kenney O'Sullivan, autobio., p. 158. Also quoted in Deutsch, "Reconceiving the City," p. 211.

[134]Regarding Woods, see: Kenney O'Sullivan, autobio., p. 158; for Keir Hardie's visit to Boston in the fall of 1895, see: Kenney O'Sullivan, autobio., p. 143. When Hardie came to Boston, Frank Foster wrote that "While this paper has little sympathy with many of the economic conclusions of Keir Hardie, it yet believes that every school of thought is entitled to a respectful hearing." *Labor Leader*, Nov. 9, 1895.

[135]Kenney O'Sullivan, autobio., pp. 141–142, pp. 182–183.

[136]Kenney O'Sullivan, autobio., pp. 173–175. See also: Blewett, *Men, Women, and Work*, p. 290.

[137]WEIU, Report of the Committee on Domestic Reform, No.1, "The Effort to Attract the Workers in Shops & Factories to Domestic Service," April 1898, p. 3, Schlesinger Library, Radcliffe College, Cambridge, MA.

[138]On domestic service see: Dudden, *Serving Women* and Katzman, *Seven Days a Week*.

[139]Glendower Evans papers, Schlesinger Library, unpublished autobiographical essay, p. 1, n.d.

[140]Obituary, *Boston Globe*, Dec. 13, 1937.

[141]Elizabeth Glendower Evans, "What Do You Know of the Children After They Leave Your Home or Institution? Do You Supervise Them?" *Proceedings of the Thirty-Fourth National Convention of Charities and Corrections* (1907): pp. 274–278. Glendower Evans served as a trustee from shortly after her husband's death in 1886 until 1914.

[142]Kenney O'Sullivan, autobio., p. 155. Also cited in Deutsch, "Reconceiving the City," p. 211.

[143]See previous discussion of Mary Morton Kehew's contributions during the 1895 rubber workers' strike. See also: Mary Blewett's description of the assistance native-born shoeworkers received from Brahmin Bostonians during the 1895 strike, in *Men, Women, and Work*, pp. 279–280.

[144]Philippa Strum, *Brandeis: Beyond Progressivism* (Lawrence: University Press of Kansas, 1984), p. 24.

[145]*Boston Globe*, 23 Sept., 1902; *The Pilot* [Boston], Sept. 27, 1902; *American Federationist*, Nov. 1902.

[146]Kenney O'Sullivan, autobio., p. 186.

[147]Kenney O'Sullivan, autobio., p. 188.

[148]Proceedings of the 17th Annual Convention of the Massachusetts State Branch, American Federation of Labor (1902), p. 50.

[149]Regarding the Lawrence textile industry, see: Cameron, *Radicals of the Worst Sort*; on the Essex County shoe industry, see: Blewett, *Men, Women, and Work*. For a general overview, see: Dublin, *Transforming Women's Work*.

CHAPTER 3

For Those "Willing to Assist"
The Formation of the National Women's Trade Union League

They met over lunch, the young, wealthy settlement house worker and the nearly forty-year-old veteran labor organizer. Together, William English Walling and Mary Kenney O'Sullivan created the National Women's Trade Union League. Brought together by the annual AFL convention, held that year in Boston, these two very different people sought to shape an organization which would address their mutual goal: trade unionism for wage-earning women. During a lengthy lunch at Boston's Revere House, Walling and Kenney O'Sullivan worked out the details. They became so engrossed in their planning that they failed to notice they were the last guests in the dining room. Only an impatient waiter remained. As Kenney O'Sullivan later recalled:

> Suddenly we realized we had been there for hours. Mr. Walling remembered he had only a $270 check that he could not get cashed. President Gompers and all the others that knew him had gone to the convention hall. He left the table to find someone to cash his check and he came back to the table without his watch.[1]

As a concerned social reformer, Walling was willing to sacrifice his watch to assist in the organization of women. Kenney O'Sullivan, having spent more than a dozen years in that same effort, was no less determined.

If for no other reason, the sheer increase of women in the workforce demanded action. By 1900, over 20% of all American women were earning wages. Participation rates for young women, immigrant women and African American women were even higher.[2] The percentage of women in the total workforce was a result of the growth of American industrialization. Thus, while almost one-quarter of wage-earning women still worked as domestics, an almost equal number worked in manufacturing, especially in textiles and garments.[3] Concentrated in the large cities and single-industry towns of the industrial Northeast and Midwest, these women were clustered in the low-paying, low-skilled facets of production. In Illinois and New York, the vast majority of women worked in Chicago and New York City and were concentrated in the garment trade.[4] In Massachusetts, it was not garment making but the production of the cloth itself which employed vast numbers of women. More than 46% of the Commonwealth's 329,000 wage-earning women worked in manufacturing. Of those 151,340 women, almost 40% worked in the textile mills, producing cotton and woolen cloth, primarily in Fall River, Lawrence, and Lowell. Another 16% worked in the boot and shoe industry, based in Lynn. No one industry truly dominated the state's largest city, Boston. In 1900, however, 29% of women working in the factories of Boston were employed in the garment industry.[5]

Statistically, the majority of wage-earning women were young immigrants or the daughters of immigrants, contributing to their families' household income. After 1900, however, a sharp increase of the number of married women in the workforce occurred. On the national level, in 1900 3.9% of female wage earners in non-agricultural work were married; by 1910 that number had risen to 6.8%. In some cities, married women's participation rates were even higher. In the Massachusetts textile center of Fall River, 23% of working women were married.[6] Married or single, regardless of age, all women could expect low wages and regular periods of unemployment.

In a study conducted by the Women's Educational and Industrial Union (WEIU) in 1901, weekly wages were compared with food and housing costs. One hundred women who worked in a variety of occupations across the state were interviewed.[7] According to the survey, the average weekly wage for domestic servants was $3.99 a week, while shoe workers earned $10.45 a week. Given that the domestic servant would typically live with her employer, she would not incur any housing or food costs. The shoe worker's room and board costs were found to be $4 a week, leaving that worker with an "excess" of $6.25 a week. The report noted that the so-called excess would be needed to cover other living costs such as clothing, carfare, medical treatment, recreation, and support of dependent family members. Perhaps even more important, the excess income of the woman shoe worker was "more apparent than real because of the irregularity of employment at full time."[8]

Thus, wage-earning women whether single or married received wages that barely allowed for survival. Generally, women who worked in manufacturing earned half a man's wage.[9] But soaring immigration and increased mechanization drove men's wages down too. Coupled with regular but often unpredictable periods of unemployment and rising food costs, many working-class families relied on the wages of several family members just to make ends meet.[10] The sanctity of the family wage earned by a male breadwinner was increasingly challenged by the harsh economic reality of industrial America as it entered the twentieth century.

In his report to the AFL convention of 1901, Samuel Gompers acknowledged the threat industrial capitalism posed to the concept of the family wage. The solution was two-fold: stronger child labor laws and the extension of "the benefits of organization" for women.[11] Nonetheless, these women remained, for the most part, unorganized. Admitting that "[f]igures for union membership are notoriously unreliable," historian Alice Kessler-Harris hazards the guess that just over three percent of women industrial workers were members of trade unions in 1900.[12] To be sure, male industrial workers were not overly represented in unions either. Although union membership in the United States quadrupled between 1897 and 1904, most of that increase was among white, male, native-born, and skilled workers.[13] Women were seen as special cases, frequently unorganizable, by virtue of their age and ethnicity, as well as because of their temporary and unskilled status within the workforce.

Until recently, many labor historians agreed that most women worked only before marriage, in semi- or unskilled jobs, and that women's identity was not shaped by their work but rather by their potential or actual status as wives and mothers. Thus, many scholars concurred with the contemporary assessment that women themselves were to blame for their low union participation. But some labor historians have begun the process of reshaping the question first asked by Theresa Wolfson in 1925: "Where are the organized women workers?"[14] Fifty years later Alice Kessler-Harris took the question to another level: "When we stop asking why women have not organized themselves, we are led to ask how women were, and are, kept out of unions."[15] Even more recently, Ava Baron has probed more specifically: "Rather than ask: Why have women been difficult to organize? [we should ask]: What assumptions about gender have been structured into unions?"[16]

The experiences of Mary Kenney O'Sullivan as a woman bookbinder and a woman organizer highlight the pervasiveness of these hostile gender assumptions. The notion of a family wage earned by a male breadwinner in effect dictated, to employee and employer alike, that a woman's wage could and should be less than a man's. Further, their perceived temporary status as workers justified segregating women in the unskilled facets of production. By the end of the nineteenth century, increased mechanization had raised the demand for cheap, unskilled labor, a demand which would be met by immigrants and women. Women were even more attractive as employees because of the socially sanctioned view that they were, or at least should be, compliant when confronted with male authority, be it father, husband, or boss. Trade unionists also shared these gender assumptions.[17] Yet at the same time, woman's presence in the industrial workforce, not to mention the economic necessity of her participation, indicated a basic inadequacy in the gender concepts of the day. Moreover, it created an ambiguity which unions were forced to confront.

During the summer of the 1902 the AFL newspaper, the *American Federationist*, published a series of articles by John Stafford entitled "The Good That Trade Unions Do." Only through trade unionism would men earn higher wages, wages sufficient to remove women and children from the work place. According to Stafford, "When girl wage-earners decrease, competition between wage-earners decreases also. . . . This leads to higher wages." Women as well as men would benefit from fewer wage-earning women. If they were no longer required to work outside of the home, women's health would improve and they would have more of "an opportunity to learn housework" too. Perhaps most important in Stafford's opinion, "Fewer girl wage-earners means less prostitution."[18]

While the low wages women received were seen by many as the cause of prostitution, Stafford argued that "the obscene conversation and forced evil association in factories and shops, with girls or men who have become depraved is apt to cause their ruin." Not surprisingly, then, "Respect for women is apt to decrease when they are compelled to work in the factory or the store. . . . More respect for women brings less degeneration and more marriages."[19] For Kenney O'Sullivan, and for millions of other women like her for whom employment was a necessity, respectability could be found within the trade union movement. Whether or not she read Stafford's article, she would have likely agreed much more with the sentiments expressed in an article by the Iowa Commissioner of Labor Arthur Holder that appeared in the same issue of the *American Federationist*. Separated by only a few pages, these two articles are indicative of the conflicting views of the AFL regarding the role of women in the workplace and the trade union movement.

Holder agreed with Stafford that "[t]he greatest peril of the age is the very low wages of our women." But Holder's solution was not the removal of women from the workplace through higher wages for men. Rather,

> Woman must protect woman, whether she be affluent or needy. The strong must help the weak, the intelligent must interest themselves in the condition of the helpless. . . . How can this be brought about the easiest and the quickest? **Organize them!**[20]

Holder stressed that these actions must be gender-based and must cross class lines. When he urged women to "be sisters in deed as well as name," Holder could have been describing the Women's Trade Union League (WTUL).

Founded in Great Britain in 1874 by Emma Paterson, a former bookbinder, the WTUL sought "to accustom the women to the idea of organization."[21] In its first dozen or so years, it was known as the Women's Protective and Provident League and managed to organize at most 2,500 women. But after 1890, with a change of name and a new leader, Lady Emilia Dilke, the WTUL began a much more aggressive campaign to bring women into existing British trade unions. By 1901, almost 6% of the English female labor force was organized. This achievement reflected not only the efforts of the British WTUL. The historian Robin Miller Jacoby claims "[t]he British labor movement was considerably more receptive than the American to the inclusion of unskilled and semi-skilled workers."[22]

Despite their different views regarding trade unionism for the semi- or unskilled of either gender, the AFL was hardly unaware of the British WTUL and its accomplishments in organizing women workers. In 1899, the *American Federationist* printed a letter from AFL president Samuel Gompers to British WTUL president Lady Emilia Dilke commending her and her organization for their success. Some months earlier, two fraternal delegates from the British Trade Union Congress had attended the 1898 AFL convention and spoke of the British WTUL and its achievements before a special committee. Gompers informed Lady Dilke that the committee reported back to the convention that "[w]e . . . commend her example to the women of America for emulation."[23] Three years later, in 1901, the AFL newspaper ran a short piece on the British WTUL, outlining its history and its accomplishments.[24] A year later, the Stafford series would appear, offering a very different view. Organized labor's rhetorical seesaw was evident on the state and local level as well. At its 1902 convention, the Massachusetts State Branch of the AFL (MSB) discussed the necessity of organization for women. In his annual report, MSB out-going president and Boston cigarmaker Frank McCarthy noted the "constant increasing of the number of women engaged in the different lines of industry, with no corresponding increase in their membership in labor organizations." According to McCarthy, "Women can organize as well as men, and will organize when they understand more thoroughly the aims and objects of trade unionism."[25] However, when the Committee on the President's Report responded to the full convention, that committee recommended that the question of women's labor **not** be addressed.

Instead, the convention did adopt a resolution put forward by Joseph Jackson of Fall River. Jackson introduced the resolution seeking support of a ban on women's and children's labor between 6 p.m. and 6 a.m.. For Jackson, and many other trade union men, night labor for women and children was "a disgrace to the state of Massachusetts, and against the moral, physical and intellectual interests of those so employed."[26] Championed by male trade unionists and female social reformers alike, such legislation adds yet another layer to the ambiguity regarding women and their place within the work force and the trade union. In seeking state protection of women workers during the Progressive Era, the advocates of such legislation were tacitly acknowledging women's lack of union protection. At the same time, such laws reflected women's socially proscribed role as "mothers of the race" in need of special protection.[27] Admittedly, protetcive labor legislation did seek to ameliorate some of the harsh work conditions faced by all workers. Yet these laws sometimes limited women's access to certain skilled or semi-skilled occupations, especially within the printing and bookbinding industries.[28]

At its next annual convention in 1903, MSB President James R. Crozier, a Carriage and Wagon Workers Union official from Boston, also discussed in his report the need of organization for women wage earners. Noting that "women have entered upon the industrial field to stay," Crozier said that the only way women could earn the same wages as men was through unionization. He then went on to say:

> We often hear that the wife is at work in the factory while the husband walks the streets in idleness, and sometimes there is much truth in this statement. The most effective remedy is to elevate the wages of the women, and this can be done only through organization.[29]

In effect, the MSB was acknowledging the widely-held view that the only reason employers preferred women was that they were a cheaper source of labor. Crozier goes on to relate "an experiment" in a Peabody, Massachusetts tannery. There, after some initial trials, women were found capable of lifting the hides during the tanning process. Soon women were hired at $6 or $7 dollars a week, replacing men who had earned $10 to $12 a week for the same work. As Crozier wryly pointed out, "The purpose of this corporation in making this change is something other than having the society of women in their factory."[30]

Perhaps in response to this anecdote, the President's position regarding the organization of women was endorsed. Unlike the previous year, when no action was taken, in 1903 the Committee on the President's Report recommended that the "incoming Executive Council [of the MSB] be empowered to apply a corps of women organizers and place them in such localities as in their judgement they may deem best."[31] Just a month later, the WTUL would be organized to do just that. However, it would be another six years before the MSB annual convention would again recognize the necessity of trade unionism for women.[32] The MSB, like its parent organization the AFL, demonstrated far more enthusiasm for the formation of Woman's Union Label Leagues.

The Union Label first came into use in San Francisco in 1874. There, American-born cigarmakers sought protection against cheaper cigars produced by non-union Chinese immigrants. Quite intentionally, the label was white, signifying that "the cigars were made by white labor, as opposed to the yellow of the Orient."[33] Although it was argued that the label and "the box to which it was attached contained cigars made by a first-class workman, **under sanitary conditions**," the racialized meaning was clear.[34] Demand for products bearing the union label increased as the movement spread across the country.[35] The Boston Letter Carriers' Association pledged to wear only those uniforms bearing the United Garment Workers Label. In 1903, the Boston Central Labor Union (BCLU) "voted that all carriages and vehicles appearing in Labor Day parade must bear union label and all horses must wear union label shoes."[36] Twenty-five years after its introduction, after several other trades had adopted a union label, the concept had become gendered as well as racialized.

In 1899, Sarah Crossfield of Muncie, Indiana organized the Woman's Union Label League. Explaining the purpose of this group to AFL president Samuel Gompers, Crossfield wrote:

> This league is composed of the wives, mothers, and daughters of laboring men and working girls and was organized for the purpose of helping

weak union men to stand up for their rights and to educate the workmen's wives in the labor movement. This is a woman's union, and our
main object is to **agitate** for the union label.[37]

Here, finally, was a place for woman within the house of labor, not as a
producer, but as a consumer of union goods.[38] As one union label advocate wrote, "The mistress of the household represents the 'purchasing
power.'" She can not go on strike, but she can obviate the necessity of
striking by demanding the union label."[39] While recognition of the need
of union protection for working women undermined the notion of the
family wage earned by a male breadwinner, limiting women's power to
that of consumer served to support that concept. This limitation also
meshed nicely with the socially prescribed attributes of manhood, helping to make "weak union men" stronger when they finally achieved their
"rights". One of those rights was the right to earn a wage sufficient to
support a family.

In 1904, the *American Federationist* ran a contest, seeking essays on
the benefits of the trade union label. In his first-place entry, Walter

Mary Kenney O'Sullivan and her three children, Mary Elizabeth, Mortimer, and
Roger, circa 1903. Schlesinger Library, Radcliffe College.

MacArthur saw in woman's character much that would align her with the union label. He wrote:

> The instincts of woman and the interests of labor are conjoined in the union label. Both stand for cleanliness, morality, the care of the young, the sanctity of the home; both stand against strife and force. The union label makes woman the strongest, as she is the gentlest, of God's creatures."[40]

As the guardian of the home, woman could play a role in the trade union movement. Her power was to derive from consumption, not production.

As both a producer and a consumer, Mary Kenney O'Sullivan had long been an advocate of the union label. As a bookbinder in Chicago, she worked in a trade which strongly supported the union label movement. She was not above checking the hats of male companions, making sure they wore only those with a union label. Kenney O'Sullivan later recalled:

> I once found President Gompers wearing a bogus union label in his hat. In Chicago we only used products that had the union label. . . . When I showed Mr. Gompers the false label he was a very much surprised man.[41]

Kenney O'Sullivan's actions were in no way meant to be a substitute for women's direct participation within organized labor but simply as a way of propagating the union message and thereby improving the conditions of labor for all. In January, 1904 the Boston Woman's Union Label League was formed with Kenney O'Sullivan as the organizing secretary. Although it had the blessings of the MSB, and its first informational tract was printed on the BCLU letterhead, the Boston Woman's Union Label League had its headquarters at Denison House.[42] Thus, as she had done throughout the 1890s, Kenney O'Sullivan continued to rely on both the labor and social reform communities. But while she fully supported the union label movement as an educational tool, her primary goal remained the organization of wage-earning women. According to Kenney O'Sullivan, trade unionism for women was their "economic, as well as their moral responsibility."[43]

When she began the Union for Industrial Progress [UIP] in 1894 [see Chapter 2], Kenney O'Sullivan envisioned it as a vehicle of education as well as a mechanism through which trade unionism would be encouraged. Having secured the use of the Women's Educational and Industrial Union [WEIU]'s front door, the UIP continued to hold regular meetings throughout the 1890s. Yet the reform-minded, Brahmin-led WEIU did not formally associate itself with the UIP until 1903. When it finally did so, it was in such a way as to not merely associate with the UIP, but to swallow it whole.

Until that time, the UIP maintained its emphasis on trade unionism for women. In its statement of support for an AFL resolution in favor of the organization of women in 1898, the voice of UIP president Kenney O'Sullivan is clear. The UIP statement, as reproduced in the *American Federationist*, concluded that:

> We strongly urge all women who work for wages, of whatever occupation, to join in or form trade unions of their respective crafts, to the end that their sex will be no bar to honorable employment, or compel them to accept a lower wage than men performing similar labor.[44]

When he spoke at a UIP gathering in early 1902, the veteran Boston labor leader George McNeill delivered a similar message.[45]

Speaking to one hundred women UIP members, McNeill reviewed the labor reform efforts during the previous century in both the U.S. and in England. He emphasized that "the trade unions had done more than legislation" in improving work conditions.[46] While it is likely that Kenney O'Sullivan would have agreed with McNeill, it is unlikely she attended his talk. In January, 1902, she was a month away from giving birth to her third child in four years.[47] Whether or not Kenney O'Sullivan heard McNeill speak, certainly some WEIU members did as the UIP continued to hold its meetings in the WEIU hall on Boston's Boylston Street. Given the WEIU emphasis on education and reform rather than trade unionism, McNeill's remarks might not have been looked upon favorably by many WEIU members.[48] The WEIU preference for education and legislative reform may also have played a part in the WEIU's decision to dramatically alter its relationship to the UIP the following year.

On November 17, 1903, the WEIU Board of Governors met to discuss affiliation with the UIP. According to WEIU president Mary Morton Kehew, because the UIP embraced "very many of the [WEI]Union employees," and because its apparent purpose was "similar to that of the [WEI]Union, it would seem wise to bring the two organizations into closer relations."[49] Those relations had been strained in the past. Now the WEIU sought to co-join the two groups as their aims seemed similar. The affiliation became official in March, 1904. The WEIU Board adopted Kehew's plan as presented. Kehew's proposal included a restructuring of the UIP and a clarification of its purpose. Henceforth, a WEIU member would sit on the UIP executive board and the WEIU president would serve as UIP president as well. Lectures would be coordinated between the two groups and one-fifth of the UIP members' dues would go to the WEIU. In exchange, the WEIU would provide the UIP with what space it needed.[50]

In many ways, this was more an usurpation than an affiliation. Further, the object of the UIP would now be

> [t]o encourage working women to study the principles of economics and good citizenship. [And] [t]o encourage among all women a spirit of sociability, sisterhood, and hearty desire for each other's best interests.[51]

This had been the goal of the WEIU since its founding in 1877: "to increase fellowship among women, in order to promote the best practical methods of securing their educational, industrial, and advancement. . . . to help women helping themselves."[52] For the members of the WEIU, sisterhood across class lines could be powerful. Certainly, their organization is an excellent example of what the historian Kathryn Kish Sklar has defined as "women's political culture."[53] There were, however, within the WEIU and the settlement house movement which Sklar focuses on, limits to that culture. The third and final objective of the reconfigured UIP clarifies the limitations:

> To encourage organization among working women believing that organization, **if properly used**, tends to elevate the character and improve the condition of the worker; believing also that in the growth of character, which comes from union and mutual sympathy and respect, will be found the surest claim to justice, and the safest path toward a fuller life.[54]

The influence of Kenney O'Sullivan can be seen in much of the above. For her, the organization of women would bring improved working conditions as well as a measure of respectability as a worker. Trade unionism could only lead to industrial justice. In her decade-long association with Kenney O'Sullivan, WEIU president Kehew had demonstrated her commitment to the same philosophy. Yet Kehew and the WEIU still felt it necessary to qualify that commitment, giving their support to trade unionism only when "properly used."

The WEIU Board of Governors had debated the merits of appointing Kenney O'Sullivan a board member in 1895, fearing that as a trade union woman she would automatically be associated with a "radical element."[55] The WEIU continued to seek to distance itself from any hint of radical trade unionism eight years later. Demonstrating its commitment to "pure and simple" trade unionism, the WEIU moved to form a company union for its more than 200 employees.[56] Now willing to have a union within its very midst, the WEIU had indeed evolved over the years, perhaps in part due to the continued presence of Kenney O'Sullivan. But more than just the passing of the years played a role in the WEIU's decision to formally affiliate itself with the UIP in its now modified state. At the same time that Mary Morton Kehew proposed this action, Mary Kenney O'Sullivan was just a few blocks away, proposing a very different association. What Kenney O'Sullivan hoped to create was an organization of women in which trade unionism was to be the primary, not secondary, goal.

On the evening of November 14, 1903, several delegates to the annual American Federation of Labor convention made the short walk from their meeting place in Boston's Faneuil Hall into the city's North End. There they attended a meeting at the Civic Service Settlement House. The mostly male trade unionists were joined by Mary Kenney O'Sullivan and several settlement house workers, including William English Walling. That night, the National Women's Trade Union League was born.

It was no coincidence that the League would take shape in a settlement house. Seen since as the "neglected child of the settlement houses" and a "step-child of the AFL," the WTUL was the coming together of these two constituencies.[57] The seeds of cooperation between labor and social reform had been planted years earlier, from Chicago's Hull House to Boston's Denison House.[58] However, as the ethnicity of the South End settlement changed from Irish to Italian, Syrian and Greek, Denison House pulled away from active participation in the labor movement.[59] Yet Denison House continued to support the concept of trade unionism, at least in the abstract.

In her Head Worker's Report for 1901, Helena Dudley stressed that better public schools, improved housing, and additional recreation facilities were needed. According to Dudley, "the most important factor, however, in improving conditions is the great struggle made by the working people themselves to obtain higher wages and shorter hours." Dudley continued:

> With this struggle, as expressed by the Trade Unions, we are heartily in sympathy, although we,—with the more intelligent workers among them,—must regret some hasty and ill-judged actions.[60]

Just what those hasty and ill-judged actions were remains unclear. What is clear is the continued reluctance of Denison House to actively support trade union efforts in their neighborhood, aside from "an occasional public talk on labor matters or the use of our rooms by the smaller unions."[61]

Again, much like the AFL, Denison House rallied behind the Woman's Union Label League movement. When a League was organized in Boston, Denison House founder and Wellesley professor Vida Dutton Scudder became president, and Head Worker Dudley served as vice-president. In her report for 1904, Dudley hastened to point out that the Label League was "not in any sense an enterprise of Denison House." Nonetheless, Dudley added:

> The officers [of the Boston Woman's Union Label League] hope that such a league, organized expressly to emphasize and assist the humane and idealist aspect of the achievement of the labor unions, may help. . . . to keep to the fore that aspect of the great labor movement.[62]

Kenney O'Sullivan was also an officer of the Label League. But she was much more a pragmatist than an idealist. When Kenney O'Sullivan talked about the necessity of organization for women, she did not mean in an auxiliary to trade unionism. As Denison House no longer appeared to support her efforts, it should come as no surprise that the WTUL was born in another settlement house. Admittedly, that settlement, the Civic Service House, was just a few blocks from the AFL convention. Yet it was more than proximity which caused Civic Service House to welcome the organizers of the WTUL.

Founded in 1901 by Boston philanthropist Pauline Aggasiz Shaw, the Civic Service House "purposed to reach a constituency approaching or within the privileges of citizenship."[63] Even before passage of the Nineteenth Amendment granting women the right to vote, American women enjoyed some of the privileges of citizenship.[64] Lacking the vote, however, working-class women were in many respects non-citizens and thus certainly in need of the protection and rights that trade unions could provide.[65] Therefore, within a year of its opening, Civic Service House was actively organizing the female immigrant garment workers of Boston's North and West End neighborhoods.

Much of this union activity was under the direction of Philip Davis, the House assistant head resident. A recent graduate of Harvard College, Davis had come a long way from his birth in a Russian shetl twenty-six years earlier.[66] Born Feivel Chemerinsky, Davis emigrated alone as a teenager and settled with family members in Chicago. There, Davis

found work in a garment factory and became active in the labor movement. He began attending English classes at Hull House and, with financial assistance provided by Jane Addams, went on to the University of
Chicago. While finishing his undergraduate work at Harvard, Davis
"went back to the slums, by choice."[67] Although his tuition was paid for,
he needed living expenses. Becoming an assistant head resident at the
newly opened Civic Service House provided Davis with a small income
as well as room and board. It also provided the former garment worker
and labor organizer with a way "to share the benefits of his education
with others of the slum dwellers."[68]

Davis set to work among his neighbors, primarily women immigrants who toiled in the small garment sweatshops nearby. By the fall of
1902, he had helped organize dozens of women into three separate locals. Within the first year, the membership of the Waist-makers', the
Wrapper-makers' and the White-Goods Workers' locals totalled more
than 500 women.[69] An unsuccessful strike in the fall of 1903 left the locals' meager treasuries depleted and caused Davis much dismay. He was,
however, to find some good in that failed strike. Almost fifty years later,
Davis wrote in his autobiography that "[u]nwittingly, they [the employ-
ers] had encouraged the formation of a formidable foe—the National
Women's Trade Union League. . . ."[70]

As an immigrant and former garment worker turned social reformer,
the now very Americanized Davis could readily see the potential of an
organization such as the WTUL. Social reformers could and did provide
timely financial support, a place to meet, and even a level of middle-class
respectability, but if the WTUL was to effectively organize women, it
needed the active participation of trade union leaders. In its formative
stages, the WTUL appeared to have both of these ingredients that Kenney O'Sullivan, given her experiences of the 1890s, had realized were so
necessary.

Most accounts, contemporary and historical, note the critical role
William English Walling (1877–1936) played in assisting Kenney
O'Sullivan in forming the WTUL.[71] Walling, known as English to his
friends, was the precocious and charming son of a wealthy Kentucky
doctor. After graduating from the University of Chicago in 1897 at the
age of nineteen, Walling entered Harvard Law School, only to return to
Chicago after one year to study political economy with Thorstein Veblen.
He was soon moving in the same circles in which Kenney O'Sullivan had
moved earlier in the 1890s. Part of the Hull House group, Walling
attended union meetings and worked for the state of Illinois as a factory

inspector until 1901. He then moved to New York, joining the resident staff of the University Settlement House. There Walling led one of the settlement's many "study circles," his being devoted to "Labor and Social Movements."[72]

Through Walling, the New York City Central Federation of Labor began meeting at the University Settlement. A trip to England in 1903 introduced him to the British Women's Trade Union League.[73] As a former factory inspector and a settlement house worker, Walling knew well the often horrific conditions under which women labored. As an advocate of trade unionism, he was intrigued by the possibilities an organization such as the WTUL might have for the millions of American women who worked for low wages and long hours and who frequently fell outside the pale of traditional trade unions. Thus, he went to the 1903 AFL convention hoping to find willing partners in establishing a similar group in the United States.

In a sense, Walling worked the convention, sharing his idea of an American model of the British WTUL with any delegates who would listen. His fellow University Settlement resident, Ernest Poole, had traveled to Boston with him and later remembered the energy Walling put into spreading the word:

> Through [Walling] I found my way into hotel bedrooms filled with smoke and delegates in shirt-sleeves, and listening there I soon began to feel the many forces at work behind the convention hall. . . . I was present in that small room and recall how large a part he played in the first work of organizing what later spread all over the country—the National Women's Trade Union League.[74]

Walling was introduced to Kenney O'Sullivan soon after he arrived in Boston for the AFL convention. Although neither were delegates, both were much in evidence in and out of the convention's meeting place in Boston's Faneuil Hall. Walling was on a mission and Kenney O'Sullivan was a recognized labor organizer and the honored widow of one of the AFL's most-admired organizers, John O'Sullivan. A year earlier, the AFL convention had marked O'Sullivan's recent death with the recommendation that the Executive Council contribute to the memorial fund established by the BCLU.[75] At the 1903 convention in her home town, Kenney O'Sullivan was surely greeted warmly by many, including her old friend Samuel Gompers. Whether it was through Gompers or through their mutual friends in the settlement house movement, Walling and Kenney

O'Sullivan met and together, over a long lunch in Boston's Revere House, thrashed out the details of what was soon to be the WTUL.[76] The wealthy male social reformer and the female working-class labor organizer must have made an interesting pair. Walling was full of youthful enthusiasm for an organization devoted to trade unionism for women and, as Samuel Gompers would later remember, "Mary Kenney O'Sullivan's quick mind caught the possibilities of the suggestion."[77]

Philip Davis invited Walling and Kenney O'Sullivan to hold a preliminary meeting at the Civic Service House.[78] They were joined by several delegates to the AFL convention, including John O'Brien, president of the Clerks International Protective Union, who chaired the meeting. Kenney O'Sullivan and Davis agreed to visit the various Boston settlements in the next few days in the hopes of generating more support from the social reform community. Kenney O'Sullivan was also appointed to the committee charged with drafting a constitution for the WTUL. She was joined by Walling and Mrs. Nellie Parker from Galensburg, Illinois. Parker was in town representing her local Trades and Labor Assembly, one of the four women delegates out of the 496 delegates to the 1903 AFL convention.[79]

Three days later, on November 17th, the WTUL organizers met again, this time in Faneuil Hall, at the site of the AFL convention itself. Even more settlement workers were in attendance, including Robert Woods, head of the South End House, and Helena Dudley and Vida Scudder, representing Denison House. It was certainly not a coincidence, however, that the organizers chose not to meet for a second time in a settlement house. They knew that the active participation of labor was critical if the WTUL was to have any credibility as a vehicle for trade unionism. In his autobiography, written twenty years later, Samuel Gompers recalled giving the WTUL his immediate blessings. "When they submitted to me a proposal," he wrote "I gave it most hearty approval and participated in the necessary conferences."[80] However, in her account, also written twenty years later, Kenney O'Sullivan did not list Gompers as one of the participants, nor did the secretary's report, written by Nellie Parker.[81] In Gompers' place was Max Morris, fourth vice president of the AFL, representing the Retail Clerk's Union. Also present were four delegates representing the United Garment Workers of America: Ephraim Kaufmann, Victor Altman, Walter Chuck, and T.A. Rickert. These four male union officials represented a trade in which the workforce was almost a third female.[82]

Further explanation of the British WTUL was provided by James O'Grady of the British Trades Union Congress, a fraternal delegate to the AFL convention. He told those assembled of the "very useful work accomplished by the Woman's Trade Union League of Great Britain." He said that "the organization had been of invaluable assistance to the trade union and stated that they had placed a number of paid organizers in the field." Max Morris added that "he believed the Federation of Labor would welcome the new movement and that it would prove of especial assistance to the clerks."[83] Given that the number of women working as retail clerks had grown dramatically in recent years, Morris was justified in seeing the potential benefits of the WTUL for his particular trade.[84] As for the AFL as a whole, it would soon be evident that his sentiments of support were not shared.

At this same meeting, Walling reported on the progress regarding the writing of the constitution, and two resolutions were passed stipulating that the WTUL would first communicate with an existing local or national union before organizing any women into that trade and that the WTUL "should become in some way affiliated with the central labor bodies wherever such affiliation is possible."[85] A resolution was then introduced "asking for the endorsement of the American Federation of Labor." According to the meeting report,

> [i]t was stated by several present that such an endorsement could be secured, but **it was thought advisable not to ask for it until such time as the League should have accomplished some definite work.** The resolution was tabled.[86]

In retrospect, it appears that the WTUL organizers gave up before they even started. Without the full text of that day's discussion it is difficult to pass judgement. Were the assembled social reformers and trade unionists simply being practical? Kenney O'Sullivan certainly had reason to doubt the level of support of the AFL. She knew from her own experience that the AFL was at best ambivalent, at worst hostile, to the organization of women. Kenney O'Sullivan had seen first hand the reluctance of most male trade unionists to see women not as competitors but as allies in the labor movement.

Rather than seek the endorsement of the AFL, the WTUL organizers resolved instead, through Nellie Parker, to submit a resolution to the AFL convention asking that the AFL appoint at least one woman organizer for the coming year.[87] That resolution was approved on the thirteenth and final day of the AFL convention. It would be another five years, however, before the AFL would act on that resolution.[88] The convention also passed a resolution in favor of the Woman's Union Label Leagues.[89]

In her account of the formation of the WTUL, Kenney O'Sullivan claimed that her old friend Sam Gompers asked her "to explain to the delegates the objects of the organization."[90] The historian Philip Foner cites this as well, adding that Gompers' reception of Kenney O'Sullivan was far less enthusiastic than the one he gave Martha Moore Avery, a local anti-Socialist. None of this is contained within the official proceedings nor is there any mention of Kenney O'Sullivan at the podium in the *Boston Globe*'s account of the formation of the WTUL.[91] In an undated letter probably written more than a decade later, Kenney O'Sullivan discussed the founding of the WTUL. In it she wrote, "As to attending a meeting Sam [Gompers] allowed me to announce it in Convention." She went on to say that Gompers "might also remember it [the founding of the WTUL] as I **tried** to get his cooperation at the time."[92] In all likelihood, Kenney O'Sullivan had been allowed to announce the meetings being held to form the WTUL. Formal recognition from the AFL would not be had for some time.

Even without corroboration of anecdotal evidence, it is clear that the AFL did not welcome the WTUL with open arms. The constitution of the WTUL as first written in those few days of November, 1903 reflects that reality. The object of the WTUL was simply "to assist in the organization of women wage workers into trade unions."[93] This had been Kenney O'Sullivan's purpose for twenty-five years; now, finally, it appeared she would be a part of, even a leader in an organization devoted to trade unionism for women. Yet even as the organization was evolving, it was apparent to all that relying solely upon organized labor would not be enough. Social reformers "willing to assist those trade unions already existing, which have women members, and to aid in the formation of new unions of women wage workers" would be welcomed as members too.[94]

In his autobiography, Gompers explained the dangers, in his mind, of a cross-class alliance such as the WTUL. In 1925, he wrote:

> To these efforts of women helping women, interested women of means contributed funds. This sort of subsidizing created a problem of control—whether wage-earning women or those interested in wage-earning women should guide the movement. I had to be on guard constantly to help maintain the balance for trade unionism. . . . The friendly outsider may contribute advice and assistance, but there is no opportunity for him to play a conspicuous part.[95]

The problem of control would be an issue in the years ahead—the work of Nancy Schrom Dye, Elizabeth Anne Payne, and Robin Miller Jacoby attests to that.[96] Women's political culture, as somewhat glowingly described by Kathryn Kish Sklar in her recent work, had its limits—class limits to be exact.[97] Kenney O'Sullivan's experiences in Boston, particularly with the Brahmin-run WEIU, are indicative of those limits. At the same time, however, these "interested women of means contributed funds," as well as a level of support not generally found among the male-dominated trade union movement. True, that support brought with it an inherent tension caused by class difference, resulting in a problem of control which would plague the WTUL for its entire fifty years of existence.

On November 19th, the WTUL organizers met for a third and final time. The constitution was accepted as written by Walling, Kenney O'Sullivan, and Parker. Officers and an executive board were elected, the composition of which barely met the constitutional requirement that a majority of the board be trade union members. Mary Morton Kehew, the socially prominent and socially minded president of the WEIU and a long-time supporter of Kenney O'Sullivan, was elected president while Jane Addams was elected vice-president. Kenney O'Sullivan was elected secretary and Mary Donovan, a shoe worker from Lynn who also served as treasurer for that city's Central Labor Union, was elected treasurer.[98] The other executive board members were Mary MacDowell, a Chicago University Settlement House worker; Lillian Wald, founder of the Henry Street Settlement House in New York; Mary Freitas, a Lowell textile worker; Leonora O'Reilly of New York, a former garment worker and now organizer; and fellow garment workers' organizer, Ellen Lindstrom of Chicago.[99] These nine women—five trade unionists and four "allies"—now faced the difficult task of moving this organization out of a Faneuil Hall meeting room and into the communities they hoped to serve. Given the geographic distribution of the members and the high concentration of women wage earners in those cities, the WTUL established local branches in Boston, New York, and Chicago within a few months.[100]

William English Walling, although not an official member of the Board, was not quite ready to step back. Six days after their final meeting, Walling wrote to WTUL Board member and Chicago settlement house resident Mary MacDowell. He wanted to "venture a few words about the policy followed at the Boston meeting in the election of officers." He wrote that

> Mrs. Kehew was selected for the presidency on account of her influence and sincere friendship to the trade union movement. It was not expected that she or any other of the non-union members of the Executive Board

would be able to give the new organization the time necessary to get it
in working order.

As president of the WEIU and an active supporter of Denison House, as
well as a frequent appointee to city and state committees, Kehew was admittedly not in a position to devote herself exclusively to the WTUL. Nor
could Jane Addams, whose first allegiance was to the settlement house
movement, of which she was a nationally recognized leader. As for the
working-class women on the WTUL Board: they, according to Walling,

> while they may be expected to give considerable time to the work of
> the league, are not so well adapted for that work as they are for the ac-
> tual organization of the workers themselves. . . . [101]

This young man who had never worked for wages in his life easily assumed that trade union women would not be capable of running their
own organization. In the WTUL, as Walling saw it, "women of college
education were to give ideas, women of social position to use their influence to create a social sensitiveness and the women in the trades to supply practical information." [102]

Thus, Walling felt that "Mrs. O'Sullivan with her long years of experience and enthusiasm is undoubtedly adapted for a permanent position in
the movement." [103] In Walling's mind, even Mary Kenney O'Sullivan was
not necessarily capable of leading the WTUL however permanent her position might be. She could, however, "supply practical information" if only
as an old friend of AFL president Gompers. Her participation during the
early years of the WTUL was crucial in another way as well. As a working-
class woman and an experienced organizer, she added a sense of legitimacy to the WTUL while its relation to the AFL remained tenuous at best.

The Boston branch of the WTUL had its first meeting February 14,
1904. National WTUL president Mary Morton Kehew presided and national secretary Kenny O'Sullivan took the minutes. Those present appointed a local executive committee. Wellesley professor Emily Green
Balch was named chair and Typographers' Union representative Mary
Haskell was to be secretary for the Boston WTUL. Other executive committee members included Miss Kaiser[?], Miss Stodard[?], and Rosa
Scully, a tobacco stripper from Roxbury who was active in her union
local and had been a delegate to the 1903 AFL convention. [104]

Mary Haskell and Kenney O'Sullivan agreed to print up two information circulars and Kenney O'Sullivan took on the task of preparing

membership cards. Before adjournment, it was agreed to invite Jane Addams to speak in Boston "at [a] meeting in which sympathizers were to be invited."[105] Presumably the circulars would be passed out to working women as they left their places of work. "Sympathizers" would more likely be attracted to a meeting at which a nationally recognized woman of their class was to speak.

Little more than a month later, Jane Addams did come to Boston when the National WTUL executive board held its first meeting. Addams was joined by the other executive board members Kehew, Kenney O'Sullivan, Mary Donovan, Lillian Wald, and Leonora O'Reilly. Some of the local branch officers attended including William English Walling, now secretary of the New York branch, and Balch and Haskell, representing the Boston League. Also present were John Tobin, president of the Boot and Shoe Workers' Union, and Dennis Driscoll, a union farrier by trade and now president of the BCLU and secretary-treasurer of the MSB.[106]

They met on Sunday morning, March 20th, breaking only for lunch. There was much to discuss and act upon. Local leagues had been established in New York, Chicago and Boston, but it was decided to make those local branches as state-wide as possible. Dennis Driscoll made a motion to establish a closer relationship with the Woman's Union Label Leagues, which was carried. Driscoll and John Tobin also debated whether the WTUL should focus on factory investigation or organizing. Driscoll favored investigation, claiming that making public "the bad conditions permitted by a lack of organization," the necessity of organization would be made clear.[107] Tobin, on the other hand, felt that conditions had been investigated enough and that the WTUL should concentrate on union organizing.

No official motion was made regarding the debate between the two male trade unionists. Yet much of the rest of the discussion focused on the need for a paid organizer. Kenney O'Sullivan, as national secretary, was directed to write Samuel Gompers regarding the yet-to-be-acted-upon resolution of the last AFL convention. That resolution stipulated that at least one woman organizer be put in the field. According to the minutes, "The consensus of opinion was that given the cordiality of the AFL toward the League, we should affiliate ourselves as closely as possible through **our** paid agent."[108] However cordial the AFL may or may not have been, the National Board of the WTUL recognized early on that if a woman organizer was to be appointed, not to mention paid, it would be not through the AFL, but through the WTUL.

The WTUL, nonetheless, wanted desperately to create a working relationship with the AFL. In that vein, it was decided that Kenney O'Sullivan should write Samuel Gompers, asking permission for the local branches of the WTUL to affiliate with the Central Labor Unions in their respective cities and states. Interestingly, before such a letter could be mailed, much less responded to, the BCLU voted later that same day to admit the Boston WTUL as a fraternal, non-voting delegate.[109] It would be another several years before the MSB would follow suit.

The National Board of the WTUL met seven months later, again in Boston, on October 7th. The local leagues reported on their activities. A strike in the Stockyards had kept the Chicago WTUL busy arranging "social receptions, with dancing, reports, and speeches."[110] Walling reported that the New York WTUL had "about fifty members, got by correspondence, and carefully chosen. They [were] all sympathizers."[111] The Boston WTUL had been swept into the Fall River Textile strike [to be discussed in Chap. 4], despite the absence of its sympathizers over the summer. Still trying to chart its course, the WTUL Board again discussed the need for organization as well as for investigation. Given the continued lack of recognition from the AFL, the League decided to take matters into its own hands.

After Kenney O'Sullivan "reported that President Gompers had not yet found it **practicable** to include a woman among the organizers" for the AFL, the WTUL appointed its own.[112] Gertrude Barnum, a judge's daughter from Chicago, was appointed as a national organizer for the WTUL.[113] She was to be paid $75 a month, with each local branch contributing a third of her salary. Apparently, despite Walling's opinion that the working-class members of the WTUL would be ideally suited for organizing, none were now to be found. While Kenney O'Sullivan might have been the obvious choice, her personal circumstances at that time would not permit it. As a widow with three young children, it would have been difficult, if not impossible, for her to take such a position which would demand constant travel. Kenney O'Sullivan did, however, manage to attend the 1904 AFL convention, held a month later in San Francisco. She went as a fraternal delegate representing the National WTUL, hoping to gain the formal recognition denied it at the 1903 AFL convention in Boston. For that task, too, Kenney O'Sullivan was the obvious choice.

A continent away and a year later, the now established WTUL presented itself to the AFL delegates. Two male delegates from the Amalgamated Meatcutters and Butcher Workmen's union introduced the resolution seeking admittance of the WTUL to the annual AFL conventions. The two men claimed that as the WTUL had "rendered the Labor Movement a great service in assisting the women involved in the recent strike of Butcher Workmen [in Chicago] and the existing strike of the Textile Workers [in Fall River]," the WTUL should be granted "one Fraternal Delegate with one vote."[114] The Committee on Resolutions recommended against the resolution. A motion from the floor was made in its favor. Perhaps sensing defeat was at hand, or possibly forewarned, Kenney O'Sullivan offered an amendment to the resolution.

She moved that "the resolution be adopted, with the exception of that part which granted a vote."[115] A shrewd negotiator, Kenney O'Sullivan was willing to give up that one convention vote, out of the almost 16,000 which were allotted, for official recognition of the WTUL. Knowing full well that the AFL appeared to be much more supportive of the Woman's Union Label Leagues, she also moved that that organization be included in the resolution. The compromise as offered by Kenney O'Sullivan, however, was not enough. Frank Foster, a member of the Committee on Resolutions, spoke sharply against his fellow Bostonian's amendment and the resolution itself. Foster said:

> I believe we should have the cooperation of every organization whose sympathies are in accord with the trade union movement, but their fraternal delegates should be by the choice of the Convention, not by a mandatory resolution forcing them upon us whether we wish them or not.[116]

Perhaps Foster was merely putting into practice his personal philosophy of "collective individualism," refusing to be forced into accepting just any fraternal delegate. Maybe it was a completely personal act against the widow of the man who while alive had eclipsed Foster in terms of organizing abilities, popularity, and level of friendship with Samuel Gompers. Possibly, Foster was simply acting as organized labor had for decades, limiting its official membership to those bona fide members of the trade movement rather than mere "supporters."[117] Perhaps it was a combination of all of this. In any case, Kenney O'Sullivan must have been hurt by the lack of support from Foster. He had known her for a dozen years, had seen her in action, and had regularly reported her organizing achievements in his paper, the *Labor Leader*. It certainly did not help the WTUL's efforts to achieve formal recognition from the AFL. Kenney O'Sullivan's amendment was voted down and the Convention delegates voted to accept the Committee's report that the resolution be denied. Despite her best efforts, the WTUL remained outside of the AFL.

Kenney O'Sullivan had been much more successful two days earlier, on November 17th, when she introduced a resolution which easily

passed the convention. Along with James Duncan, secretary-treasurer of
the Granite Cutters' Union and first vice-president of the AFL, Kenney
O'Sullivan offered the following resolution:

> That the best interests of labor require the admission of women to full
> citizenship as a matter of justice to them and as a necessary step toward
> insuring and raising the scale of wages for all.[118]

While the AFL may not have been willing to grant the WTUL membership, full or otherwise, within its organization, organized labor could
support women's suffrage. It would appear that justice for women might
come at the ballot box before it entered the AFL Convention hall.

The following day, November 18th, Kenney O'Sullivan spoke out in
favor a resolution granting economic relief to the strikers of Fall River.
As president of the United Textile Workers, John Golden put forward a
motion asking for a one-cent assessment on the entire AFL membership for three weeks. It was estimated that the assessment would send
$75,000 to Fall River's textile workers, out on strike since July. Admit-
tedly, that would translate to only $3 for each of the 25,000 strikers, but it
was a dramatic gesture of solidarity towards a workforce which was less
than one third unionized and 60% women and children.[119] Several delegates from Massachusetts spoke on behalf of the assessment, including
Frank Foster and Dennis Driscoll.

But it was Kenney O'Sullivan "whose speech. . . . on the condition
of the strikers at Fall River, Mass., caused hundreds of men to burst into
tears and won thunders of applause."[120] According to the *San Francisco
Examiner*, "in a voice ofttimes shaken by emotion, but audible in every
part of the spacious convention hall," she spoke of the suffering of the
women strikers, of the hunger of thousands of children. "To safeguard
the virtue of these unfortunate women," reported the *Boston Globe*, "and
protect the health and perhaps the life of the children," Kenney O'Sullivan urged organized labor to send immediate financial aid to Fall
River.[121]

Kenney O'Sullivan's request was met. Yet the next day, when she attempted to win recognition for the WTUL, she did not receive the standing ovation she was given the day before. Nor did she win a place for the
WTUL within the organized house of labor. While the AFL could readily
sympathize with and offer financial support to hungry women and children during a strike, allowing a cross-class alliance of women dedicated
to trade unionism to join their ranks was not possible.

Nonetheless, the WTUL would forge ahead. The League engaged in strikes and organizing, educational programs and investigation of work conditions. Initially, the WTUL carried out these activities through its three original branches. For the Boston WTUL, the first challenge was the Fall River textile strike. There the Boston League did not seriously attempt to organize the strikers; rather, they sought to transform them into domestic servants. It was, it would turn out, an unfortunate decision made by those willing to assist.

NOTES

[1]Mary Kenney O'Sullivan, unpublished autobiography, n.d., c. 1920s, Schlesinger Library, Radcliffe College, Cambridge, MA., microfilm edition, the papers of the Women's Trade Union League and Its Principal Leaders, Smaller Collections Reel 1, p. 201; hereafter, Kenney O'Sullivan, autobio..

[2]In 1900, the U.S. Census found the following percentages of women at work:

Native born, of native born parents, 21–24 years old: 21%
Native born, of immigrant parents, 16–20 years old: 40%
Immigrant women, 16–20 years old: 57%
African American women, 16–20 years old: 50%
African American women, 55–64 years old: 41%

All figures from Dept. of Commerce and Labor, Bureau of the Census, *Statistics of Women at Work* (Washington, D.C.: Government Printing Office, 1907), p. 12.

[3]According to figures based on the 1900 Census, a growing number of white native-born women were entering the clerical field. The largest growth rates for white women both native-born and immigrant were found in manufacturing where increased mechanization—leading to deskilling of production and decreasing wages—facilitated the entry of women. For example, between 1890 and 1900, the number of women glovemakers increased by 109%; women shirt, collar, and cuff makers, 90%; women candy makers and knitting mill operatives, both 61% For the same period, the number of women working as domestics increased only 6%. *Statistics of Women at Work*, p. 32, p. 39.

[4]Of the almost 59,000 women who worked in manufacturing in Illinois, almost 45,000 of them did so within Chicago; of those women, about 38% worked as garment makers. See: U.S. Bureau of the Census, *Twelfth Census* (1900), Vol. 8, Part 2, p. 171, p. 173, p. 181.

A similar situation was found in New York. Out of that state's 230,000 female factory workers, more than 132,000 worked in New York City, almost 40% of them in the garment trade. See: *Twelfth Census* (1900), Vol. 8, Part 2, p. 597, p. 623, p. 631, p. 637. See also: Nancy Schrom Dye, *As Equals and As Sisters: Feminism, the Labor Movement, and the Women's Trade Union League of New York* (Columbia: University of Missouri Press, 1980), p. 17.

[5]*Twelfth Census*, Vol. 8, Part 2, p. 365, p. 367, p. 371, p. 373, p. 383, p. 389, p. 391. See also: Thomas Dublin, *Transforming Women's Work: New England Lives in the Industrial Revolution* (Ithaca: Cornell University Press, 1994), p. 252.

[6]Joseph A. Hill, *Women in Gainful Occupations, 1870– 1920*, U.S. Bureau of the Census, Monograph No. 9 (Washington, D.C.: Government Printing Office, 1929), pp. 75–76; p. 133.

[7]"Social Statistics of Workingwomen," *Massachusetts Labor Bulletin* No. 18 (May 1901). The one hundred women comprised the following occupations and locations: 20 retail workers in Boston; 20 textile workers in Lowell and Fall River; 20 waitresses from Boston; 20 shoe workers from Haverhill and Lynn; and 20 domestics from the Boston area.

[8]"Social Statistics of Workingwomen," p. 40.

[9]Alice Kessler-Harris, *A Woman's Wage: Historical Meanings and Social Consequences* (Lexington: University Press of Kentucky, 1990), p. 8.

[10]Ardis Cameron, *Radicals of the Worst Sort: Laboring Women in Lawrence, Massachusetts, 1860–1912* (Urbana: University of Illinois Press, 1993), pp. 98–99; Dublin, *Transforming Women's Work*, p. 255; Dye, *As Equals and As Sisters*, p. 21.

[11]*Proceedings of the Twenty-first Annual Convention of the American Federation of Labor*, (1901), p. 187.

[12]Alice Kessler-Harris, *Out to Work: A History of Wage-Earning Women in the United States* (New York: Oxford University Press, 1982), p. 152 and "'Where are the Organized Women Workers?'," *Feminist Studies* 3 (Fall 1975): p. 92.

[13]Much of this growth occurred in the AFL-affiliated unions; independent unions, such as the railroad brotherhoods, grew at a much slower pace. Leo Wolman, *The Growth of American Trade Unions, 1880–1923* (New York: National Bureau of Economic Research, Inc., 1924), p. 34.

[14]Theresa Wolfson, "Where are the Organized Women Workers?" *American Federationist* 32 (June 1925): p. 455.

[15]Kessler-Harris, "'Where are the Organized Women Workers?" p. 94.

[16]Ava Baron, "Gender and Labor History: Learning from the Past, Looking to the Future," in *Work Engendered: Toward a New History of American Labor*, Ava Baron, ed. (Ithaca: Cornell University Press, 1991), p. 13.

[17]Kessler-Harris, " 'Where are the Organized Women Workers?' " pp. 94–95.

[18]John Stafford, "The Good That Trade Unions Do," *American Federationist* 9 (July 1902): p. 358.

[19]Stafford, *American Federationist* 9 (Aug 1902): p. 423.

[20]Arthur E. Holder, "Woman in Economics," *American Federationist* 9 (July 1902): p. 367, emphasis added.

[21]Quoted in Gladys Boone, *The Women's Trade Union Leagues in Great Britain and the United States of America* (New York: Columbia University Press, 1942), p. 23. On the formation of the British WTUL see also: Betty Askwith, *Lady Dilke: A Biography* (London: Chatto & Windus, 1969); Harold Goldman, *Emma Paterson: She Led Woman into a Man's World* (London: Lawrence & Wishart, 1974); and Robin Miller Jacoby, *The British and American Women's Trade Union Leagues, 1890– 1925* (Brooklyn, NY: Carlson Publishing, Inc., 1994).

[22]Jacoby, *The British and American Women's Trade Union Leagues*, p. 21.

[23]*American Federationist* 6 (June 1899).

[24]*American Federationist* 8 (April 1908): pp. 135–136.

[25]*Proceedings of the Seventeenth Annual Convention of the Massachusetts State Branch, American Federation of Labor* Oct. 6–9, 1902 (Boston: Foster's Union, 1902), pp. 10–11.

[26]*Proceedings . . . MSB* (1902), p. 37. For discussion of night work laws, see: Alice Kessler-Harris, "The Paradox of Motherhood: Night Work Restrictions in the United States," in *Protecting Women: Labor Legislation in Europe, the United States, and Australia, 1880-1920* Ulla Wikander, Alice Kessler-Harris, and Jane Lewis, eds. (Urbana: University of Illinois Press, 1995), pp. 337–357. In Massachusetts, night work laws were aimed at women and children in the textile industry. After seventeen years of agitation by male trade unionists and female social reformers, a law banning the employment of women and minors in textile mills between 6 p.m. and 6 a.m. was finally passed in 1907. See: Clara M. Beyer, *History of Labor Legislation for Women in Three States* Women's Bureau Bulletin No. 66 (Washington, DC: Government Printing Office, 1929), pp. 49–54.

[27]Historical treatments of protective labor legislation directed at women wage-earners are numerous. For example, see: Judith A. Baer, *The Chains of Protection: The Judicial Response to Women's Labor Legislation* (Westport, CT: Greenwood Press, 1978); Ava Baron, "Protective Labor Legislation and the Cult of Domesticity," *Journal of Family Issues* 2 (1981): pp. 25–38; Nancy S. Erickson, "Muller v. Oregon Reconsidered: The Origins of a Sex-based Doctrine of Liberty of Contract," *Labor History* 30 (1989): pp. 228–250; and Susan Lehrer, *Origins of Protective Labor Legislation for Women, 1905-1925* (Albany: State University of New York, 1987).

[28]In 1914, women bookbinders in Philadelphia and New York City complained that recently-passed state laws, which banned nightwork for women, in effect meant longer hours for less pay. As nightwork in binderies paid twice that of a day wage, women had to work six days for what they could earn working just three nights. See Barbara M. Klaczynska, "Working Women in Philadelphia, 1900–1930" (Ph.D. diss., Temple University, 1975), p. 119, and Lehrer, *Origins of Protective Labor Legislation for Women*, pp. 128–129.

[29]*Proceedings of the Eighteenth Annual Convention of the Massachusetts State Branch, American Federation of Labor* (Boston: Suffolk Press, 1903), p. 16. See also Maurine Weiner Greenwald, "Working-Class Feminism and the Family Wage Ideal: The Seattle Debate on Married Women's Right to Work, 1914–1920," *Journal of American History* 76 (1989): pp. 118–149.

[30]*Proceedings . . . MSB* (1903), p. 17. See also: Kessler-Harris, *A Woman's Wage*, p. 21.

[31]*Proceedings . . . MSB* (1903), p. 77.

[32]*Proceedings of the Twenty-fourth Annual Convention of the Massachusetts State Branch, American Federation of Labor* (Boston: Allied Printing, 1909), p. 13; the MSB did not recognize the existence of the WTUL until 1911, and then only as a "fraternal delegate." See *Proceedings of the Twenty-sixth Annual Convention of the Massachusetts State Branch, American Federation of Labor* (Boston: Feinberg & Sons, 1911), pp. 78–79.

[33]P.H. Shevlin, "Second Prize Essay," [Union Label Essay Contest] *American Federationist* 11 (July 1904): p. 576.

[34]M.A. Tierney, "A Union Label Talk," *American Federationist* 9 (July 1902): p. 365.

[35]In 1885 the Hatters' union and the Iron Molders both developed a union label. Six years later, the United Garment Workers and the Printers followed suit. By 1900 many other crafts, including Shoemakers, Custom Tailors, Horseshoers, and Brewers also used a union label.

[36]Regarding the Letter Carriers, see: *Thirty-second Annual Report of the Massachusetts Bureau of Statistics of Labor* (Boston: Wright & Potter Co., 1902), p. 40; regarding the Labor Day parade, see: *Thirty-fourth Annual Report of the Massachusetts Bureau of the Statistics of Labor* (Boston: Wright & Potter Co., 1904), p. 340.

[37]Quoted in Philip S. Foner, *Women and the American Labor Movement: From Colonial Times to the Eve of World War I* (New York: The Free Press, 1979), p. 240.

[38]For an excellent discussion of the gendered and racialized components of the trade union label, albeit a generation later, see Dana Frank, *Purchasing Power: Consumer Organizing, Gender, and the Seattle Labor Movement, 1919–1929* (New York: Cambridge University Press, 1994), esp. Chaps. 8 & 9.

[39]Walter MacArthur, "First Prize Essay," in the Union Label Prize Contest in *American Federationist* 11 (July 1904): pp. 573–574.

[40]MacArthur, "First Prize Essay," p. 573.

[41]Kenney O'Sullivan, autobio., p. 86.

[42]"The Boston Woman's Union Label League," in Vida Dutton Scudder papers, box 2, folder 15, Sophia Smith Collection, Smith College, Northampton, MA. In Jan., 1903, the MSB Executive Committee voted to organize a Woman's Union Label League. See *Thirty-fourth Annual Report of the Massachusetts Bureau of the Statistics of Labor* (1904), p. 335.

[43]Mary Kenney O'Sullivan, "Occupations Opened to Women," *Boston Globe*, Nov. 10, 1903.

[44]"Resolutions Adopted by the Union for Industrial Progress at Boston, Mass.," *American Federationist* 6 (Sept. 1899): p. 180.

[45]On McNeill, see: Robert R. Montgomery, "'To Fight This Thing Till I Die': The Career of George Edwin McNeill," in *Culture, Gender, Race, and U.S. Labor History*, Ronald C. Keat, et al., eds. (Westport, CT: Greenwood Press, 1993), pp. 3–23.

[46]*Boston Globe*, Jan. 27, 1902.

[47]Shortly after the death of her first son, John Kenney (1896–1898), Kenney O'Sullivan gave birth to another son, Mortimer. Yet another son, Roger, was born two years later, in 1900; Mary Elizabeth was born in February, 1902, seven months before her father's death.

[48]For a recent overview of the educational and reform emphasis of the WEIU, see Laurie Crumpacker, "Beyond Servants and Salesgirls: Working Women's Education in Boston, 1885–1915," in *Women of the Commonwealth: Work, Family, and Social Change in Nineteenth-Century Massachusetts* (Amherst: University of Massachusetts Press, 1996), pp. 207–232.

[49]Women's Educational and Industrial Union Board of Governors' Minutes, Vol. 8 (Oct.1, 1902–Oct.1, 1904), p. 60, Schlesinger Library, Radcliffe College, Cambridge, MA.

[50]WEIU Board of Governors minutes, Vol. 8, pp. 86–87.

[51]Women's Educational and Industrial Union, *Annual Report* (Boston: William B. Libby, 1904), p. 11.

[52]WEIU constitution, as reprinted in *A Report of Progress Made in the year 1905 Being the Twenty-fifth Anniversary of the Women's Educational and Industrial Union* (Boston: n.p., 1905), p. 5.

[53]Kathryn Kish Sklar, *Florence Kelley and the Nation's Work: The Rise of Women's Political Culture, 1830–1900* (New Haven, CT: Yale University Press, 1995), p. xiii. For an extremely perceptive review of Sklar's important biography of Kelley, see Dana Frank, "A Small Circle of Friends," *The Nation* (June 5, 1995): pp. 797–800. My thanks to Mary Blewett for pointing this out to me.

⁵⁴WEIU, *Annual Report* (1904), p. 11.

⁵⁵See Chap. 2.

⁵⁶WEIU, *Annual Report* (1904), p. 12.

⁵⁷"Neglected child" quote from William L. O'Neill, *Everyone Was Brave: A History of Feminism in America* (New York: Quadrangle Books, 1971), p. 98; "step-child" quote from Judith Becker Ranlett, "Sorority and Community: Women's Answer to a Changing Massachusetts, 1865–1895" (Ph.D. diss., Brandeis University, 1974), p. 180.

⁵⁸Allen F. Davis, "The Women's Trade Union League: Origins and Organization," *Labor History* 5 (Winter 1964): p. 3. See also: "What Trade Unionists Think of Settlements," *The Commons* 7 (Sept. 1902): pp. 13–14, and Philip Davis, "The Social Settlement and the Trade Union," *The Commons* 9 (April 1904): pp. 146–147.

⁵⁹See Chap. 2, p. 36.

⁶⁰College Settlements Association, *Twelfth Annual Report* (1901), p. 54, Sophia Smith Collection, Smith College, Northampton, MA.

⁶¹CSA, *Annual Report* (1901), p. 54.

⁶²College Settlement Association, *Fifteenth Annual Report* (1904), p. 37, Sophia Smith Collection, Smith College, Northampton, MA.

⁶³Robert A. Woods and Albert J. Kennedy, eds., *Handbook of Settlements* (New York: Russell Sage Foundation, 1911), p. 108.

⁶⁴Linda K. Kerber, "A Constitutional Right to be Treated like American Ladies: Women and the Obligations of Citizenship," in *U.S. History as Women's History: New Feminist Essays*, Linda K. Kerber, Alice Kessler-Harris, and Kathryn Kish Sklar, eds. (Chapel Hill: University of North Carolina Press, 1995), p. 18.

⁶⁵More than thirty years ago, Joseph Huthmacher argued that the working class, as much as the middle class, was directly behind the period of reform known as the Progressive Era. If nothing else, it was working-class voters who carried reform initiatives in urban elections. See: Huthmacher, "Urban Liberalism and the Age of Reform," *Mississippi Valley Historical Review* 49 (Sept. 1962): pp. 231–241. More recently, David Montgomery has made the same point. See Montgomery, *Citizen Worker: The Experience of Workers in the United States with Democracy and the Free Market During the Nineteenth Century* (New York: Cambridge University Press, 1994), pp. 159–160. For women workers, the notion of citizenship much less its application, was truncated, thus the turn to protective legislation. See Kessler-Harris, "The Paradox of Motherhood," pp. 352–353. Another route for those outside the pale of citizen, could be protection through trade unionism.

⁶⁶This account of Davis's life is based on his autobiography, *And Crown Thy Own Good* (New York: Philosophical Library, 1952).

[67]Davis, *And Crown Thy Own Good*, p. 117.

[68]Davis, *And Crown Thy Own Good*, p. 117.

[69]Davis, *And Crown Thy Own Good*, p. 137. See also: *Thirty-fourth Annual Report of the Massachusetts Bureau of Statistics of Labor* (Boston: Wright & Potter Printing Co., 1904), p. 335.

[70]Davis, *And Crown Thy Own Good*, p. 140.

[71]Davis, "The Women's Trade Union League," p. 7; see also: Boone, *The Women's Trade Union Leagues*, p. 43; Dye, *As Equals and As Sisters*, pp. 14–17; Foner, *Women and the American Labor Movement* (1979), p. 298; Jacoby, *The British and American Women's Trade Union Leagues*, p. 13; and Elizabeth Anne Payne, *Reform, Labor, and Feminism: Margaret Dreier Robins and the Women's Trade Union League* (Urbana: University of Illinois Press, 1988), pp. 45–46. Contemporary accounts include Samuel Gompers, *Seventy Years of Life and Labor: An Autobiography* Vol. I (New York: E.P. Dutton, 1925), p. 490; Kenney O'Sullivan, autobio., p. 201. Biographical sources on Walling include David Shannon, William English Walling," *Dictionary of American Biography* Vol. XI, Supplement Two (New York: Charles Scribner's Sons, 1958), pp. 689–690; his obituary in the *New York Times*, Sept. 13, 1936 as well as in *The Crisis* 43 (Nov. 1936): 334–335; see also: Anna Strunsky Walling, et al., *William English Walling: A Symposium* (Philadelphia: The Telegraph Press, 1938). Walling went on to be one of the founders of the NAACP; see David Levering Lewis, *W.E.B. DuBois: Biography of a Race* (New York: Holt & Co., 1993), passim. Along with several other wealthy reformers, Walling was briefly profiled in "Our Millionaire Socialists," *Cosmopolitan* (Oct. 1906), p. 599, copy in the William English Walling Papers (microfilm edition, 1977), State Historical Society of Wisconsin, reel 2, frame 444. A recent, full-length biographical treatment of Walling and his wife only briefly mentions the formation of the WTUL. See: James Boylan, *Revolutionary Lives: Anna Strunsky & William English Walling* (Amherst: University of Massachusetts Press, 1998), pp. 62–63, p. 71.

[72]*University Settlement Bulletin* (Dec. 1902), the Walling Papers (microfilm edition, 1977), reel 2, frame 332.

[73]As Allen Davis pointed out in his article, "The Women's Trade Union League," written over three decades ago, the WTUL "is an interesting example of the cross-fertilization of reform ideas between the United States and Great Britain," p. 9, note 24. Other scholars have emphasized the connection as well. See Jacoby, *The British and American Trade Union Leagues* for a comparison of the two Leagues. Vivien Hart, *Bound by Our Constitution: Women, Workers, and the Minimum Wage* (Princeton, NJ: Princeton University Press, 1994), compares wage reform efforts in the U.S. and Great Britain.

[74]Strunsky Walling, et al., *Symposium*, p. 23.

[75]Interestingly, the initial resolution called for five minutes of silence during the AFL convention as a tribute to O'Sullivan. Instead, Dennis Driscoll of Boston urged that the recommendation of the Committee on Resolutions be accepted. Rather than five minutes of silence, the more tangible remembrance of contributions to the memorial fund was approved, and much appreciated by his widow, Kenney O'Sullivan. See: *Proceedings of the Twenty-second Annual Convention of the American Federation of Labor* (1902), p. 107.

[76]Kenney O'Sullivan, autobio., p. 201.

[77]Gompers, *Seventy Years of Life and Labor* Vol. 1, p. 490. See: Allen Davis, *Spearheads for Reform*, p. 141, for what he described as the coming together of "the grandson of a Kentucky millionaire and the daughter of an Irish peasant."

[78]Davis, "The Women's Trade Union League," p. 10.

[79]*Proceedings of the Twenty-third Annual Convention of the American Federation of Labor* (1903), p. x. See also: "Reports of Meetings Held for the Purpose of Organizing the Woman's Trade Union League," papers of the Women's Trade Union League, Mary Dreier Robins Collection, microfilm edition, reel 8, frames 221–222; Davis, "Women's Trade Union League," pp. 10–11; Foner, *Women and the American Labor Movement*, p. 298. In its coverage of the opening sessions of the 1903 AFL convention, the *Boston Globe* printed a telling picture on the third page of its Nov. 11th evening edition. Under the headline: "The Great Convention of the A.F.L. in Session," is a photograph showing a sea of white, male faces. Three pages later, on p. 6, can be found a photograph of the "Women as Labor Delegates." There was actually a fifth woman in attendance. However, as a fraternal delegate representing the Church Association for the Advancement of the Interests of Labor, Harriete Keyser was a non-voting attendee.

[80]Gompers, *Seventy Years of Life and Labor*, Vol. 1, p. 490; also quoted in Davis, "The Women's Trade Union League," p. 11, and Foner, *Women and the American Labor Movement*, p. 298.

[81]Kenney O'Sullivan, autobio., p. 200; "Reports of Meetings, MDR papers, reel 8, frame 222.

[82]In 1910, the earliest year for extant figures, men and women were employed in the garment industry as follows:

> Men: 71,163
> Women: 31,809
> Total: 102,972

Percentage of union membership of this workforce in 1910 was:
> Men: 21.9%
> Women: 11.2%
> Total: 16.9%

All figures from Wolman, *The Growth of American Trade Unions, 1880–1923*, p. 147.

[83]"Report of Meeting," MDR papers, reel 8, frame 223.

[84]According to the 1900 Census, the number of women sales clerks had increased from 57,171 in 1890 to 146,577 in 1900, an increase of 156.4%; see: *Statistics of Women at Work*, p. 39.

[85]"Reports of the Meeting," MDR papers, reel 8, frame 223.

[86]"Reports of the Meetings," MDR papers, reel 8, frame 224.

[87]*Boston Globe*, Nov. 20, 1903.

[88]*Proceedings . . . AFL*, 1903, p. 249; Kessler-Harris, *Out to Work*, pp. 155–156.

[89]*Proceedings . . . AFL* (1903), p. 119. In his opening remarks, Gompers had taken the National Consumers' League (NCL) to task for their issuance of labels to workplaces deemed by the NCL as "sanitary" regardless of whether those workplaces were unionized. He went on to state that the matter having been brought to the NCL's attention, Gompers was certain that "this unintentional injury" would cease. *Proceedings . . . AFL* (1903), p. 23. On the NCL, see: Kathryn Kish Sklar, "Two Political Cultures in the Progressive Era: The National Consumers' League and the American Association for Labor Legislation," in *U.S. History as Women's History: New Feminist Essays*, Kerber, Kessler-Harris, & Kish Sklar, eds., pp. 36–62.

[90]Kenney O'Sullivan, autobio., p. 20.

[91]*Boston Globe*, Nov. 18, 1903.

[92]Mary Kenney O'Sullivan to Alice Henry, n.d., c. 1914, Papers of the National Women's Trade Union League, microfilm edition, reel 17, frame 396, Library of Congress, emphasis added.

[93]WTUL constitution as reprinted in Boone, *The Women's Trade Union Leagues*, p. 250. See also: Davis, "The Women's Trade Union League," p. 11, and Foner, *Women and the American Labor Movement* (1979), p. 300.

[94]WTUL constitution, Boone, *The Women's Trade Union Leagues*, p. 250.

[95]Gompers, *Seventy Years of Life and Labor*, Vol. 1, p. 490–491.

[96]Dye, *As Equals and As Sisters*, pp. 51–52; Payne, *Reform, Labor, and Feminism*, p. 61; Jacoby, p. 58. Working-class organizer and WTUL Executive Board member Leonora O'Reilly was so infuriated by class conflicts within the WTUL that she briefly resigned in 1905, only to permanently resign in 1915. See: Mary J. Bularzik, "The Bonds of Belonging: Leonora O'Reilly and Social Reform," *Labor History* 24 (1983): pp. 60–83.

[97]Sklar, *Florence Kelley and the Nation's Work*, esp. Part III; the limitations of women's political culture also included those of race and ethnicity. I agree with Dana Frank's observation that "The evidence presented in the book suggests,

however, that only a small circle of rich white women gained power," "A Small Circle of Friends," p. 798.

[98]Mary Donovan, related to a Lynn shoe manufacturer, played a leading role in the divisive 1903 shoeworkers' strike. According to historian Mary Blewett, as local secretary of the increasingly conservative Boot and Shoe Workers Union, Donovan sided with the AFL-affiliated union rather than that of the women strikers who were represented by the Lady Stitchers' Assembly, a Knights of Labor affiliate. See: Blewett, *Men, Women, and Work*, p. 308. In a sense, this strike was an example of the still on-going battle between the Knights and the AFL, a battle which most historians see as won by the late-1880s. See: Leon Fink, *Workingmen's Democracy: The Knights of Labor and American Politics* (Urbana: University of Illinois Press, 1985), p. 199; Bruce Laurie, *Artisans into Workers: Labor in Nineteenth-Century America* (New York: The Noonday Press, 1989), Chap. 6; Richard J. Oestreicher, *Solidarity and Fragmentation: Working People and Class Consciousness in Detroit, 1875–1900* (Urbana: University of Illinois Press, 1989), Chap. 6. Not surprisingly, Kenney O'Sullivan also sided with the AFL, sharply criticizing the Lady Stitchers' strike in an article which appeared in the *Boston Globe*, Jan. 25, 1903. According to Mary Blewett, the position taken by Kenney O'Sullivan, Donovan, and the AFL, doomed the WTUL in its efforts to reach the women stitchers north of Boston. See Blewett, *Men, Women, and Work*, p. 314.

[99]Walling paid for the telegrams sent to those Executive Board members not present, informing them of their appointment. Kenney O'Sullivan to Alice Henry, n.d., c. 1914, National Women's Trade Union League papers, Library of Congress, microfilm edition, reel 17, frame 936. Alice Henry, an Australian journalist and social reformer, came to the U.S. in 1906 and went to work for the National WTUL. In 1914, she was preparing to write a book on Women and trade unionism and it was likely then that she contacted Kenney O'Sullivan for background information. The resulting publication was *The Trade Union Woman* (New York: Appleton, 1915). On Henry, see: Diane Kirkby, *Alice Henry: The Power of the Pen and Voice, The Life of an Australian-American Labor Reformer* (New York: Cambridge University Press, 1991).

[100]On the National WTUL see: Susan Amsterdam, "The National Women's Trade Union League," *Social Service Review* (June 1982): pp. 259–272; Boone, *The Women's Trade Union Leagues*; Davis, "The Women's Trade Union League,"; Jacoby, *The British and American Women's Trade Union League*; Kirkby, *Alice Henry*, and "'The Wage Earning Woman and the State': The National Women's Trade Union League and Protective Labor Legislation, 1903–1923," *Labor History* 28 (1987): pp. 54–74; Payne, *Reform, Labor, and Feminism*. Substantial treatments of the WTUL, on the national level, can be

found in the following general works: Foner, *Women and the American Labor Movement* (1979), Chaps. 16, 17, 23, and 26; James J. Kenneally, *Women and American Trade Unions* (Montreal: Eden Press, 1981), Chaps. 5 and 6; Kessler-Harris, *Out to Work*, Chaps. 5–7.

Less attention has been paid to the local branches. On the New York WTUL, see: Dye, *As Equals and As Sisters*; Gary E. Endelman, *Solidarity Forever: Rose Schneiderman and the Women's Trade Union League* (Ann Arbor, MI: University Microfilm International, 1979); and Annelise Orleck, *Common Sense and a Little Fire: Women and Working-Class Politics in the United States, 1900–1965* (Chapel Hill: University of North Carolina Press, 1995). On the Chicago League, see Sandra Conn, "Three Talents: Robins, Nestor, and Anderson of the Chicago Women's Trade Union League," *Chicago History* 9 (1980–1981): pp. 234–247, and Colette A. Hyman, "Labor Organizing and Female Institution-building: The Chicago Women's Trade Union League, 1904–1924" in *Women, Work, and Protest: A Century of U.S. Women's Labor History*, Ruth Milkman, ed. (New York: Routledge & Kegan Paul, 1987).

The Boston WTUL has been examined only in the post-1912 era. See Stephen H. Norwood, "From 'White Slave' to Labor Activist: The Agony and Triumph of a Boston Brahmin Woman in the 1910s," *The New England Quarterly* 65 (1992): pp. 61–92; Norwood, *Labor's Flaming Youth: Telephone Operators and Worker Militancy, 1878–1923* (Urbana: University of Illinois Press, 1990); and Norwood, "Reclaiming Working-Class Activism: The Boston Women's Trade Union League, 1930–1950," *Labor's Heritage* Vol. 10 (Summer 1998): pp. 20–35.

[101]William English Walling to Mary MacDowell, Nov. 25, 1903, Papers of the National Women's Trade Union League, Library of Congress, microfilm edition, reel 17, frame 53.

[102]As quoted in Dye, *As Equals and As Sisters*, p. 34.

[103]Walling to MacDowell, Nov. 25, 1903.

[104]Handwritten minutes, "The first meeting of the New England members of the National Women's Trade Union League," Feb. 14, 1904, Mary Kenney O'Sullivan papers, Schlesinger Library, Radcliffe College, Cambridge, MA.

[105]"The first meeting," Feb. 14, 1904.

[106]Handwritten minutes, "First meeting of the National Board of the Women's Trade Union League," March 20, 1904, Kenney O'Sullivan papers.

[107]"First Meeting of the National Board," March 20, 1904, p. 4.

[108]"First Meeting of the National Board," March 20, 1904, p. 5, emphasis added.

[109]*Boston Globe*, March 21, 1904.

[110]Handwritten minutes, "Second Meeting," Oct. 7, 1904, p. 2, Kenney O'Sullivan papers.

[111]"Second Meeting," Oct. 7, 1904, p. 3.

[112]"Second Meeting," Oct. 7, 1904, p. 1, emphasis added.

[113]Melvyn Dubofsky, "Gertrude Barnum," in *Notable American Women, 1607–1950* (Cambridge, MA: Belknap Press, 1971), pp. 93–94; see also: Ann Schofield, *"To do and to be": Portraits of Four Women Activists, 1893–1986* (Boston: Northeastern University Press, 1997), pp. 20–49.

[114]*Proceedings of the Twenty-fourth Annual Convention of the American Federation of Labor* (1904), p. 161.

[115]*Proceedings . . . AFL* (1904), p. 161.

[116]*Proceedings . . . AFL* (1904), p. 161.

[117]It should be noted, as recorded in the annual AFL *Proceedings* that fraternal delegates from the British Trades Union Congress did have voting privileges at the AFL conventions during this period.

[118]*Proceedings . . . AFL* (1904), p. 147.

[119]*San Francisco Examiner*, Nov. 19, 1904, copy in the Kenney O'Sullivan papers.

[120]*San Francisco Examiner*, Nov. 19, 1904.

[121]*San Francisco Examiner* and *Boston Globe*, both Nov. 19, 1904.

CHAPTER 4

"The Fight for Subsistence"
The Early Years of the Boston Women's Trade Union League

Despite the outpouring of support from the recent AFL national convention, many in Fall River had little if anything to be grateful for at Thanksgiving 1904. The *Boston Globe* reported that although promises of AFL strike fund assistance were encouraging, "it was a gloomy Thanksgiving at best."[1] Local charities tried to help make the day a bit brighter. The Salvation Army, as it had been doing for several weeks, fed soup to 500 children and 250 adults. A former Fall River priest now serving a parish on Cape Cod sponsored a dinner for 1000 children at Anawam Hall.[2] Organized labor offered some holiday relief as well. The Textile Council, representing all the Fall River textile unions, spent $2000 sending out food baskets for 250 families. But, given that upwards of 25,000 Fall River textile workers had been out on strike for four months, the combined relief efforts barely scratched the surface of the needs of an increasingly desperate and hungry community engaged in a collective "fight for subsistence."[3]

The recently-created coalition of trade union leaders and social reformers known as the Women's Trade Union League joined in this struggle. In its first strike, the WTUL had much to learn about both labor organizing and organized labor. Most of all, the WTUL would come face to face with the limitations of its own organization as it attempted to put into practice its goals for wage-earning women. These limitations were structural as well as sentimental. They impacted on how the WTUL evolved as an organization and shaped its tenuous relationship with the AFL. These limitations, of both structure and sentiment, certainly shaped the WTUL response to the Fall River strike of 1904. Six years later, a more experienced WTUL would apply some of the lessons learned in Fall River to a much smaller but more successful strike by carpet weavers in Roxbury.

For a number of reasons, the strike that began in Fall River on July 25, 1904 was a long time in coming. A recession in the cotton industry, brought on by high prices for raw cotton and declining revenues from the finished product, had prompted the owners of Fall River's giant textile mills to cut wages by 10% in November 1903. Weavers were under additional strain from the growing intensity of the work itself as manufacturers increased the number of looms the average weaver tended from eight "to ten, twelve, even fourteen."[4] With more looms to tend simultaneously, weavers were actually producing less cloth, which further reduced their wages as they were paid not by the hour but by the piece. Thus, according to the *Massachusetts Labor Bulletin*, "their weekly earning are reduced, although the amount of work they are required to do is increased."[5]

For their part, the owners also claimed to be under pressure from more than the industry-wide recession. The growing threat of Southern competition was cited by Fall River manufacturers as a burden to be shared by workers and owners alike.[6] Testifying before a Massachusetts legislative committee in 1903, industry spokesman Charles Bancroft focused on the fact that the Southern textile mills could and did pay higher stock dividends. According to Bancroft, the South enjoyed many advantages over the mills of New England. In the South could be found cheaper land, lower taxes, and fewer labor laws.[7] Seemingly the only possible response for this troubled industry was to cut wages. According to the historian John Cumbler, however, there was another potential, if partial, panacea Fall River manufacturers could have introduced.

Cumbler claims that the city's mill owners dragged their heels in introducing more technologically advanced machinery such as the Northrup and Draper looms. These automated looms increased production and allegedly made the weaver's job less stressful. According to Cumbler, the mill owners' reluctance to introduce new technology stemmed from the "interlocking directorships" so common in the relatively small business community of Fall River. Textile mill owners also had controlling interests in local companies which produced the older looms and thus had little incentive to shop elsewhere. Rather, Fall River manufacturers "concentrated on speculating on cotton rather than investing in technology."[8] They also cut wages.

When the Cotton Manufacturers Association announced a wage cut of twelve and a half percent beginning July 25, 1904, their mills were overstocked. Therefore, they could more than afford to stop production should workers go out on strike in reaction to the latest reduction of wages. As the *Massachusetts Labor Bulletin* would later remark, "the time could hardly have been arranged more conveniently for the manufacturers."[9] The more cautious leaders of organized labor fought for time, urging the rank and file to delay any strike action.[10] At a meeting arranged by the State Board of Arbitration on July 22nd, the union-led Textile Council asked the mill owners to postpone the wage cut, due to go into effect in three days, for another two weeks. The mill owners refused, and, in any case, it was already too late. Despite recommendations from their leaders, the active rank-and-file mill workers had already voted to strike.

On July 20th three of the five unions representing at best only one-fifth of Fall River's textile workers voted to go out on strike. Of the city's 25,000 cotton workers, only between four and five thousand were union members and only 1,909 of that number actually voted, 1,513 voting to strike. While slightly more than 1,000 organized weavers voted eight-to-one in favor of a strike, the Mule Spinners' union failed to reach the necessary two-thirds majority and the Carders' union was almost equally divided. Thus, "this strike of such magnitude and far-reaching results, affecting 26,000 operatives, was declared at the will of 1,513 persons."[11] Half of those operatives were women.

Quoting the Abstract of the Twelfth U.S. Census, William Hard wrote in 1908, "If you want to see the climax of female factory industry in the United States, go to Fall River."[12] According to that same census of 1900, of the just over 13,000 women employed in Fall River, 12,000 worked in the textile industry.[13] But the numbers tell only part of the story. Those numbers were mirrored in the character, not to mention the sights and sounds, of this single-industry city:

> The girls of the cotton mills of Fall River perform a promenade on Main Street every Saturday afternoon. From half past one they walk, solid sidewalks of them reaching half a mile to the north and half a mile to the south of the post office, and plunging together in a kind of foam-crested storm-wave of hats. . . . [14]

That storm wave of hats for the most part rested upon the heads of young, single immigrant women in their late teens and early twenties. As reported by the Massachusetts Bureau of the Statistics of Labor in 1903, however, one out of five of Fall River's women textile workers was married, and the fact that the proportion of married women workers was growing was a matter of concern.

The Bureau's investigation found that only in Fall River and nearby New Bedford did the number of married women exceed 20 percent of the total female workforce of each city. But several other single-industry cities in the Commonwealth, such as the shoe cities of Brockton and Haverhill, as well as other textile centers such as Lawrence and Lowell, saw almost as high a percentage of married women working in the mills.[15] Declining wages in a constricted job market meant that the families residing in textile cities such as Fall River needed the income of several family members, including the wife and/or mother, simply to survive.[16] Thus, while the majority of women textile workers in Massachusetts continued to fit the stereotypical mold of young, single women, a shift can be seen. Increasingly, the new industrial woman of the early twentieth century was not a young woman nor was she a single, self-supporting individual. She was certainly most likely to be an immigrant or the child of immigrants, especially if this new industrial woman lived in Fall River.

In 1900 "Fall River had a higher percentage of foreign-born inhabitants than any other city in the United States."[17] A steady stream of immigrants had poured into the city since the nineteenth century. As William Hard wrote in 1908:

> . . . the Portuguese in Fall River are now supplanting the French-Canadians in the lower forms of mill work, just as the French-Canadians undermined the Irish and English, just as the English and Irish got in beneath the native New Englanders. . . .[18]

With the exception of the Lancashire English, many of whom had worked in the textile industry before emigration, each successive wave of immigrants entered the mill in the least skilled and lowest-paid positions. By the time of the 1904 strike, French Canadians represented the largest immigrant group in Fall River and were beginning to move up "the industrial scale."[19] Initially unwelcome in either the mill or the union hall, by the early years of the twentieth century French Canadians had begun to enter the ranks of the skilled workers represented by a trade union.[20] Correspondingly, ethnic hostility in Fall River had shifted by 1904 to more recent arrivals: the Portuguese, who came primarily from the Azores, and growing numbers of Polish immigrants.

Viewed with contempt by the immigrants who had preceded them, the Portuguese and Poles were isolated both residentially as well as within the mill. Even on Fall River's Main Street, where the women flocked after their half-day of work on a Saturday, ethnic divisions, and even outright hostility, were in evidence. In describing one (probably fictionalized) recent immigrant from the Azores by the name of Margarida Maria Rodrigues, the reform-minded writer William Hard compared her appearance to that of a French Canadian woman. In her "neat brown tailored suit," one would hardly know that the more skilled and more highly paid weave-room worker "came from Quebec as much as five years ago." Rodrigues, on the other hand, was still "engaged, painfully but persistently, in making the transition from Portuguese to American conceits of dress."[21] While she had shed her "vivid salmon-colored skirt and a comprehensive purple shawl," Rodrigues' new American dress, with its low-cut neck and "promiscuous ruching," was viewed with disdain by her more acculturated fellow-worker:

> As [Rodrigues] comes out of the department store, the sophisticated eye of the weave-room girl runs quickly, coolly, [over Rodrigues]. . . . And if you really want to know what pain is the most hideous that . . . Rodrigues endures in the course of the week, it is the look she gets from that weave-room girl who wouldn't think of touching a drawing-frame . . .[22]

These craft and ethnic divisions were played out in more than styles of dress. They were equally present within the trade union community of Fall River.

In a series of articles submitted to the *Manchester Guardian* in 1903, British social commentator T.M. Young summed up the impact of ethnic divisions upon trade unionism in Fall River:

> The constant flow of immigrants from Europe and from Canada, many of whom cannot speak or understand English, makes any efficient union of labour in the cotton mills impossible. . . . [23]

But more than a language barrier inhibited union growth in Fall River. Craft divisions had remained even after the AFL sponsored the formation of the United Textile Workers of America (UTW) in 1901. The UTW "merged almost all of the textile unions then in existence including . . . the old cotton craft unions of New England, chiefly weavers and card room workers."[24] Only the Mule-Spinners' union remained outside of the UTW, a reflection of the strong national organization of these highly-skilled workers.

Based in Fall River, with local weaver James Tansey as its first president, the UTW was meant to be not so much an industrial as an "inter-industrial" union, representing textile workers regardless of craft. Despite its promise, however, the UTW was never able to rise above "the narrow craft conceits of the Fall River officials."[25] When, in 1899, Tansey had been appointed president of the local Textile Council, an organization meant to represent all of Fall River's textile unions, he had appeared to be a supporter of the industrial model of unionism. Thus he was the logical choice as the next president of the UTW, which was to bring that same approach to the national level. But by 1903 the UTW president had soured on the idea of "inter-industrial" unionism and was leading the exodus of organized skilled textile workers out of the UTW. Fearing that the UTW was not doing enough to "protect the skilled positions which were dominated by the English, Irish, and French Canadian workers," Tansey resigned from the presidency and the union.[26]

Ethnic divisions were certainly a major factor in the apparent triumph of craft over industrial unionism, at least among the Fall River textile workers. Language barriers were compounded by basic but virulent prejudice directed at the latest wave of immigrants to Fall River. Coming from vastly different cultures, the Portuguese and the Polish immigrants who entered the mills as unskilled, low-paid operatives were met with scorn by the immigrants who had come before them. The more skilled workers feared that this new cohort working for much lower wages would drive down the wages of all. The repeated wage cuts for all crafts in 1903 and again in 1904 seemed to prove them right. But more than ethnicity played a role in the unions' inability to coalesce into a cohesive and potentially powerful whole.

According to the British observer, T.M. Young, writing in 1903:

> . . . mule-spinning is being gradually abandoned by American mills in favour of ring-spinning, for which cheap and comparatively unskilled labour can be employed. 'The mule-spinners,' said one mill superintendent to me, 'are a tough crowd to deal with. A few years ago they were giving trouble at this mill, so. . . . [w]hen the men came back on Monday morning, they were astonished to find that there is no work for them. That room is now full of ring frames run by **girls**.[27]

Increased mechanization resulting in lesser-skilled, lower-paid positions which would be then considered appropriate for women was occurring in many industries during the nineteenth and into the twentieth century. As previously stated, an increasingly stratified gender-based division of labor resulting from technological change also occurred in bookbinding and printing. This gendered division of labor, which in the textile industry was further complicated by issues of ethnicity, made union organizing that much more difficult; in the eyes of the textile-union leaders of Fall River, half of their fellow operatives were seen as unorganizable by virtue of their ethnicity as well as their gender.[28] Such seemingly unsurmountable odds explain in large part why at best only 20 percent of Fall River's textile workers were union members when all 25,000 went out on strike in July 1904. Regardless of their union status, ethnicity, or gender, all workers had been hurt by the repeated wage cuts and accelerated work pace. Thus, despite divisions amongst the workers and a cautious leadership, the vote to strike was taken. On the morning of July 25th, when the mill whistles blew, the workers stayed out.

That first day hundreds of strikers gathered peacefully at the mill gates, jeering the handful of workers who initially did not join their striking co-workers. According to the *Boston Globe*, "Aside from a little yelling and good-natured bantering of the few who went in, the operatives made no demonstration, and it was as quiet and orderly around the other mill gates as it is on Sabbath morning."[29] Although seventy-two mills employing 26,000 workers eventually shut down for almost six months, there was little if any violence connected to the strike. It would later be reported that the number of arrests made by the Fall River Police actually decreased by twenty-five percent for the period covering the first two months of the strike.[30] Such an absence of violence was extraordinary, particularly given the sheer number of workers involved and, as time went on, the length of the strike (it would last into the next year).

Initially, there was an almost festive air to this summer-time strike. "MANY FALL RIVER STRIKERS WELCOME IDLENESS" read the headline in the *Boston Sunday Globe* six days after the strike began. According to the *Globe*, the strikers had "money in the banks and think they need a vacation anyway—few cases of actual want."[31] Below these words, the newspaper ran three large photographs of male and female strikers in bathing costumes, frolicking in the waters and strolling on Sandy Beach, a twenty-minute street car ride from downtown Fall River. Generally only able to enjoy a day at the beach on Sundays, those skilled workers with money in the bank regarded a weekday excursion as an unusual treat.

But at the end of July, no one knew that the strike would last into the next year. Even the mill owners anticipated a strike of "two weeks at the most," the *Boston Globe* reported, adding that "by that time they think that the help will be willing, if not anxious, to return to their old places at the reduced wages." At the same time, however, it was no secret that the mill owners appreciated the money that would be saved by a shutdown and, given their available finished stock, could stay closed for up to three months. Citing increased cotton prices and wages higher than in mills in New Hampshire and Rhode Island and especially the South, Fall River mill owners claimed that "it [was] impossible to do business at a profit under the old scale of wages." One cotton broker was quoted as saying that "this is a fight to the finish as far as the manufacturers are concerned."[32]

Organized labor was just as determined to see the strike through and to prevent the wage cuts which the mill owners claimed were so critically necessary. By the end of the first day of the strike, all five major unions— the weavers, spinners, carders, slashers, and loom-fixers—had met in halls not big enough to hold all who attended. In their meetings that first day, each of the unions pledged its members strike relief money within two to three weeks. That relief, however, was for members only. The 20,000 or so other striking operatives were not eligible for such aid, and by the time the strike was only a week old, union leaders worried about "keeping the non-union help in line."[33] While they were not able to share their dwindling strike relief benefits with non-union strikers, union leaders did acknowledge the importance of keeping everyone, union and non-union alike, out. According to Thomas O'Donnell, secretary of the Spinners Union who offered to go on half-pay for the duration of the strike, "The non-union operatives are with us and will stand with us until the last. . . ."[34] In mid-August, two events were planned to raise relief funds specifically for non-union strikers. The proceeds from a baseball game between the New Bedford and Fall River teams were to go to the fund as well as the admission collected at a special concert put on by two traveling theater companies, one of which was in Fall River for a production of the play, "Factory Girl."[35] Other than a few such special events, non-union strikers and their families had only private charities and limited public assistance to see them through.

According to the *Massachusetts Labor Bulletin*, "The amount of aid given to strikers by the State and City varie[d] from $1 to $2 a week, the $2 rate being given only in cases of want where there is a large family of dependents."[36] By mid-November, about $24,000 in aid had been distributed in Fall River, "wholly to the articles of subsistence, that is, groceries and provisions." Despite increased economic hardship, made only more frightening by the approaching winter, there appeared to be little more the state could do. Efforts to mediate the strike through the State Board of Arbitration had started even before the strike began and continued throughout, but to no avail.[37] No amount of mediation by the state seemed capable of breaking the impasse between labor and capital in Fall River in 1904.

While capital was sustained by its profit motive and a sizable stock-pile of cloth already produced, labor was motivated to continue its strike by sheer anger. According to the *Fall River Herald*, it was the women operatives in particular who started the strike and saw it to its finish six hungry months later. Three weeks into the strike, the *Herald* reported that the women strikers "are thoroughly steeped in anger and are heard from at times in a way that leaves the settlement of the strike a very questionable matter for weeks to come." Quite simply, they were angry because they were being asked to tend more machines for lower wages. These women were not labor activists; indeed, as the *Fall River Herald* put it:

> many of them are not members of unions, and those who are, do not attempt to take any active part in the proceedings. They are patient and tractable operatives who are seldom disturbers, who did not rebel in their work until a climax has been reached in a long series of petty grievances.[38]

Normally seen as docile employees—one of the reasons often cited by employers for hiring women—as strikers these women were pushing the bounds of acceptable female behavior, even for women of the working class.

It was generally acknowledged that women seldom initiated labor actions, but "once involved in strikes [they] usually proved more persistent, often more so than the men." According to the labor investigators John B. Andrews and W.D.P. Bliss, the willingness of women to continue a strike once started

> has been attributed by some to the belief that working women hold that they are not likely to remain permanently in the industrial field. This belief gives them, in the opinion of many [union] secretaries, a somewhat lessened sense of responsibility and a greater willingness to venture more.[39]

The notion that women were only temporarily employed in textile production was increasingly inaccurate. Indeed, the sympathetic reporter for the *Fall River Herald* pointed out that just before the strike started, supervisors had fired several of the women "who had passed middle life and were still compelled to make a living at the loom." The firings were justified on the grounds that the speedups demanded that women be "young and vigorous"—and potentially more "tractable" than seasoned hands who had worked under different, somewhat better conditions.[40]

The supportive *Herald* reporter further argued:

> Since the strike began, those women, or many of them, have been actively engaged in strike work not dictated by the unions but prompted wholly by the womanly desire to fight as long as they can and prevent as much suffering as they can. No man can understand the true situation in the city at this time who does not try to interview a few of these women and ask them why they are striking.[41]

The vast majority of women strikers were not union members, and thus their involvement in the strike was motivated not by union solidarity but by the desire to improve the conditions of their daily labor. That is not to say that the women were unwilling to be part of the trade union community, but like the recently arrived Portuguese and Polish immigrants, the women strikers—many of whom also belonged to these ethnic groups— were unwelcome in that community. Thus their anger, and the potential for change that anger contained if channeled into an organized and collective response, went untapped by the Fall River unions. John Golden, UTW president and the official leader of the Fall River strike, was particularly unable to understand the needs of the women strikers, trade union members or not.[42] Golden left any systematic organization of women strikers to the WTUL.

The New England members of the NWTUL had organized themselves in February, 1904.[43] By the summer of that same year, the League was an active participant in the Fall River strike.[44] Since many of the strikers were women, the League saw this as a wonderful opportunity to respond to the plight of women wage-earners. This concern led the Boston WTUL to organize a "strike time experiment." While the success of the experiment is debatable, it indicates the limitations of this labor/reform coalition's ability to eliminate the barriers of class and ethnicity despite a shared identity predicated on gender. Further, by not actively engaging in any effort to organize the thousands of women strikers into the existing textile unions, the WTUL also demonstrated its unwillingness to challenge the position of the AFL and its affiliated craft unions regarding women workers.

Instead, in the fall of 1904 the League recruited 130 women strikers to come to Boston to work as domestics.[45] In explaining the experiment, the NWTUL secretary and upper-class ally Gertrude Barnum wrote: "Distressed mistresses, searching for servants ask constantly, 'Why do not factory girls change their hard lot by taking up housework.' "[46] But there were several "difficulties" which the WTUL had to overcome to put its plan into action. The potential for homesickness, lack of money for transportation or for lodgings in Boston before a presumably live-in position as a domestic could be secured, and a lack of training were all cited by Barnum as obstacles the WTUL had to deal with in order to begin its strike-time experiment. Those challenges met, Barnum readily admitted that the greatest obstacle of all "was the prejudice, arising from the social stigma which attaches to 'going out to service,' a stigma which is not imagined but real."[47] The difficulties in convincing more than a handful of the thousands of women strikers to exchange their limited autonomy as mill workers for the restricted and lower paid life of a servant was not limited to this Fall River strike-time experiment.[48]

While recognizing the difficulties, Barnum was reluctant to admit the experiment failed. She did, however, admit that several women returned to Fall River. Also, "a very large group is working in paper mills in Rumford Falls, Maine." Finally, Barnum concluded, "Seventy or more are still in domestic service, though not more than twenty are happy about it." She was cognizant of the women's "grievances"—"the servility of their positions, the isolation, and the long hours 'on duty'."[49] In another article, Barnum herself provided the testimony of one former textile worker turned servant, which gives ample evidence of why the WTUL experiment failed. "Mary" was one of the 130 women sent to Boston, leaving family and friends and an entire way of life behind. Barnum quoted "Mary" as saying:

> Some of the girls that's workin' out in Boston, they ain't much stuck on it. They say it's terrible lonesome. You ain't as good as the people you live with, and you get terrible hours—you're just never through . . . 'Taint like Fall River, where you know people. **I don't see as there is much hope unless the unions get us up in some way.**[50]

"Mary" recognized that her only chance of dignity as a woman wage-earner was through trade unionism—not through conversion to domestic servant. Nonetheless, there is no suggestion from WTUL ally Gertrude Barnum that the organization of domestic workers or the thousands of Fall River women still on strike should be next on the League's agenda.

More than just the 130 women recruited into domestic service left Fall River during the strike. In December of 1904 the *Massachusetts Labor Bulletin,* a monthly publication of the state's Bureau of the Statistics of Labor, reported the "departure of about 18,000 persons" from Fall River. According to the *Labor Bulletin,* "A large number of those leaving were French Canadians, who, in a great many instances, returned to their homes."[51] Such a return home was not as likely an option for the more recent immigrants from Poland or the Azores, for whom the distance was too great and the cost of travel too much. They and their families remained in Fall River as the strike dragged on and winter approached.

Organized labor on both the state and national level sought to provide support for the strikers and their families who stayed in Fall River. But rather than offer striking women employment as domestics, organized labor resorted to more traditional forms of support—public statements and monetary assistance. In early October, when the strike was about ten weeks old, AFL president Samuel Gompers spoke at a rally sponsored by the textile workers' unions in Fall River. Gompers urged the striking union members "to stand up against the degradation of slavery."[52] During its annual convention in mid-October, the Massachusetts State Branch of the AFL (MSB) passed two resolutions regarding the striking textile workers in Fall River. The MSB resolved to send a number of speakers to Fall River as well as to ask the AFL, at its convention the following month, to approve strike benefits for the textile workers.[53] The AFL did so, as already noted, after an impassioned speech by Mary Kenney O'Sullivan, caused "hundreds of men to burst into tears" when the AFL met in San Francisco in November.[54]

Back in Fall River, just as the AFL convention was getting under way, the city's manufacturers announced that they would re-open the mills on November 14th at the reduced wage rates announced the previous July. Most likely, excess stock had been sold off and the usual busy season for the production of cotton cloth was about to begin.[55] When the mill owners announced their intentions to re-open, the unions urged the strikers, union and non-union alike, to stay home. Neither the mill owners nor labor leaders were sure how the increasingly hungry strikers would react. After sixteen weeks without work, even the thrifty had depleted their savings and only trade union members could rely on strike benefits. The vast majority of the strikers had to rely upon the very limited amount of aid from stingy public sources and overburdened private charities. Nonetheless, all but a handful of strikers stayed home on November 14th. As one manufacturer reported to the State Board of

Arbitration, when "he opened his mill . . . the response was disappointing; he therefore shut it down."[56]

Other mill owners did not give up so readily, hoping at the very least that the unskilled recent immigrants would be forced to return to work at any wage. The manufacturers knew full well that the vast majority of their striking workforce was by now destitute. But it would appear that the timing of the strike assessment approved at the AFL convention, coming just days after the announced re-opening, was a critical factor in sustaining union and non-union strikers alike. Thanks in large part to Kenney O'Sullivan's speech, "a thousand dollars a day [soon] came into the city from trade unions around the country, especially in New England."[57] By early December, those mills that had re-opened shut down once again. As one year ended and another began, one of the nation's largest and longest strikes to date continued into its sixth month.[58]

By mid-January, 1905 the city of Fall River was also in the midst of a record-breaking cold spell. According to the *Boston Globe*, the strike in Fall River now suffered its first casualty. On January 15th, after reading a newspaper account of the previous day's failed strike talks, fifty-three year old striking textile worker John Neville slashed his throat in front of his crippled wife. That same day, three other weavers nearly succeeded in committing suicide at their Fall River boardinghouse, having turned on the gas from the room's light fixture.[59] As this evidence of the hardship caused by a prolonged strike in a single-industry town was reported, the recently sworn-in governor William L. Douglas stepped into the fray.[60]

Douglas, a shoe manufacturer from Brockton "whose factory turned out more shoes with the union label than any other in Brockton," had run against the incumbent John L. Bates as a friend to labor.[61] Such a claim was not difficult given the anti-labor position of Governor Bates, who in 1904 had vetoed a Massachusetts State Branch of the AFL-sponsored bill outlawing night work for women and children textile workers. Seeing this veto as "a crime against human progress," the MSB was successful in its resolve to "use their influence to defeat" Bates in the 1904 election.[62] Within days of taking office, and on the same day that the *Boston Globe* reported the suicide of one striker and the attempted suicide of three others, now-Governor Douglas called a conference of strike leaders and mill owners at the State House in Boston. Within two days, on January 18th, two representatives of the Fall River textile manufacturers appeared before the State Board of Arbitration. The two announced "that through the mediation of Governor Douglas a settlement of the cotton strike had been effected and the help was to return forthwith."[63]

The settlement which the governor negotiated required that the strikers return to work at the reduced wage offered twenty-six weeks earlier. Governor Douglas did stipulate that the manufacturers would pay their workers a five-percent dividend based on the average profit margin (yet to be determined) earned between January and April, 1905.[64] In other words, once the governor decided what margin of profit was reasonably due Fall River's mill owners, textile workers would then receive five percent of any amount over that. The strikers, however, were to suffer no penalties regarding employment because of the strike and, further, weavers would now be required to work no more than ten looms at a time, as opposed to twelve or more before the strike. Thus, as the historian John Cumbler has argued, "Both sides claimed victory. The mills got their reduction, but the workers got a promise of better wages in the future."[65]

Almost immediately, organized labor admitted that "the terms secured [were] not all that [was] desired."[66] The concerted power of the Cotton Manufacturers Association had seen to that. The intervention of Governor Douglas put 25,000 striking textile workers back to work, albeit at reduced wages. But the great strike of 1904 was over and as one somewhat sympathetic son of a prominent Fall River family later observed:

> smoke again poured from the factory chimneys, the whirr of the spindles and the ceaseless clatter of shuttles were again joyful sounds within the factory walls; at the bell hour the army of the dinner-pail again responded to rollcall,—the long strike was ended.[67]

The commentator neglected to mention that those joyful sounds were heard, however, by workers returning to work at lower wages after six months of unemployment.

At the second meeting of the WTUL National Executive Board, held in Boston on October 7, 1904, the then still-ongoing Fall River strike took up much of the report from the Boston branch. Gertrude Barnum gave the report for Boston, citing the efforts to bring Fall River female strikers north as domestics as well as the local league's continued work in making sure the Boston dailies published favorable accounts of the strike. It appeared, though, that the initial response of the Boston WTUL had been hampered, as most of the middle- and upper-class allies had "been absent during the summer." Further, given that "the Fall River situation may be due to the inevitable decline of the cotton mills in New

England," there was little more for the WTUL to do other than "to arouse sympathy for the Fall River work[er]s."[68]

Mary Kenney O'Sullivan, in attendance at the October 7 meeting held in her home town, did not comment on "the Fall River situation." She did note during the general discussion that AFL "President Gompers had not yet found it practicable [sic] to include a woman among the organizers for the American Federation of Labor."[69] Despite Gompers' visit to Fall River during which he witnessed thousands of women textile workers on strike and still unorganized, he continued to hold Kenney O'Sullivan and her organization at bay.

Two months after the Fall River strike ended, Kenney O'Sullivan spoke to the first National Conference on Women in Industry, held in New York City on March 26, 1905. She followed several speakers, including Samuel Gompers and Hull House founder and NWTUL vice-president Jane Addams.[70] As national secretary of the WTUL and a labor organizer who appreciated the contributions of middle- and upper-class allies, Kenney O'Sullivan still wanted to make clear the terms of those contributions:

> Women of opportunity who understand that they receive much and give little in real service, in comparison to their wage earning sisters, **if true to that understanding**, will give invaluable service in bringing about a more just condition.[71]

Perhaps Kenney O'Sullivan was responding in part to Gertrude Barnum's article, "Fall River Mill Girls in Domestic Service," which had appeared shortly before the conference. Certainly, she had been aware of Gertrude Barnum's "experiment" and very likely found it an unsatisfactory response to the strike and to the conditions of labor which brought on the strike. According to historian Meredith Tax, Barnum, the daughter of a Chicago judge, was "one of the allies least sensitive to class issues."[72] She also lacked much understanding of the issues of ethnicity within Fall River, as she demonstrated when she spoke to the Twentieth Century Club in Boston during the strike. The Chicago-based *Union Labor Advocate* quoted Barnum as saying, "In Lowell they have so mixed the nationalities that the trades unions are overcome, which, thank God, is not the case in Fall River."[73]

For Kenney O'Sullivan, an experiment in which striking textile workers were to be converted into domestic servants, an occupation even more poorly paid and potentially exploitative, was not the way in which to effect "a more just condition." Instead, "[t]horough organization would give these women courage, independence, and self-respect." While appreciative of the assistance given by "women of opportunity" in achieving the organization of wage-earning women, Kenney O'Sullivan specified what sort of women should be involved as allies:

> We need faithful, sincere, and unselfish women, who are courageous and full of integrity. Organization built through the efforts of such women will endure . . . If you believe 'Thy Will be done on earth, as it is in heaven,' practice it, come in and **co-operate, educate, and organize**.[74]

Such were the goals of the WTUL itself—education about the conditions of women's labor, the organization of wage-earning women, and increasingly the establishment of protective labor laws, all through the active cooperation of working-class women and their middle- and upper-class allies. As the WTUL sought to establish itself, both nationally and within specific American cities, Kenney O'Sullivan continued her efforts to ensure that the WTUL would remain true to its stated goals, particularly her long-held goal of organization for women.

Samuel Gompers also spoke at the National Conference on Women in Industry. Since Gompers was president of the AFL, his blessings were crucial if the WTUL was to achieve its goals. Although denied official status as a voting member of the AFL at the labor organization's 1904 convention, the WTUL did not give up in its attempts to win such recognition.[75] Thus, Gompers' remarks at the WTUL-sponsored gathering in late March, just four months after the first AFL rejection, must have been listened to closely by all WTUL leaders, Kenney O'Sullivan included. But all that Gompers promised his listeners that day was "the co-operation of the American Federation of Labor" and little more.[76]

Gompers began by assuring his audience that their work regarding the organization of women was indeed important. According to Gompers, "Modern industry has brought in its wake conditions that have taken the woman, the girl and the wife from her home and brought and dragged her into the factory and workshop and the store." But he went on to say that, despite such conditions, "No intelligent man here will deny the right of women to work." Gompers made plain that women, like men, had the right to work—but not under such conditions. The only hope for all wage-earners was trade unionism, and therefore the work of the WTUL was to be applauded.

Gompers emphasized all that trade unions had already done for women workers within "the full limit of their ability and power," especially regarding "equal pay for women and men for equal work done." Claiming that equal pay for equal work was a central principle of the AFL, he reminded his listeners that "trade unionists, **the men**, have borne sacrifices and burdens and have been compelled to make a fight to try and make this principle effective."[77] In other words, the WTUL was joining an on-going struggle in which the rules of engagement had already been worked out by the AFL during its almost quarter century of existence.

Much like Kenney O'Sullivan, Gompers sought to define the role of those who "sympathize[d]" with the cause of trade unionism. According to Gompers, the efforts of the WTUL were not to be "a work of Charity!" Rather, the WTUL was "instituted so that the girls and women may be placed in a position where they may be helped to help themselves. What working men want, is less charity and more rights."[78] While Gompers did not go into just what it was that working women might want, he did direct yet another barb at well-meaning social reformers. To those good Progressives who championed a myriad of causes, many of which were seemingly shaped by the social concern of the moment, Gompers said:

> You, ladies and gentlemen, who are in this great work, who may give it your sympathetic support, do not let this work of trade union organization among women become a mere fad. There is no greater wrong than the fad that will have its vogue for a day or a week or a year and then pass out of the lives of the women wage earners . . . to inspire hope into them to organize . . . then . . . leave them to the tender mercies of their employers.[79]

That warning given, Gompers closed by pledging "the sincerest cooperation" of the AFL and wished the WTUL "every success."

But that cooperation, however sincere, did not extend to granting the WTUL's request for one fraternal delegate *with a vote* in the AFL convention. While the British Trades Union Congress had attended AFL conventions for several years, sending two voting delegates, and the Canadian Trades and Labor Congress sent one voting delegate, this privilege was not granted to the American WTUL, despite repeated requests. Just before the AFL was to gather in Pittsburgh for its twenty-fifth national convention in 1905, Gompers wrote Gertrude Barnum reiterating the AFL position regarding the WTUL:

I but repeat the views of many active men in the trade union movement
when I say to you that they believe this idea of fraternal delegates with
either voice or vote may go too far in upsetting the American Federation of Labor. . . . [80]

For Gompers, and for the AFL which he had helped create, the issue was
not one of gender but of class. Gompers had long been critical of the
Knights of Labor for a variety of reasons including the Knights' membership requirements, which did not necessarily prohibit middle-class reformers from joining the order. In Gompers' mind, this meant that the
Knights became "a hodge-podge with no basis of solidarity."[81] The AFL
was not to take this route—it was to be strictly a federation of trade
unions. The presence of "sympathizers" within the WTUL meant that, as
far as Gompers and the AFL were concerned, the WTUL was a cross-
class alliance and not a trade union federation devoted to the interests of
women. As the historian Elizabeth Anne Payne put it, "In the eyes of the
Federation's leaders, the League never lost its philanthropic cast."[82]

In their efforts to put into action their concept of industrial feminism,
Kenney O'Sullivan and the other working-class members of the WTUL
were frequently frustrated on multiple levels. They had to confront the ambivalence of the AFL regarding the organization of women and the Federation's class bias towards the women social reformers. At the same time, the
working-class WTUL members had to work with women reformers whose
actions were often shaped by their class bias. It would appear that in her attempt to build a national coalition between the male-dominated labor community and the predominately-female social reform community, Kenney
O'Sullivan was taking on a near impossible task.

Nor were efforts of the Massachusetts WTUL at coalition building
going any more smoothly on the state or local level. While the Chicago
branch had gained recognition from the local and state labor federations
in the form of a voting delegate, the Massachusetts WTUL had at best
merely cordial relations with the Boston Central Labor Union (BCLU)
and the Massachusetts State Branch of the AFL (MSB).[83] It was probably due to Kenney O'Sullivan's many years of active labor organizing in
the Boston area, as well as her position as widow of one of the state's
most revered trade unionists, that her old friend and BCLU organizer
Harry Lloyd agreed to speak at a WTUL-sponsored meeting in Boston's
Perkins Hall during the fall of 1905.[84] Perhaps, however, as long as Kenney O'Sullivan's old nemesis Frank Foster held sway over organized
labor in Massachusetts, which he would do until his death in 1909, even

her connections could not help gain the Boston WTUL a place of respect, not to speak of power, within the local or state labor bodies.[85]

Nonetheless, the Massachusetts WTUL continued its efforts to include the male leaders of the local and state labor communities within their organization. Lacking the financial resources to host its own national convention and unwelcome for the most part at the annual AFL conventions, the NWTUL organized in 1907 three simultaneous "interstate" conferences, held in Boston, New York and Chicago July 14, 1907.[86] Held on a Sunday so wage-earners as well as sympathizers could attend, the three conferences each revolved around a theme relevant to the issues regarding women and trade unionism. According to the *Boston Globe*, that city's conference posed the question "How may women's unions best be strengthened?"[87] President of the Massachusetts WTUL Mary Morton Kehew introduced the first speaker, Arthur M. Huddell, international vice-president of the steam engineers union and president of the BCLU. Other male trade unionists included cigar-maker and BCLU secretary Henry Abrahams, Collin Cameron of the carpenters' union, and Henry Sterling of the typographers union. They, along with the League's vice-president, Kenney O'Sullivan,

> all declared that one of the surest means of assisting in the organization of trade unions of women would be the solid and constant support by women of the crafts of various organizations as, frequently having charge of the purchases of the family, the women are able to make them in such directions as to assist all trade unions.[88]

Invoking woman as consumer rather than producer was a traditional response of organized labor and social reformers alike. As noted earlier, Kenney O'Sullivan herself had long been an advocate of buying only products with the union label and had helped organize the Boston Woman's Union Labor League in January, 1904. She did so, however, in large measure as a response to the Massachusetts Consumers League label campaign, which she felt was not sufficiently pro-union.[89]

In any case, there was more to the Boston WTUL Interstate Conference than talk of label leagues. Wages, specifically equal wages for equal work, framed most of the speakers' remarks. According to Arthur Huddell, "There can not be two standards in unions, the same wages for women as for men should be the watchword in the industrial world."[90] Huddell was quoted in a three-page piece written by WTUL founder and then vice-president of the Illinois league Mary MacDowell, which appeared in the AFL monthly, *American Federationist*. Such prominent coverage of the WTUL was usually not to be found in the pages of the *Federationist*. Generally, the AFL-sponsored journal reported on issues regarding women wage-earners on its own terms. In September of 1905, the journal began "a series of articles written by eminent men and women upon the subject of woman's labor and the organization of women in trade unions" at the request of the WTUL itself.[91]

The series would continue through June of 1906, and while the WTUL may have requested the series, there was little if any mention of the work of the league even in the lead article by WTUL co-founder William English Walling, who wrote on the "Field Organization for Women." Several articles followed on women in specific trades, such as the garment industry, bakery and candy workers, and waitresses. Even an article written by then NWTUL president Ellen M. Henrotin neglected to mention the WTUL except when identifying the author. In addressing the need for the "Organization for Women," Henrotin invoked rhetoric more indicative of her long association with the General Federation of Women's Clubs, of which she had been a past president, than of the organization she now led.[92]

Though not part of this series, the five-page article entitled "Wage-Working Women" that appeared in the December 1906 issue of the *Federationist* was perhaps the official AFL position towards the WTUL and its middle- and upper-class female sympathizers. Written by Gompers' staunch ally, Eva McDonald Valesh, the article summed up once again where wage-earning women should look for assistance:

> When club women ask what has been done to make life more livable for wage-earning women, the answer is that so far the American Federation of Labor is the **only** force in society which has concerned itself to any great extent with active and **practical** work for the advancement of wage-earning women.[93]

Valesh did not once mention the WTUL, perhaps because in her mind such a cross-class organization was incapable of organizing working women in a "practical" way. In the recent histories of the WTUL, much has been made of the failure of the organization to cross class lines but generally as evidenced by class and ethnic tensions between working-class members and their allies.[94] While that was often certainly the case, the class bias of the AFL was a further stumbling block for the WTUL and is usually mentioned only in passing.

Yet for the working-class leaders of the WTUL such as Kenney O'Sullivan, the class bias of male trade unionists was extremely problematic. For more than twenty years, she had confronted the boundaries of class in her dealings with social reformers. Nonetheless, she continued to find more support for her efforts to organize working women in that community than in the labor community. At the same time, she was not just a woman, but a **working-class** woman. It was this identity which shaped her association with a cause increasingly taken up by the WTUL, the cause of woman suffrage.

On February 15, 1906 Kenney O'Sullivan spoke before a U.S. House of Representatives' committee then hearing testimony regarding the proposed Constitutional amendment for woman suffrage. Part of a delegation of over two hundred women from the National Equal Suffrage Association, she was introduced by her old friend from Chicago, Florence Kelley, who was now living in New York and serving as head of the National Consumers League.[95] Kenney O'Sullivan began her remarks by explaining who she was:

> I come to ask you for my right as a citizen, as a member, and as a producing member of society, to ask you for the right, not only for myself, but for the people of whom I am a part—the working women and the common people.[96]

Eschewing "the philosophical and theoretical side" of the suffrage debate, Kenney O'Sullivan stated quite simply why women, especially wage-earning women such as herself, needed the vote: "I know that the working women of this country are not receiving the highest wages because they have not a vote." Citing women employed in the Federal bookbindery who did not receive equal pay for equal work, she accused the government of taking "advantage of the women of my class because they have not a vote and are not full-fledged citizens."

Kenney O'Sullivan argued that it was entirely appropriate as a "producing member" of society to claim the vote, not as a privilege but as a right.[97] Invoking the language of early-nineteenth-century male laborers who made similar claims, this wage-earning woman sought to extend that argument to working-class women.[98] Middle- and upper-class women leading the revived woman suffrage movement of the early twentieth century also relied upon the woman-as-producer theme in their quest to gain the vote. They did so as a way to emphasize the contributions women made to society as mothers, social reformers, and wage-earners. But it was also part of the suffrage movement's conscious campaign to enlist the support of working-class women in a cause which, for a variety of reasons, tended to be seen as and often indeed was a very middle-class movement.[99]

According to NWTUL historian Robin Miller Jacoby, the League considered itself to be "the industrial branch of the woman suffrage movement."[100] Given that many of the WTUL allies were also involved in that movement, such a characterization of the WTUL should come as no surprise. Nancy Schrom Dye, in her examination of the NYWTUL, argues that the league's efforts in the woman suffrage movement focused not so much on the leadership of the AFL and its affiliated unions but on the "rank and file." Dye claims that many male trade union members in New York, especially those who were also immigrants, feared the positive impact woman's suffrage would have on the growing temperance movement. Further, according to Dye, many rank-and-file men were suspicious of a movement which had the support of the well-to-do.[101]

For its part, the AFL had ratified a resolution in support of woman's suffrage at each annual convention since 1890. On more than one occasion the resolution was introduced by Kenney O'Sullivan. At the 1904 convention, although they declined to approve the WTUL's request for admission as a voting delegate, the AFL delegates voted unanimously

> [t]hat the best interests of labor require the admission of women to full citizenship as a matter of justice to them and as a necessary step toward ensuring and raising the scale of wages for all.[102]

Apparently, allowing women to become full citizens of the polis was less threatening than allowing the WTUL to have a voice within the AFL. Even the Massachusetts State Branch of the AFL agreed that woman suffrage was needed but did so in quite maternalist language. In 1906, the annual convention of the MSB voted that the ballot was "necessary for women, in order that they may defend and safeguard the home and the civil and political rights of themselves and their children."[103]

Although this was an argument far removed from Kenney O'Sullivan's, which emphasized the need of women to defend their wages and thus by extension perhaps safeguard their homes and children, all the rhetoric in support of woman suffrage played a part in its eventual realization—even when that rhetoric was based upon the gendered, ethnic, or racial arguments of the day. The resolution which Kenney O'Sullivan introduced at the 1906 AFL convention was devoid of justification on any grounds. The resolution passed and simply stated that the Congressional committee which had heard the testimony of Kenney O'Sullivan and several others should make a favorable report to the rest of the Congress regarding the woman suffrage amendment.[104]

She had less success in getting the 1906 convention to consider separately another resolution she introduced, a resolution addressing the need for a paid woman organizer. When the Committee on Resolutions made its report, it recommended that the resolution be combined with several other resolutions requesting that the AFL Executive Council appoint organizers in various specific trades. Kenny O'Sullivan had probably proposed that her resolution be considered separately as a way to highlight what she saw as a vital need. Although Kenney O'Sullivan "spoke at some length in favor of the appointment of a woman organizer," the motion failed and the appointment she proposed would not be made for another two years.

In 1908, the AFL Executive Council appointed Annie Fitzgerald, president of the Women's International Union Label League, as a paid organizer but, according to one of the earliest historians of the WTUL, limited Fitzgerald's appointment to only "a short period."[105] Perhaps even more important than the brevity of Fitzgerald's appointment, the first since Kenney O'Sullivan held the post in 1892, was the organization with which Fitzgerald was closely associated. By appointing a leader of the Label League, was the AFL relegating the organization of women to that of consumer rather than that of producer? Fitzgerald's appointment as woman organizer was too brief to achieve much or to leave any record which would indicate the AFL's intent. Although it regularly claimed that it could not afford to keep sufficient organizers in the field, the AFL's ambivalence regarding the organization of women explains its position far more accurately than its strapped finances.[106]

For almost thirty years, Kenney O'Sullivan had continued to organize women wage-earners despite the lack of consistent support from the AFL and the constraints of the social reform community to which she frequently turned. By 1906, personal considerations also hampered her work. During the 1890s Kenney O'Sullivan had had the support of her husband, who was more than happy to be in charge at home so that his wife could speak at yet another meeting or go to yet another strike; the situation was different after 1902 when Jack O'Sullivan died. As the Worcester-based *Labor News* told its readers in 1906, Kenney O'Sullivan's organizing was confined to the Boston area, "where she can be near her three children." According to the *Labor News*, "but for them she could become a national organizer; a mother's love keeps her near her little family."[107] Still, Kenney O'Sullivan was able to attend AFL conventions held in distant cities and was present in 1907 when the AFL convened in Norfolk, Virginia. There too the NWTUL gathered for what has been alternately referred to as its "First National Convention" and "an informal gathering of only seven delegates," including Kenney O'Sullivan.[108] The Norfolk convention marked the debut of recently elected NWTUL president Margaret Dreier Robins. As president for the next fifteen years, Robins, based in Chicago, with the assistance of her sister, Mary Dreier, a leader in the NYWTUL, used her considerable personal wealth as well as her great charm to oversee the League during its most dynamic period.[109] She apparently even charmed Samuel Gompers sufficiently to be seated next to him at the AFL Executive Council banquet held during the Norfolk convention—which she attended as a **non-voting** delegate representing the WTUL.[110] Within two years of assuming the presidency, Robins also relied upon the force of her personality to settle ongoing disputes within the Boston League, disputes in which Kenney O'Sullivan was involved.

While neither the New York or Chicago leagues were free of internal conflict, the Boston WTUL was especially contentious.[111] In its first five years of existence, the Boston branch went through five executive secretaries and three presidents. The 1911 election of the fourth local president was also an occasion of conflict in which Kenney O'Sullivan was personally involved; this will be discussed in the next chapter. But the coming and going of BWTUL secretaries in the league's early years is worthy of brief examination in that it highlights the ever-present dilemma over direction which all the local branches faced. That dilemma was between focusing on organizing or agitating for protective labor legislation through outreach aimed at middle- and upper-class supporters.[112]

The executive secretary's job was not an easy one. In Boston, the position was initially held by Mary Haskell, a member of the Boston Typographers' union. By 1905, the young Edith Abbott, who would go on to become Dean of the School of Social Work at the University of Chicago, came to Boston to serve as secretary. Originally from a comfortable middle-class background, Abbott had just completed her Ph.D. at the University of Chicago and was thus the quintessential ally—middle class and educated. Apparently her position as secretary of the Boston League, which she held only for a few months, was overwhelming. Shortly after arriving in Boston, Abbott wrote her sister:

> I am expected to meet labor committees, arrange meetings for those interested in the work, be ready to speak at women's clubs and so forth,

help organize women in different trades, investigate sanitary conditions or anything that comes along in that line. I am afraid I am too conservative for the Labor people. I shall get on alright [sic] with Mrs. Kehew and the League but I am very much afraid of the other side of it. . . . I feel as if I am walking on eggs . . . [113]

Not only was Abbott overburdened by the variety of her responsibilities, but she never felt comfortable with the Boston labor community and soon returned to Chicago. After her departure, the BWTUL went through two more secretaries—Mabel Gillespie, who held the position only temporarily in 1906 (though she would return as secretary in 1909 and remain until her death in 1923), and Mary Crawford, a graduate of Radcliffe College and later a writer of historical romance novels.[114]

In 1908, Emily Greene Balch, professor of economics at Wellesley College, was elected the new president of the BWTUL, succeeding the venerable Mary Morton Kehew.[115] Kenney O'Sullivan remained vice-president of the local League and was very likely comfortable with the new president, whom she had known since her early days at Denison House. It appears that shortly after Balch assumed the presidency, Mary Crawford resigned as secretary. While she professed to "know only a little" about trade unionism, Crawford was a staunch advocate of organization, claiming that "women in industry will receive just treatment and fair wages only if they ally themselves with the Trade Union Movement."[116] Balch, on the other hand, appears to have preferred the legislative route as the most effective means to address the conditions of labor for women. She was a veteran of several state investigatory commissions and long an active member of the Massachusetts Consumers League. Six months after becoming BWTUL president, Balch was appointed to the State Commission on Industrial Education in June, 1908.[117]

At the same time that Balch's appointment to the Industrial Commission was announced, the Executive Board of the NWTUL met in Boston. Several of the Board's members were in town anyway, attending the annual convention of the General Federation of Women's Clubs. While Balch had reported to NWTUL president Robins in April that "we have got onto a business-like and economic basis," by June the Boston WTUL was teetering on the edge of collapse.[118] According to the minutes for June 26th:

Boston reported a season of readjustment which became necessary through a variety of circumstances. The League there is for the present

> without a paid secretary in charge . . . A paid assistant secretary gives
> half time. The writer's work has been chiefly of a propaganda nature.[119]

The "variety of circumstances" mentioned above was very likely the
election of Balch to the presidency, followed by the resignation of Mary
Crawford. Without a secretary actively engaged in organizing, and with a
president who leaned toward legislative remedies, the BWTUL appeared
to be floundering.[120] The League was also temporarily homeless, camped
out for the time being in the office of Kenney O'Sullivan, who was then
working part-time as a rental agent for the Cabot family.

It appears that NWTUL President Robins stepped in to stem the tide
of potential dissolution in Boston. Perhaps it was at her suggestion, possibly even her insistence, that Josephine Casey of Chicago was sent to
Boston as the new secretary/organizer. Casey, who was praised by Kenney O'Sullivan as a "railroad man" who understood first hand the benefits of trade unionism, had been instrumental in the formation of the
Chicago Elevated Railway Employees Union.[121] Casey had been active
in the Chicago WTUL and was well-liked by labor and allies alike. The
discord in Boston was no secret, and local ally Anne Withington urged
Robins to warn the young organizer:

> May I implore you not to let our dear Miss Casey come on without a
> word of warning as to our peculiarities. I have seen three secretaries
> sacrificed and I hope never to see another. Tell her to keep in the mid-
> dle of the road and she will be able to do her work without getting into
> any of these wholly extraneous rows which the poor old League has
> been blighted by for four years . . . I hope Miss Casey will make us
> into a League at last.[122]

While the BWTUL pulled out all the stops in welcoming Casey to
Boston, including a "monster reception" at which 150 or so guests officially greeted the new secretary, she too lasted only a few months.[123]

In her short stint, Casey established a library in the new quarters of
the BWTUL and began a series of weekly talks by local labor leaders and
social reformers. But while she was quoted as promising to "induce the
women to join such unions as are already organized and in the future organize more unions," Casey's most successful organizing was in the formation of a working women's singing group, the "Eight-Hour
Chorus."[124] By early February 1909, Robins was back in Boston trying
once again to keep that branch from caving in upon itself.

On February 2nd she wrote her husband Raymond Robins that she had arrived safely in Boston "with Josephine in charge and we are about to tackle the G— P— great problem! Some of the union girls are coming and this is but a word!" Two days later Robins was writing her husband again: "These are strenuous and effective days! Mrs. Woods and Josephine have resigned and Boston is temporarily lost."[125] Apparently the forces supporting a more educational and legislative approach had won.[126] Casey's natural inclinations to organize had been stymied, whether intentionally or not, by the Boston leadership—specifically local president Emily Greene Balch.

According to the historian Alice Meehan Clement, "The direction that the league took for the rest of its existence was formulated by the convention of 1909. . . . [and] the priorities that emerged as paramount favored the legislative activists."[127] In many of her other comments at the NWTUL conference which began in Chicago on Sept. 27, 1909 and lasted for five days, Kenney O'Sullivan made clear that trade unionism for wage-earning women rather than legislation was her primary goal—and hopefully the goal of the WTUL as well. She especially objected to one component of the legislative directive. When discussing what would become the official WTUL legislative program, which included demands for the eight-hour day, safe and sanitary work conditions, and a minimum wage for women in

National Women's Trade Union League second biennial conference delegates, Chicago, 1909. Schlesinger Library, Radcliffe College.

the "sweated" trades, Kenney O'Sullivan requested that the provision banning night work for women be struck from the list. As a former bookbinder and as the mother of dependent children, Kenney O'Sullivan had first-hand experience of the economics and the personal realities involved.

In many trades, including bookbinding, night work paid better than daytime hours. Such a prohibition could also be the opening wedge in keeping women out of certain trades altogether, such as the often lucrative (but frequently morally questionable) trade of bartending. Further, while she might be exhausted from a night of work, such a schedule would allow a mother to be home during her child's waking hours. Thus, Kenney O'Sullivan told her fellow NWTUL convention delegates, "I don't believe we can afford to go on record as prohibiting night work. . . . I mean we as women who are seeking the ballot."[128] By reminding her listeners that they were seeking woman suffrage as a way to become full citizens, she pointed out the potential contradiction in supporting legislation which would limit women's options as workers.

Upon her re-election as vice-president of the NWTUL, Kenney O'Sullivan stated quite plainly what she saw as the League's purpose:

> We are here to organize, and as I understand our purpose it is to organize all workers of various trades according to their trades. . . . That principle has been my religion, is my religion, and will be my religion so long as I have the opportunity to think and to talk.[129]

In language that any trade unionist, male or female, could easily comprehend, Kenney O'Sullivan now made her stand apart from the organization which she had helped form. As the NWTUL began to consciously move away from organizing, it sealed the breach between itself and the AFL. In other resolutions debated at the 1909 convention the League sought to further distance itself from the AFL, coming out against the extension of the Chinese Exclusion Act and in support of a Labor party.[130] On these two issues, Kenney O'Sullivan was divided—following AFL policy, she advocated extending the prohibition against Chinese immigration, but she also spoke in favor of establishing a Labor party.

The resolution in favor of recommending to the AFL at its next annual convention that a third party based on the interests of labor be formed was drafted and submitted by the Boston delegation to the NWTUL convention. It appears to have been instigated by Kenney O'Sullivan's close friend, the wealthy WTUL ally Elizabeth Glendower Evans. Evans had just returned from a long sojourn in England where she had became friends with many Fabian Socialists, including Ramsey MacDonald and John and Katherine Bruce Glazier. It was probably the author H.G. Wells who actually converted Evans, for in her travel diary she notes that after spending "a red letter day with Wells" the next day she "somewhat rashly perhaps" joined the Fabian Society herself.[131] Evans reported to the 1909 NWTUL convention what she had seen while in England: "I saw the perfectly immense power of the labor party, with only thirty-six members in Parliament but with the endorsement of the trade unions." Claiming that the "labor party has got to come" to America, Evans then deferred to her friend Kenney O'Sullivan.[132]

For her part, Kenney O'Sullivan reminded her listeners that "men of the American Federation of Labor" would definitely not be interested in any third-party movement, even one associated with the cause of labor. Kenney O'Sullivan herself had loyally adhered to Gompers' anti-politics position throughout the 1890s as the AFL argued this point on the state and national level (see Chapter 2). But in 1909, she was ready to shift her position, perhaps in response to how little had changed during her two decades of organizing. Connecting her argument to the fight for woman's suffrage, Kenney O'Sullivan said that, when given that right, "we women [will] want a new political party."[133]

The 1909 NWTUL Convention was more than just a turning point at which the NWTUL accepted its permanent lack of connection to the

WTUL *Seal from* Life and Labor, *January 1911.*

AFL by advocating positions directly opposed to the interests of the Federation. It also can be seen as the point at which Kenney O'Sullivan began to sense the inability of the WTUL to overcome the many obstacles it faced. She continued nonetheless to remain in leadership positions both on the national level and within the Boston League. Increasingly, though, it was through her friend Glendower Evans that Kenney O'Sullivan remained involved. This would be particularly evident during the 1910 strike of carpet weavers in Roxbury, Massachusetts.

By all accounts, the strike at the Roxbury Carpet Company was a successful effort that won the women weavers a restoration of a twelve-and-a-half-percent wage cut and the right to union representation.[134] This strike of only 128 women workers received little attention in the Boston papers, although the work stoppage put more than six hundred employees out of work from February to the end of April. Ten weeks into the strike, the *Boston Globe* reported that Pauline Newman, a working-class leader of the New York WTUL, spoke in a Roxbury church. While Newman's subject was the massive New York shirtwaist-makers' strike, she very likely encouraged the small band of Roxbury carpet weavers in their efforts.[135]

During the three-month-long strike, the weavers had not only the support of the WTUL but also the financial support of the Boston Central Labor Union. Under the aegis of the BWTUL, the women strikers formed Carpet Weavers Local 721 and affiliated with the United Textile Workers of America (UTW). John Golden, president of the UTW, represented his new members at the several meetings called by the State Board of Arbitration.[136] Glendower Evans chronicled the strike in a short piece for *The Survey*, a liberal journal of the day. Though omitting her own leadership, she praised Golden as "intelligent [and] sober-minded." In her words, however, "the heroines of the Boston strike" were the women weavers, who also happened to be "American born and bred." They were not those "poor creatures" who appeared, unsuccessfully, as the "strikebreaker—[the]Armenian, Pole, or Greek."[137]

How vastly different this strike in Roxbury was from the Fall River strike of 1904–1905. In its sheer size alone, the Roxbury strike was at the very least more manageable, involving slightly more than a hundred strikers as opposed to 25,000. Furthermore, in the five years since its debut in Fall River, the BWTUL had matured somewhat. It had built a base, however tenuous, within the Boston labor community. Nor did it have to worry during a springtime strike about summer vacations preventing the participation of its allies. The ethnic differences, however, were critical and worthy of note even at the time.

All these factors combined to make this strike a far more positive experience for the strikers and for the BWTUL. Unlike Fall River, the originally unorganized Roxbury strikers became part of a union, the strike demands were met, and the strikers returned to their jobs. In "the fight for subsistence," of the women it sought to assist, the WTUL had learned much as it fought for its own survival as an organization. The League members could take some satisfaction from their achievements. However, the victory at Roxbury would be followed only two years later by the "smash-up" in Lawrence during the Bread and Roses strike of 1912.

NOTES

[1]*Boston Globe* Nov. 25, 1904.

[2]As one historian of Fall River has noted, "By December, 1904, the suffering had become unbearable. . . . For the first time in Fall River history the Roman Catholic clergy were moved to side openly with the operatives." See Philip Thomas Silva, "The Spindle City: Labor, Politics, and Religion in Fall River, Massachusetts, 1870–1905" (Ph.D. diss., Fordham Univ., 1973). 630–631.

[3]Anne Withington, "The Fight for Subsistence at Fall River," *The Commons* 9 (Nov. 1904): pp. 556–557.

[4]John T. Cumbler, *Working-Class Community in Industrial America: Work, Leisure, and Struggle in Two Industrial Cities, 1880–1930* (Westport, CT: Greenwood Press, 1979), p. 201. See also: "Strike of Cotton Operatives in Fall River," *Massachusetts Labor Bulletin* 34 (Dec. 1904): pp. 322–323.

[5]*Massachusetts Labor Bulletin* (Dec. 1904): p. 323. See also: Louis Galambos, *Competition and Cooperation: The Emergence of a National Trade Association* (Baltimore: John Hopkins University Press, 1966).

[6]Thomas R. Smith, *The Cotton Textile Industry of Fall River, Massachusetts: A Study of Industrial Localization* (New York: King's Crown Press, 1944), p. 105. While the rhetoric surrounding the Southern threat may have begun in the 1890s, Cumbler, *Working-Class Community*, p. 138, claims that the actual negative impact on Fall River stock dividends was not serious until the mid-1920s.

[7]Charles Bancroft, testimony on Sept. 8, 1903 before the Massachusetts Committee on Relations between Employer and Employee, typescript of hearings before the Committee, Aug. 18–Nov. 7, 1903, pp. 182–193, Massachusetts State House Library, Boston.

[8]Cumbler, *Working-Class Community*, p. 137.

[9]*Massachusetts Labor Bulletin* (Dec. 1904): p. 323.

[10]Cumbler, *Working-Class Community*, p. 203.

[11]*Massachusetts Labor Bulletin* (Dec.1904): p. 321; see also: Cumbler, *Working-Class Community*, pp. 203–204.

[12]William Hard, "The Woman's Invasion," *Everybody's Magazine* 19 (Nov. 1908): p. 580.

[13]According to the Twelfth Census, Vol. 8, p. 383, in 1900 Fall River reported the following numbers of people employed:

> All men, 16 years and older: 17,686
> All women, 16 years and older: 13,374
>
> Men working in cotton textiles: 12,587
> Women working in cotton textiles: 12,162

In other words, while 80 percent of Fall River's workforce labored in the city's several textile mills, more than 90 percent of the women wage-earners were concentrated in that one industry.

[14]Hard, "The Woman's Invasion," p. 582.

[15]Commonwealth of Massachusetts, *Thirty-Third Annual Report of the Bureau of the Statistics of Labor* (Boston: Wright & Potter, 1903), p. 256. Indeed the trend was growing. By 1908, the number of married women working in the Massachusetts textile industry had risen to almost 30 percent. See Charles P. Neill, *Report on the Condition of Woman and Child Wage-Earners in the United States, Volume I: Cotton Textile Industry* (Washington,DC: GPO, 1910), p. 129.

[16]Regarding the family wage economy, see Thomas Dublin, *Transforming Women's Work: New England Lives in the Industrial Revolution* (Ithaca, NY: Cornell University Press, 1994), p. 235. On the decline of wages in the Fall River textile industry, see *Massachusetts Labor Bulletin* (Dec. 1904): p. 324.

[17]Based on the Twelfth Census of the United States, as reported in Commonwealth of Massachusetts, *Forty-first Annual Report of the Statistics of Labor* (Boston: Wright & Potter, 1911), p. 277.

[18]Hard, "The Woman's Invasion," p. 583.

[19]*Forty-first Annual Report*, p. 278.

[20]Cumbler, *Working-Class Community*, p. 198.

[21]Hard, "The Woman's Invasion," p. 584.

[22]Hard, "The Woman's Invasion," pp. 584–585.

[23]T.M. Young, *The American Cotton Industry* (New York: Charles Scribner's Sons, 1903), p. 3.

[24]Robert W. Dunn and Jack Hardy, *Labor and Textiles: A Study of Cotton and Wool Manufacturing* (New York: International Publishers, 1931), p. 179.

[25]Dunn and Hardy, *Labor and Textiles*, p. 206.

[26]Cumbler, *Working-Class Community*, pp. 196–197.

[27]Young, *The American Cotton Industry*, p. 4, emphasis added.

[28]Neill, *Report on the Condition of Woman and Child Wage-Earners*, p. 611.

[29]*Boston Globe*, July 25, 1904.

[30]*Massachusetts Labor Bulletin* (Dec. 1904): p. 331.

[31]*Boston Sunday Globe*, July 31, 1904.

[32]*Boston Globe*, July 25, 1904.

[33]*Boston Globe*, Aug. 2, 1904.

[34]*Fall River Globe*, Sept. 21, 1904, as quoted in Cumbler, *Working-Class Community*, p. 205.

[35]*Fall River Herald*, Aug. 16, 1904.

[36]*Massachusetts Labor Bulletin* (Dec. 1904): p. 330.

[37]Massachusetts State Board of Conciliation and Arbitration, Daily Log of Hearings, 1886–1923 (LA4, 535x) Volume II, July 22, 1904–Jan. 18, 1905, Massachusetts State Archives, Boston.

[38]*Fall River Herald*, Aug. 16, 1904.

[39]John B. Andrews and W.D.P. Bliss, *Report on the Condition of Woman and Child Wage-Earners in the United States: Volume X: History of Women in Trade Unions* (Washington, DC: Government Printing Office, 1911), pp. 205–206.

[40]*Fall River Herald*, Aug. 16, 1904.

[41]*Fall River Herald*, Aug. 16, 1904.

[42]Cumbler, *Working-Class Community*, p. 206.

[43]Minutes of Feb. 14, 1904, Kenney O'Sullivan Papers, SL, MC340, box 1, folder 6.

[44]*Charities* 13 (4 Feb., 1905): p. 414.

[45]Anne Withington, "The Fight for Subsistence," *The Commons* 9 (Nov. 1904): p. 557.

[46]Gertrude Barnum, "Fall River Mill Girls in Domestic Service: A Strike Time Experiment," *Charities* 13 (4 Mar., 1905): pp. 550–551, cited in Meredith Tax, *The Rising of the Women: Feminist Solidarity and Class Conflict, 1880–1917* (New York: Monthly Review Press, 1980), p. 340, note 34.

[47]Barnum, "Fall River Mill Girls," p. 550.

[48]See for example: "Social Statistics of Workingwomen," *Massachusetts Labor Bulletin* (May 1901): pp. 29–49, and "Trained and Supplemental Employees for Domestic Service," *Thirty-Seventh Annual Report of the Bureau of the Statistics of Labor* (Boston: Wright & Potter, 1907), pp. 89– 123 for contemporary studies.

[49]Barnum, "Fall River Mill Girls," p. 551.

[50]Gertrude Barnum, "The Story of a Fall River Mill Girl," *The Independent* 58 (Feb. 21, 1905): p. 243, emphasis added.

[51]*Massachusetts Labor Bulletin* 34 (Dec. 1904): p. 330.

[52]Quoted in Cumbler, *Working-Class Community*, p. 207.

[53]Massachusetts State Branch, American Federation of Labor, *Proceedings of the Nineteenth Annual Convention* (Boston: Foster's Union Print, 1902), p. 43, p. 49.

[54]*San Francisco Examiner* and *Boston Globe*, both Nov. 19, 1904.

[55]*Massachusetts Labor Bulletin* 34 (Dec. 1904): p. 323.

[56]State Board of Conciliation and Arbitration, Vol. II, p. 436.

[57]Cumbler, *Working-Class Community*, p. 209.

[58]*Massachusetts Labor Bulletin* 34 (Dec. 1904): p. 320.

[59]*Boston Globe*, Jan. 16, 1905.

[60]Contrast the magnitude of suffering during a strike in a single-industry town such as Fall River with the somewhat lesser impact in a slightly more diversified community such as Troy, New York. There, according to the historian Carole Turbin, female collar workers and male iron workers, many of whom were related by blood and/or marriage, often timed their job actions so as not to coincide thus insuring the continuation of some family income as well as the organized support of one group of workers for another. See Turbin, *Working Women of Collar City: Gender, Class, and Community in Troy, New York, 1864–1886* (Urbana: University of Illinois Press, 1992).

[61]Henry F. Bedford, *Socialism and the Workers in Massachusetts, 1886–1912* (Amherst: University of Massachusetts Press, 1966), p. 206.

[62]*Proceedings* (1904), p. 37.

[63]State Board of Conciliation and Arbitration, Daily Log, Vol. II, p. 456. See also: *Boston Globe* (Evening edition), Jan. 18, 1905 and Cumbler, *Working-Class Community*, p. 208.

[64]*Boston Globe*, Jan. 18, 1905.

[65]Cumbler, *Working-Class Community*, p. 208. A year later, this rather convoluted scheme was still in dispute, challenged by the textile unions and the manufacturers alike according to the *Annual Report of the State Board of Conciliation and Arbitration* (1906), pp. 20–22. In their discussion of the Fall River strike settlement, authors Robert Dunn and Jack Hardy claimed that the sliding scale of wages tied to profits "actually meant a reduction" and that "[m]any of the best workers were blacklisted" despite the agreement that there would be no penalty against workers for their part in the strike. See Dunn and Hardy, *Labor and Textiles*, p. 218.

[66]Samuel Gompers, "The Fall River Strike," *American Federationist* 12 (March 1905): p. 139.

[67]Jonathan Thayer Lincoln, *The City of the Dinner-Pail* (Boston: Houghton Mifflin Co., 1909), p. 93.

[68]Woman's Trade Union League, Minutes of the second meeting of the National Board, Oct. 7, 1904, p. 2, Margaret Dreier Robins papers, NWTUL microfilm edition, reel 8, frame 235.

[69]Minutes, NWTUL Board, Oct. 7, 1904, p. 1.

[70]Minutes of the Third meeting of the WTUL, Mar. 26, 1905, MDR papers, reel 8, frames 245-251.

[71]Kenney O'Sullivan, "The Need of Organization Among Working Women," MDR papers, reel 8, frames 257-265, p. 8, emphasis added. Two other versions of the same speech are also available, one appears to be a transcript taken that day (Mar. 26, 1905) and can be found in the NWTUL papers, box 1, Library of Congress, microfilm edition; the other version can be found in the *Union Labor Advocate* 5 (April 1905). I have chosen to rely the version found in the MDR papers as that appears to have been the original text with annotations by Kenney O'Sullivan.

[72]Tax, *The Rising of the Women*, p. 110.

[73]"The Strike of the Textile Workers in Fall River," *Union Labor Advocate* 5 (Feb. 1905): p. 14.

[74]Kenney O'Sullivan, "The Need of Organization Among Working Women," p. 9, emphasis added.

[75]*Proceedings of the Twenty-fourth Annual Convention of the American Federation of Labor* (1904), p. 161.

[76]Samuel Gompers, "Address to the National Conference of the Women's Trade Union League," March 26, 1905, NWTUL papers, Library of Congress, microfilm edition, reel 17, frame 85.

[77]Gompers, "Address to the National Convention," NWTUL papers, Library of Congress, reel 17, frame 84, emphasis added.

[78]Gompers, "Address to the National Conference," NWTUL papers, Library of Congress, reel 17, frame 84.

[79]Gompers, "Address to the National Conference," NWTUL papers, Library of Congress, reel 17, frame 85.

[80]Samuel Gompers to Gertrude Barnum, Oct. 12, 1905, NWTUL papers, Library of Congress, box 1; also quoted in Philip S. Foner, *Women and the American Labor Movement: From Colonial Times to the Eve of World War I* (New York: The Free Press, 1979), p. 318.

[81]Samuel Gompers, *Seventy Years of Life and Labor: An Autobiography*, edited with an introduction by Nick Salvatore (Ithaca, NY: ILR Press, 1984), p. 76. See also: Salvatore, "Introduction," p.xix. In her examination of the WTUL, with an emphasis on the role of Margaret Dreier Robins who assumed

the national presidency in 1907, Elizabeth Anne Payne claims that Robins was likely influenced by the example of the Knights of Labor. See: Payne, *Reform, Labor, and Feminism: Margaret Dreier Robins and the Women's Trade Union League* (Urbana: University of Illinois Press, 1988), p. 105. In an act of probably unintentional symbolism, when the report of the Credentials Committee was accepted, thus seating Robins as a non-voting delegate to the 1907 AFL convention in Norfolk, the gavel used was one just presented to AFL president Gompers by the former Knights of Labor leader Terence V. Powderly. See the draft of an article for the *Union Labor Advocate*, Dec. 1907, in the NWTUL papers, Library of Congress, reel 17, frame 121.

[82]Payne, *Reform, Labor, and Feminism*, p. 97; see also: Foner, *Women and the American Labor Movement*, p. 318; Robin Miller Jacoby, *The British and American Women's Trade Union Leagues, 1890–1925: A Case Study of Feminism and Class* (Brooklyn, NY: Carlson Publishing, 1994), p. 75.

[83]Gladys Boone, *The Women's Trade Union Leagues in Great britain and the United States of America* (New York: Columbia University Press, 1942), p. 71.

[84]"The Women's Trade Union League, Massachusetts Branch," *Union Labor Advocate* 6 (Jan. 1906), p. 15. Five years after his death, John O'Sullivan was still being honored, if only in passing. The annual MSB convention of 1907 passed a resolution requiring that organized labor speak only to reporters with a union card in respect to "such men as John F. O'Sullivan." *Proceedings of the Twenty-second Annual Convention of the Massachusetts State Branch of the American Federation of Labor* (Boston: Union Print, 1907), p. 39.

[85]Gladys Boone, official historian of the WTUL, cites the success of the Roxbury strike as the reason the BWTUL was finally accepted by the BCLU. While that strike and its outcome were certainly a major factor in the BCLU— and the MSB as well—granting the BWTUL recognition in 1911, as will be discussed in Chapter 5, the passing of Frank Foster, I believe, played a part too.

[86]Boone, *The Women's Trade Union Leagues*, pp. 67–68; Jacoby, *The British and American Women's Trade Union Leagues*, p. 74. See also *Union Labor Advocate* 8 (Sept. 1907).

[87]*Boston Globe*, July 15, 1907.

[88]*Boston Globe*, July 15, 1907.

[89]Eileen Boris, *Home to Work: Motherhood and the Politics of Industrial Homework in the United States* (New York: Cambridge University Press, 1994), pp. 91–92.

[90]Mary E. McDowell, "Red Letter Day," *American Federationist* 14 (Sept. 1907): p. 679.

[91]*American Federationist* 12 (Sept. 1905): p. 625.

[92]Henrotin, "Organization for Women," *American Federationist* 12 (Nov. 1905): pp. 824–826.

[93]"Wage-Working Women," *American Federationist* 13 (Dec. 1906): p. 963, emphasis added.

[94]Nancy Schrom Dye, *As Equals and As Sisters: Feminism, the Labor Movement, and the Women's Trade Union League of New York* (Columbia: University of Missouri Press, 1980), pp. 55–60; Payne, *Reform, Labor, and Feminism*, pp. 60–61.

[95]*Boston Globe* Feb. 16, 1906; "Mrs. Mary Kenney O'Sullivan's Plea for the Ballot," *Union Labor Advocate* 6 (Aug. 1906). In her autobiography, Kenney O'Sullivan claims that while lobbying for the 1893 Illinois Factory Bill, she also assisted in the passage of a woman's suffrage bill in Illinois ["the first women's suffrage victory in the history of Illinois."] (p.110). Neither Sklar nor Tax collaborate this.

[96]*Union Labor Advocate* 6 (Aug. 1906).

[97]Working-class leader of the NYWTUL, Leonora O'Reilly, would use similar rhetoric in her remarks before a Congressional hearing six years later. See: Susan Ware, *Modern American Women: A Documentary History* (Belmont, CA: Wadsworth Publishing Company, 1989), pp. 142–146.

[98]Sean Wilentz, *Chants Democratic: New York City and the Rise of the American Working Class, 1788–1850* (New York: Oxford University Press, 1984).

[99]Ellen Carol Dubois, "Working Women, Class Relations, and Suffrage Militance: Harriet Stanton Blatch and the New York Woman Suffrage Movement, 1894–1906," *Journal of America History* 74 (June 1987): pp. 34–58; Sharon Hartman Strom, "Leadership and Tactics in the American Woman Suffrage Movement: A New Perspective from Massachusetts," *Journal of American History* 62 (Sept. 1975): p. 303; Michael McGerr, "Political Style and Women's Power," *Journal of American History* 77 (Dec. 1990): p. 878.

[100]Jacoby, *The British and American Women's Trade Union Leagues*, p. 82. See also: Dye, *As Equals and As Sisters*, Chap. 6, "The Suffrage Campaign," which focuses on New York.

[101]Dye, *As Equals and As Sisters*, p. 134.

[102]*Proceedings . . . AFL* (1904), p. 147.

[103]*Proceedings of the Twenty-first Annual Convention of the Massachusetts State Branch, American Federation of Labor* (Boston: Union Print, 1906), p. 33.

[104]The resolution introduced by Kenney O'Sullivan, no. 81, was identical to an earlier resolution, no. 62, introduced by James Duncan of the Granite Cutters' union and it was actually that resolution passed by the convention; Kenney O'Sullivan's resolution was tabled as the matter had already been decided. See

Report of the Proceedings of the Twenty-sixth Annual Convention of the American Federation of Labor (Washington: The Graphic Arts Printing Company, 1906), pp. 127, 131, 161, & 163.

[105]*Proceedings . . . AFL* (1906), p. 171; "Dinner for Miss Annie Fitzgerald," *Union Labor Advocate* 8 (Mar. 1908): p. 16; Boone, *The Women's Trade Union Leagues*, p. 70.

[106]Kessler-Harris, "'Where Are the Organized Women Workers?'," *Feminist Studies* 3 (Fall 1975): pp. 92–110.

[107]*Labor News*, Dec. 29, 1906.

[108]Boone, *The Women's Trade Union Leagues*, p. 68, p. 70. The other six delegates to the NWTUL "convention" in attendance were: Mary Dreier, Helen Marot, Agnes Nestor, Anne Nicholes, Ida Rauh, and Margaret Dreier Robins. Of those, only Nestor, representing the Glove Workers, was a voting delegate to the AFL convention; Robins was a non-voting fraternal delegate representing the WTUL.

[109]On Robins, in addition to Payne, *Reform, Labor, and Feminism*, and Alice Meehan Clement, "Margaret Dreier Robins and the Dilemma of the Women's Trade Union League: Organization versus Legislation," (Ph.D. diss., University of California at Davis, 1984) see also: Mary E. Dreier, *Margaret Dreier Robins: Her Life, Letters, and Work* (New York: Island Cooperative Press, 1950).

[110]Payne, *Reform, Labor, and Feminism*, p. 96.

[111]After a change in the NWTUL constitution in 1907, the Massachusetts branch changed its name to the Boston WTUL. See: Boone, *The Women's Trade Union Leagues*, p. 64, note 1.

[112]Diane Kirkby, "'The Wage Earning Woman and the State': the National Women's Trade Union League and Protective Labor Legislation, 1903–1923," *Labor History* 28 (Winter 1987): pp. 54–74.

[113]Quoted in Lela B. Costin, *Two Sisters for Social Justice: A Biography of Grace and Edith Abbott* (Urbana: University of Illinois Press, 1983), p. 29.

[114]Stephen H. Norwood, *Labor's Flaming Youth: Telephone Operators and Worker Militancy, 1878–1923* (Urbana: University of Illinois Press, 1990), p. 106. A brief interview with Crawford in *The Labor News*, Dec. 28, 1907, reports that she "was reared in intellectual surroundings, a college graduate."

[115]On the election of Balch, see: Mary Crawford, secretary, BWTUL to Margaret Dreier Robins, n.d., c. Jan. 1908, NWTUL papers, Library of Congress, box 1, and *Union Labor Advocate* 8 (Feb. 1908).

[116]*The Labor News*, Oct. 12, 1907; Sept. 14, 1907.

[117]*The Labor News*, June 27, 1908.

[118]Emily Greene Balch to MDR, April 11, 1908, NWTUL papers, Library of Congress, box 1.

[119]Minutes of the Meeting of the Executive Board of the NWTUL, held at Boston's South End House, Fri., June 26, 1908, NWTUL papers, Library of Congress, box 1.

[120]Clement, "Margaret Dreier Robins and the Dilemma of the Women's Trade Union League," p. 108.

[121]Kenney O'Sullivan quote, *Union Labor Advocate* 9 (Dec. 1908); see also: "Interview with Miss Casey," *The Labor News*, Jan. 30, 1909.

[122]Anne Withington to MDR, Aug. 17, [1908] MDR papers, reel 51, frames 404–5.

[123]*The Labor News*, Nov. 7, 1908 reported 500 in attendance while the *Union Labor Advocate* reported in its Dec. 1908 issue only about 150 guests.

[124]*The Labor News*, Nov. 14, 1908; Jan. 30, 1909.

[125]MDR to Raymond Robins, MDR papers, reel 52, frame 585, frame 589. See also: *Union Labor Advocate* 10 (Mar. 1909).

[126]"Minutes of the Executive Board meeting of the NWTUL, March 9, 1909, held in Chicago," NWTUL papers, Library of Congress, box 1.

[127]Clement, "Margaret Dreier Robins and the Dilemma of the WTUL," p. 113.

[128]Proceedings of the 1909 Convention, NWTUL papers, Library of Congress, reel 20, frames 49–50.

[129]Proceedings of the 1909 Convention, NWTUL papers, Library of Congress, reel 20, frames 35–36. In its Feb. 22, 1908 edition, *The Labor News* reported under the heading "Poor Little Heathens" the following tidbit: "Mrs. Mary Kenney O'Sullivan, vice-president of the Massachusetts WTUL, is adored by her three children, and brings them up in her own faith. Once her four-year-old daughter came home from school and said to her mother, with round eyes of surprise, 'Just think, mamma, those children don't know anything about labor!'"

[130]Boone, *The Women's Trade Union Leagues*, p. 75.

[131]Elizabeth Glendower Evans Trip Diaries, Vol. II, Dec. 30 & 31, 1908, Schlesinger Library, Radcliffe College, Cambridge, MA. On Evans' continued friendship with the Bruce Glasiers, which included a substantial gift of money, see: Laurence Thompson, *The Enthusiasts: A Biography of John and Katherine Bruce Glasier* (London: Victor Gollancy Ltd., 1971), pp. 159–161. On Fabian Socialism in general, see: Norman and Jeanne MacKenzie, *The Fabians* (New York: Simon and Schuster, 1977).

[132]Proceedings of the 1909 Convention, NWTUL papers, Library of Congress, reel 19, frame 977.

[133]Proceedings of 1909 Convention, NWTUL papers, Library of Congress, reel 19, frame 980.

[134]In addition to *The Survey* piece cited below, see: *Union Labor Advocate*, April and June, 1910 and *The Labor News*, July 23, 1910. On the carpet industry,

see: Arthur H. Cole and Harold F. Williamson, *The American Carpet Manufacture: A History and an Analysis* (Cambridge, MA: Harvard University Press, 1941). On earlier labor action within the carpet industry, see: Susan Levine, *Labor's True Woman: Carpet Weavers, Industrialization, and Labor Reform in the Gilded Age* (Philadelphia, PA: Temple University, 1984).

[135]Boston *Globe*, April 11, 1910.

[136]*Annual Report of the State Board of Arbitration and Conciliation* (1910), p. 31–32. See also: *Union Labor Advocate* 11 (June 1910).

[137]Evans, "The Roxbury Carpet Factory Strike," *The Survey* 24 (28 May, 1910): pp. 337–338. In its June 11th issue, *The Survey* responded to criticism of Glendower Evans' article as too "anti-capitalist" by pointing out not only her wealth but also the role she played in mediating the strike, to the benefit of employee and employer alike.

CHAPTER 5

"A General Smash-Up"
The Boston Women's Trade Union League Comes of Age

"EFFORT TO UNIONIZE GIRL EMPLOYES [sic] OF RAZOR WORKS CAUSES THE ARREST OF TWO WOMEN" read the headline in the June 9, 1910 morning edition of the *Boston Globe*. The day before, Elizabeth Glendower Evans and Mabel Gillespie had been arrested while handing out leaflets to women on their way to work at the Gillette Safety Razor Company in South Boston.[1] Evans was there as a socially prominent member of the Boston Women's Trade Union League (BWTUL), while Gillespie was acting in her capacity as organizing secretary of the BWTUL, having succeeded Josephine Casey in 1909.

Unlike Casey, Gillespie was a member of the middle class, raised in Concord, Massachusetts by an aunt after the death of her parents.[2] She attended Radcliffe College for two years before becoming a social worker in 1900, the same year she moved into Boston's Denison House. In 1903, she became secretary of the Boston Association of Charities but held that position for only a year before her appointment as the executive secretary of the Buffalo branch of the New York Consumers' League and the Child Labor Commission. In 1906, she briefly held the position of organizing secretary for the BWTUL. Gillespie permanently returned to that job in 1909 and would remain until her death in 1923.

While four other women had held that position in the first five years of the BWTUL, Gillespie's comparatively long reign as organizing secretary represented a turning point for the Boston league. It was evidence of, and at the same time responsible for, a certain level of institutional stability within the Boston branch of the WTUL. It also represented a critical shift, in both direction and personnel, which would finally result in what was referred to as "a general smash-up" during the Lawrence Bread and Roses strike of 1912.[3] Nevertheless, before the smash-up came a short period in which the Boston WTUL achieved that which Kenney O'Sullivan intended—the organization of women into viable trade unions.

Fresh from its victory in the relatively small 1910 strike of the Roxbury carpet weavers, the Boston WTUL entered the ongoing labor dispute at the Gillette Safety Razor Company with a certain amount of confidence. The frustrations of Fall River appeared to be a thing of the past. As in Roxbury, there were only several hundred workers involved in the Gillette dispute, as compared to the Fall River strike of 25,000 men and women. Also like the Roxbury strike, ethnicity did not seem to be a factor in South Boston the way it had been in Fall River.

The strike at the South Boston razor factory had started on Friday, June 3, 1910 when those men who were members of the Machinists' Union walked out in protest over wage reductions. According to the *Boston Globe*, "Many of the girls in the shop wanted to leave with the men that day, but were advised not to do so, or at least until they were organized by the machinists' officers."[4] Within just a few days, the Machinists' Union and the Boston Central Labor Union (BCLU) were cooperating with the BWTUL in an organizing drive directed specifically at the women working in the Gillette plant. By Wednesday, June 8th, Glendower Evans and Gillespie were set to hand out flyers explaining the benefits of trade unionism, particularly for women. After first addressing the fears of those women who worried that involvement with the union would lead to the loss of their jobs, the flyer went on:

> Your life depends upon your work, your hours, your pay. If you are worn out or can't make enough to live well, you can't be healthy, happy, intelligent or attractive.[5]

Shaping its appeal on the grounds of personal appearance may have had some saliency for those women actively engaged in the production of a good directly linked to one's appearance. The flyer directed at the razor factory workers, however, quickly shifted from an emphasis on personal concerns to the need for collective action:

> Union means power to say: I shall work so long each day; I must be paid enough to live; I must be free to join hands with my sisters in the shops for justice to all.[6]

Hours, wages, the right to belong to a union, and justice for workers were demands which were basic to both men and women wage-earners alike. Thus in their efforts at the Gillette plant, the WTUL would have the support of the male-led Machinists' Union as well as the BCLU.

According to one somewhat light-hearted account of the arrest of Glendower Evans and Gillespie, the two women had first gone to the local police station before handing out their flyers. *The Boston Common* reported that the police informed the two that they could not distribute their flyer on the sidewalk, which was a public way, but instead had to do so while on private property.[7] Glendower Evans and Gillespie were accompanied by Sara Conboy, a carpet weaver who had been a leader in the Roxbury strike and had just been hired by the United Textile Workers (UTW) as an organizer. The three women went to the gates of the Gillette plant, determined to hand out their flyers as the women entered work for the day.

At first they stood in nearby doorways, thus putting themselves on private property. "But," according to *The Boston Common*, "Miss Gillespie decided to defy the law to the extent of occupying the sidewalk." A policeman promptly arrived on the scene, put Gillespie under arrest, and marched her to the nearest call box so as to request the patrol wagon. Then "Mrs. Glendower Evans decided that she preferred the sidewalk to the doorway and stepped forth to distribute more freely to the fast accumulating crowd of girls."[8] She, too, was put under arrest and, along with Gillespie, put into the paddy wagon upon its arrival. But the WTUL ally was not done yet. "Mrs. Evans, declaring that she might as well get all she could out of the adventure, distributed handbills to the eager crowd [of women factory workers] from the police wagon as it jogged along."[9]

It is perhaps significant that Glendower Evans and Gillespie could risk arrest and even treat it as lightly as they did, seeing "the whole affair as a joke."[10] But Sara Conboy, who had started work at the age of eleven in a button factory, was a young widow in 1910, the sole support of her daughter. While passing out handbills, Conboy opted to stay in a doorway and stay out of jail. Not only did Conboy lack the resources of women like Evans and Gillespie, she also had a young daughter to worry about. As a paid organizer for the UTW, Conboy would devote the rest of her life to the union cause. Nonetheless, she did so within the realities of her life as a woman of the working-class.

Along with Glendower Evans and Gillespie (who were released from jail almost immediately), Conboy was on hand for a mass meeting held outside the Gillette plant at the end of the work day. Also in attendance were Pauline Newman and Rose Schneiderman, two of the New

York WTUL's most effective organizers. Newman and Schneiderman, both immigrants and wage-earners, happened to be in Boston for the annual convention of the International Garment Workers' Union.[11] These two veterans of the 1909 Shirtwaist Makers' strike, known as the "Uprising of the 30,000," urged the several hundred women in Boston not to go out on strike. Newman told the crowd, "That is not what trade unionism means. We simply want you to stop and think for a few moments over the conditions under which you work and live." Schneiderman added:

> You are earning $10 a week perhaps. Not many of you earn that, however. And what is $10 anyway? You can't live on $10. You can exist on $10, but no more—eat, sleep, work on $10; be a drudge upon $10. But what will you know of the beauties of nature, about art, literature, music; about all the things that make life worth living?[12]

According to Schneiderman, it was trade unionism that would "make life worth living." Apparently, significant numbers of the women who worked at the Gillette plant agreed. Within a few days of the arrests of Glendower Evans and Gillespie and the stirring speeches by Newman and Schneiderman, the Worcester-based *Labor News* reported that the strike had been won and "a good organization ha[d] been formed as a result of the agitation by the organizers."[13]

Throughout the rest of 1910, the BWTUL continued its efforts at organizing working women in Boston and beyond. In August the BWTUL sponsored an event which featured a talk by Rose Schneiderman before wage-earning women in Holyoke. At the end of October, a Halloween party was held at BWTUL headquarters in Boston. The efforts at gaining passage of a state minimum wage law for women, which had begun in December of 1909, also continued.[14] Mabel Gillespie was a quite active secretary for the BWTUL, but as the League entered the year 1911, yet another internal squabble threatened its precarious place within the labor community of Boston.

By the end of January 1911, the BWTUL had a new president. Sue Ainslie Clark, a native of Brooklyn, New York, moved to the Boston area in 1909 upon her marriage to Alfred Clark, an editor for the *Boston Post*. A 1903 graduate of Wellesley College, Clark had worked as Florence Kelley's assistant in the New York office of the National Consumers' League.[15] While there, she conducted investigations into the work and living conditions of women wage-earners in various New York City trades. Clark went on to co-author a series of articles based on her findings which in 1911 was published in a book entitled *Making Both Ends Meet*.[16] As a young wife, she continued her association with the social reform community in her new home, where she had connections from her days at Wellesley; in her last year at college, Clark had taken a class entitled "Social Economics" taught by Emily Green Balch.[17] Less than eight years later, the student would succeed her professor as president of the BWTUL.

Clark's election, however, was not without discord. In a letter written to her sister, Margaret Dreier Robins, Mary Dreier described her visit to Boston in late January 1911. Noting that Robins, as president of the NWTUL, would get "an official letter" from NYWTUL secretary Helen Marot, Dreier took it upon herself to focus on the personal disputes which led up to Clark's election as president of the Boston league. "Mrs. Clark, who by the way will make an excellent president," Dreier wrote, "won her presidency by one vote."[18] She described the election as a fight during which "feeling ran of course very high." According to Dreier:

> . . . . while Miss Gillespie proposed Mrs. Clark, Mrs. Kehew took her up, and it was then thought that she would be Mrs. Kehew's tool. Mrs. O'Sullivan of course wanted Mrs. Evans as president. . . .[19]

Mary Morton Kehew had been an early and generous supporter of the WTUL, and certainly her opinions regarding who should be the next president had weight. By 1911, however, Glendower Evans had become much more active than Kehew in the day-to-day activities of the BWTUL. She had participated in the Roxbury strike, faced arrest at the Gillette plant, and was increasingly involved as a leader in the Minimum Wage law campaign. And, perhaps as important, Evans was just as wealthy and well-connected as Kehew. It was not surprising that her old friend Kenney O'Sullivan would support Glendower Evans in her bid for the presidency, if only to recognize the importance of her contributions to the cause of trade unionism for women.[20] Such was not to be, however, and the lines which would be more sharply drawn a year later in Lawrence were already forming. On one side stood Glendower Evans and Kenney O'Sullivan. Opposing them, for reasons of personality as much as anything else, were Gillespie and Clark. Writing to her sister, Mary Dreier had little good to say about the Boston league. She seemed unable to understand why her attempt to solicit a yearly contribution of $2000 to $3000 from Glendower Evans failed the day after Clark, not Evans, was elected president. All Dreier could offer as an explanation was that

[t]hese good people are so very Bostonian and have more cold water in
their system than anybody I have ever heard of . . . they do not seem to
have any labor women except Mrs. Conboy and one little girl in the
Department stores.[21]

While Dreier seemed to be forgetting the presence of, not to mention the
leadership role played by, Kenney O'Sullivan, she was also forgetting other
wage-earning women who had been involved in the BWTUL for some
time, women such as Mary Woodd, a bookbinder, and Margaret Foley, a
hat maker. By 1911, both Woodd and Foley were members of the NWTUL
executive board, representing Boston along with Glendower Evans.

Dreier offered her remedy for the troubles in Boston:

I can't believe that in that group of textile workers they were not able to
find able women, and I think that instead of having the League in
Boston, they should do their work outside of Boston, and then they
might do effective work.[22]

In fact, the League would not be leaving Boston any time soon. The
BWTUL was preparing, albeit in what Dreier regarded as a rather stingy
way, to host the biennial convention of the NWTUL in June, 1911.
Dreier seemed to agree with the Gillespie-Clark faction that hosting the
1911 NWTUL convention "would give the [Boston] League the boost it
needs, and establish its standing with the other unions."[23] While the 1911
convention did not smooth over the internal disputes within the BWTUL,
it did seemingly increase its growing acceptance within the Boston labor
community.

According to the *Boston Globe*, the "Big Problems of Women Workers [were] To Be Considered" at the NWTUL's third biennial convention.[24] The convention opened on Monday, June 12th, with "music
provided by an orchestra of union women musicians."[25] NWTUL president Robins said a few words of welcome before introducing the first
speaker, Mary Kenney O'Sullivan. Robins told the 75 elected delegates
that it was "very fitting" that Kenney O'Sullivan speak first. She pointed
out that it was just a little less than eight years earlier, in that very city,
"that the National Women's Trade Union League was born," and that it
was Kenney O'Sullivan who was

one of those who were helping at that time and who saw the possibilities of this League and had the vision to look forward into the future
when we might have a gathering again like this in Boston.[26]

Despite her role in the birth of the WTUL, much less the strength of her vision, Kenney O'Sullivan claimed surprise when asked to address the convention in its opening session. Stating that she had not been formally asked to speak, she managed nonetheless to say a few words.

After first expressing her delight and gratitude at the turnout, Kenney O'Sullivan addressed one of the persistent problems the organizers of working women faced—just what role should be played by the more privileged. She reminded her listeners about the importance of the allies "who saw away ahead of the girls who work."[27] But those allies had to do more than "just talking or sending their money." According to Kenney O'Sullivan, those allies also "must do service." In her mind, "doing service," or showing support of the labor movement, meant more than just talk or money. It meant actually taking part in the day-to-day activities so vital to organization. Perhaps she had in mind the very active role of Glendower Evans, first in the Roxbury strike and then in the labor action at the Gillette plant. Much would come from this sort of participation:

> . . . to my mind service is the spirit of emancipation, and service is the spirit of building up this democratic reconstruction that comes through the trade union movement.[28]

Such "service" was key to Kenney O'Sullivan's vision of the WTUL and the benefits of trade unionism in general. Shortly after she spoke, Kenney O'Sullivan turned the podium over to the recently elected president of the Boston WTUL, Sue Ainslie Clark.

Clark spoke about problems common to all industrial workers—long hours and low wages and applauded recent state action regarding these concerns. She saw the limitation of work hours to fifty-four per week, directed only at women and children in the textile industry, as "very encouraging."[29] Clark went on to say that "that a woman from the Boston Women's Trade Union will be appointed" to the "commission for the investigation of women's wages."[30] That woman would be Glendower Evans. Interestingly, Governor Eugene Foss timed his announcement of Glendower Evans' appointment to coincide with the NWTUL convention then meeting in Boston. His letter, dated June 12, 1911, was read at the convention the next day, causing a "great demonstration" among the delegates.[31]

After "repeated calls for a speech," Glendower Evans admitted she was "almost terrified at the responsibility that has come to me, because I do want so much to make good." She went on to note that she would be relying "upon [her] comrades" but that all "must be patient if we don't seem to bring the heaven down to the earth possibly very soon."[32] Sounding very much like the Fabian Socialist she had become two years earlier, Glendower Evans was seeking human salvation through social reform. A minimum wage law for women had been under discussion in Great Britain during the several months she visited there in 1908–1909. Thus the notion that there could be a legislative remedy for the economic hardship so many women wage-earners endured as a result of their low wages was not unfamiliar.[33] It was, however, not the approach which Kenney O'Sullivan favored—she continued to seek the improvement of wages through trade unionism.

Recognition of the WTUL by the AFL and its affiliated organizations continued to be an important goal sought by Kenney O'Sullivan and others.[34] Locally, Kenney O'Sullivan had enjoyed relatively cordial relations with the BCLU for almost twenty years, even holding various offices during the 1890s. Nonetheless, the position of the female-dominated unions she attempted to bring into the central body always appeared to be ambiguous at best, causing her much professional (and probably personal) frustration. The BWTUL had similarly suffered from a lack of support from the BCLU during the League's early years when it was admitted only as a fraternal non-voting delegate. Whatever her level of frustration, however, Kenney O'Sullivan stubbornly defended the BCLU against charges levied by Sara Conboy that it had purposely altered its constitution so as to prohibit the membership of the BWTUL, even as a fraternal delegate.

In what was perhaps the most heated exchange of the NWTUL 1911 convention, these two Irish-American women sparred for several minutes regarding the intentions of the BCLU when it revised its constitution in 1910. Conboy wanted the NWTUL to know about what she saw as the calculated injustice inflicted upon the BWTUL by the BCLU through these revisions. She said, "You should have seen them snatch up the constitution and they changed it and the [WTUL] delegates were without seats in the Central Labor body until about six weeks ago when Miss Gillespie applied for **her** delegates to be once more seated."[35] Indeed, the BCLU had just recently re-admitted the BWTUL. Claiming that the apparent exclusion of the BWTUL under the revised constitution was merely an oversight soon corrected, Kenney O'Sullivan challenged Conboy's statement. But Conboy refused to back down, saying, "I know what I am talking about."[36] The two continued to argue despite an attempt by Robins to play peacemaker. Only an abrupt and complete change of topic, brought on by a totally unrelated question from the floor, ended the argument between Conboy and Kenney O'Sullivan.

Despite their growing differences, which would soon come to a head in Lawrence, the two women had much in common. Both were the daughters of Irish immigrants, had started work as children, and had worked for more than thirty years. Both had suddenly become young widows with one or more children to support. But there were critical differences as well. Conboy appears to have been a relative newcomer to organized labor, having first gotten involved in trade unionism during the 1910 strike at the Roxbury Carpet Company, where she worked as weaver. She lacked the long history that Kenney O'Sullivan had with the male-dominated labor community. She also perhaps lacked Kenney O'Sullivan's diplomatic yet dogged approach towards dealing with that community. Within a year, however, their positions vis-a-vis organized labor would be reversed. Conboy would join the upper ranks of her union, the United Textile Workers, and by extension the AFL. Kenney O'Sullivan would wind up spending the rest of her life outside of the organized labor community she had so long been, if somewhat tenuously, a part of.

Kenney O'Sullivan's disassociation actually began at the 1911 convention. Perhaps still annoyed with the outcome of the recent BWTUL election, in which even the national officers opposed her "choice" of Glendower Evans as president, Kenney O'Sullivan stepped down from her leadership role in the NWTUL. Nominated once again for the position of first vice-president, she "declined to serve."[37] Mrs. D.W. Knefler, a non-wage-earning "ally" and the president of the St. Louis League, was nominated in her place. Nominated, and soon elected, as second vice-president was Sara Conboy. Mabel Gillespie was elected to the NWTUL Executive Board.[38] In less than eight years from its founding, Kenney O'Sullivan had effectively removed herself from the organization she had helped develop.

The evidence of this transformation must rely, unfortunately, more on what was not said than that which was. In her unpublished autobiography, Kenney O'Sullivan is oddly silent about the early years of the WTUL. She only briefly describes the founding of the organization, reporting little else regarding the WTUL until the Lawrence strike of 1912.[39] Further, Kenney O'Sullivan and her friend Glendower Evans played a far less vocal role in the 1911 NWTUL convention than they did in the convention of 1909. Nonetheless, Kenney O'Sullivan's recorded remarks during the 1911 convention offer some clues to how she felt about the WTUL she had envisioned.

In perhaps her longest speech during that 1911 meeting, Kenney O'Sullivan made clear the depth of her feeling for the organization. While debating what position the WTUL should take regarding unplanned strikes by unorganized workers, she made her opinion clear. Although against "a general unorganized strike," Kenney O'Sullivan did add that "of course, if the workers are unorganized and strike before they come to the Women's Trade Union League that is another matter."[40] Ideally, however, the principles of "arbitration and conciliation" should be used whenever possible. Kenney O'Sullivan concluded:

> . . . . **if there is anybody in this room who cares more for the Trade Union League than I do, I have never seen their face.** If you care for the Trade Union League **as I understand it,** and if you care for the trade union movement, don't go on record as approving unorganized strikes.[41]

It was becoming increasingly apparent, however, that Kenney O'Sullivan's understanding of the WTUL was not in synch with those who were now assuming leadership roles within the Boston league and on the national level.

Nonetheless, the new leaders of the BWTUL accomplished that which Kenney O'Sullivan had not been able to do. At its 1911 annual convention, the Massachusetts State Branch of the AFL voted to accept the BWTUL as a fraternal delegate. Sara Conboy, representing the UTW and one of the four women present at the state convention, introduced the resolution, which was passed, 91 in favor and 16 opposed.[42] The following year, in 1912, Mabel Gillespie represented the BWTUL at the MSB convention—as she would every year after until her death in 1923.[43] Such formal recognition was critical for the WTUL as it continued to seek legitimacy within organized labor.

The reasons why the state labor organization waited almost eight years to extend the privilege of membership to the BWTUL remain unknown. Most likely, the same obstacles which the WTUL encountered on the national level regarding its position within the AFL also hampered the BWTUL goals within the Massachusetts State Federation. Equally unclear is whether or not Kenney O'Sullivan had used her personal connections as the widow of one of the organization's most-respected members to try to gain recognition before 1911. In any case, it was through the efforts of relative newcomers to the labor scene, Conboy and Gillespie, that the Boston League finally won the right to sit as a fraternal delegate within the state labor organization.

In recognition of her growing importance within the WTUL, the convention organizers asked Sara Conboy to write the foreword to the

1911 convention handbook. Beyond the numerous exclamation points, Conboy's short statement entitled "Foreword for Unionism," can be read as her personal philosophy regarding the necessity of organization. She began by saying, "Oh, the need of UNION among our women in the textile mills! That every WORKER, whatever his race, creed or color, might know the wealth of meaning in that great word, UNION, as **we understand it!**"[44] But her understanding of the necessity of trade unionism was far different from that of Kenney O'Sullivan who had entered the trade union movement a generation earlier. In 1893 when she spoke of the "necessity of organization" for women, Kenney O'Sullivan spoke of the need for "self-reliance and independence" specifically for women.[45] Almost twenty years later, Conboy appears not so concerned with issues of gender as she is with those of ethnicity and the need to impart one particular model of trade unionism to those who lacked a fundamental understanding of that model. She wrote:

> We see race after race come into the mill; we see wages cut and cut again. We know that the men and women who come from Poland, from Italy, from Armenia, do not yet understand that we and they are brothers and sisters, that we and they must stand together for what we justly earn.

Conboy continued, in an almost evangelical tone:

> We in the Union DO understand. We have seen the light and we cannot lock it up in our hearts. We must give it out to them! We are the apostles of this mighty faith of ours, that the Labor Movement is to free us all from the chains that bind unorganized, exploited workers.[46]

The WTUL also acknowledged the need to transcend ethnic differences, even passing a resolution at the 1911 convention in favor of printing organizing material in several languages.[47] But when put to the test, the disparity between rhetoric and reality would become apparent during the Lawrence strike.

The strike which began on January 11, 1912 in the textile city of Lawrence, Massachusetts remains one of the most dramatic events in American labor history. It is also one of the most well-documented and commemorated of labor actions, the very meaning of which has been a subject of both scholarly and community debate.[48] The reasons for this are many. The sympathetic journalist Mary Heaton Vorse would later remember:

Lawrence was a singing strike. The workers sang everywhere: at the
picket line, at the soup kitchens, at the relief stations, at the strike meetings. Always there was singing.[49]

Vorse was joined by scores of journalists from around the country who
witnessed more than the singing of the strikers.

The mass exodus of the children, the often brutal treatment of the
strikers by the state militia, and especially the dynamic involvement of
the Industrial Workers of the World (IWW) all seemed to point to a new
direction in worker action. Such high drama caught the attention of a
nation during a presidential election year in which much of the political
debate would focus on proposed changes in tariffs as well as debates regarding unrestricted immigration. These concerns were seen as having a
direct connection to the "labor war at Lawrence."[50]

Ironically, the strike itself began when the fifty-four hour bill went
into effect in January, 1912. This Progressive-inspired reduction in working hours (from fifty-six to fifty-four hours per week) led to a commen-
surate reduction in wages. When workers received their first pay envelope
of the new year, reflecting their loss in wages, the strike began.[51] In a
sense, the strike in Lawrence can be seen as both a product of and part of
the decline of Progressivism itself.

First and foremost, however, it was a strike of massive proportions,
involving at its peak 23,000 men, women, and child workers in a city of
which more than half of the labor force over fourteen worked in either a
woolen or cotton textile mill.[52] Thousands more were dependent upon
the wages of those out on strike, either as family members or as the
providers of auxiliary services. But there was much more than the sheer
number of strikers that added to the drama.

Lawrence was, in the words of one of its historians, an "Immigrant
City" which had by 1912 surpassed Fall River in having the greatest
number of foreign-born residents in the Commonwealth.[53] According to
the 1910 census, 86 percent of Lawrence's almost 86,000 residents were
either immigrants or the children of immigrants.[54] The largest ethnic
groups were Irish (one-third of the total) and French Canadian (one-fifth)
but increasing numbers of Italian, Polish, Russian, and Serbian immigrants had come to Lawrence in the early years of the twentieth century,
filling the textile mills' growing need for unskilled workers. Divided by
linguistic and religious differences, this diverse immigrant community
shared low wages, poor housing, and one of the highest infant mortality
rates in the nation.[55] These Lawrence workers were, for the most part, not
represented by an AFL-affiliated trade union.

According to Samuel Gompers, the immigrant and the unskilled (frequently one and the same and oftentimes female as well) went unrepresented by the AFL because they did "not speak our language, and . . . in many instances have had their suspicions and prejudices aroused by so-called radical Socialist 'intellectuals.' "[56] Language barriers and political differences were certainly compounded, however, by the prejudices of the AFL leadership against the "newer" immigrants of Eastern and Southern Europe. Such prejudices were hardly confined to trade unionists but were further justified, in their eyes, by the difficulties surrounding the organization of low-paid, unskilled workers who would be hard-pressed to pay union dues capable of supporting a viable trade union. Thus, as UTW president John Golden later admitted before a Congressional committee, when the strike began in Lawrence in January, 1912 his union could claim only 208 members out of a workforce of more than 20,000. Golden further testified that:

> We [the UTW] have over 10,000 skilled workers in the state of Massachusetts—skilled and unskilled, the majority of them between the skilled and medium skilled, and it is not any use wearying you with telling you why we have not more of the unskilled. The answer is simply the rapid changing of the nationalities.[57]

More than just those in organized labor were concerned about the increasingly diverse ethnic make-up of the nation's industrial workforce. Social reformers, too, were growing concerned that the Progressive responses they had championed for more than a decade were no longer adequate to meet the needs of these "newer" immigrants.[58] Boston settlement house pioneer Robert Woods, who so loved Mary Kenney O'Sullivan's mashed potatoes in the 1890s, had this to say about the Lawrence strike:

> There is here the most tangible recognition of a crude power of collective formation among previously unorganizable babels of laborers, which can quickly extend itself from town to town and from state to state.[59]

But these "unorganizable babels of laborers" were perhaps not so unorganized. The IWW had been active in Lawrence since at least 1910, winning a "dedicated following" of several hundred textile operatives.[60] In terms of labor organizations, the AFL and the IWW were certainly at opposite ends of a limited spectrum. Founded in 1905 as "One Big [industrial] Union," the IWW saw workers, regardless of skill level or ethnicity, in a perpetual state of war, fighting the reign of capital.[61]

Perhaps in response to the competition, the UTW had stepped up its organizing efforts in Lawrence, assisted by the BWTUL. During the summer of 1911, John Golden and Sara Conboy were joined by Kenney O'Sullivan and Glendower Evans, who "walked the streets as sandwich advertisers." But as Kenney O'Sullivan would later remember, despite at least one well-attended meeting, "how many textile workers we had we never knew. The next winter [January 1912], when the workers had a cut in their wages, the small union plus the great mass went out on strike."[62]

In the mind of John Golden, this was not a strike—it was a "revolution."[63] Two days after the strike began, Golden sent a telegram to the Massachusetts Director of Public Safety, "volunteering his services" in controlling what both this veteran labor leader and mill owners saw as a "mob."[64] When the AFL initially refused to sanction the Lawrence strike, the IWW stepped in to the void, using innovative strike tactics which included organizing workers on their basis of their native language, increased involvement of women, and the well-publicized exodus of the strikers' children.[65]

On the national as well as the local level, the WTUL leaders were divided over what their role should be in Lawrence. Despite the position of the AFL, several WTUL members felt the strike was worthy of their support. Yet, given their long, albeit tenuous, association with the AFL, it was difficult for the League as a whole to go against AFL policy. Anne Withington, middle-class ally and WTUL member from Boston, explained the initial lack of support in an article in the NWTUL paper, *Life and Labor.* "The Trade Unions," wrote Withington, "refused to take any action during the first fortnight of the strike, **while it was being led by the enemies of organized labor** . . ."[66] However, claiming that under the direction of the enemy, i.e., the IWW, the strike was about to collapse, Withington argued that the time had come for the "recognized trade organizations" to step in. On February 1st the local AFL affiliate, the Lawrence Central Labor Union, and the Boston WTUL finally set up a relief station which included the services of "a trained nurse" and small handouts of basic food stuffs.[67] The strike did not collapse as expected, but as February turned into March the BWTUL did little else than to quietly dispense much-needed charity.

One BWTUL member who did make a very public appearance in Lawrence was ally Vida Scudder. Her visit in early March caused quite a stir, especially in the Boston newspapers and on the Wellesley College campus, where Scudder had been a respected professor of English for twenty-five years.[68] As one of the founders of Boston's Denison House, Scudder had long been active in social reform, including that directed at labor. As both a scholar and a reformer, she had a particular interest in those she called her "good Italian friends."[69] Speaking at a meeting sponsored by the Progressive Women of Lawrence on the evening of March 4th, Scudder made clear her position. Although she was not a supporter of the IWW, her recent conversion to Socialism colored her remarks. She looked to "a future when, in America those of different races shall, indeed, be of one heart, one mind, one soul."[70] More concretely, Scudder also suggested the establishment of a minimum wage. According to Scudder, if the mill owners could not afford to pay wages which would "maintain men and women in health and decency, then the woolen industry has no place in Massachusetts."[71]

While Scudder's speech caused the Wellesley College Board of Trustees some alarm, the English professor's problems stemming from her Lawrence speech paled in comparison with the difficulties faced by the AFL and the WTUL. By early March, John Golden was publicly accused of misappropriating $1000 of strike relief funds.[72] Just days before, on March 4th, Golden had negotiated a separate settlement with the mills on behalf of the skilled workers represented by the UTW. He ordered the BWTUL to hand over the operation of its relief station to the UTW, who would now give out relief only to those who had agreed to return to work.[73] Given that thousands of men, women and children were still out on strike, the BWTUL was uncertain about what to do. Their uncertainty, combined with their upset over the allegations against Golden, further distressed many within the League. The possibly stolen funds were in part those raised by the Boston WTUL, and many felt used by Golden and by the AFL itself.

The NWTUL had watched from afar and was increasingly alarmed. Mary Dreier anticipated "a general smash-up." She and her sister, Margaret Dreier Robins, blamed one of their own for what happened in Lawrence. Both women accused Sara Conboy of being Golden's "tool."[74] Responding to her sister Mary's letter regarding the situation in Lawrence, NWTUL President Robins wrote:

> I wish that Boston [WTUL] had thought of asking me to go to Lawrence. I could not very well go there uninvited because I would have to go there officially and our relationship with Boston is so queer anyway . . .

Even the avowed conciliatory skills of Robins could not overcome the forces at work in Lawrence. She went on to say:

> I felt for the longest time that Golden was *N. G.* [no good], and at the [WTUL] convention last year that Mrs. Conboy was his tool if not other people's, and when the delegates elected her to the vice-presidency it made me mad then and it makes me madder today.[75]

Robins and Dreier were not alone in their frustration and outright anger at how UTW president Golden, his organizer and WTUL vice-president Conboy, and by extension the AFL itself had reacted to the Lawrence strike.

Mary Kenney O'Sullivan had her own opinions regarding the strike. According to Kenney O'Sullivan, the IWW owed its apparent success in Lawrence to

> the high-handed methods used by the three branches of the American Federation of Labor. These divisions were the Lawrence Central Labor Union, the Boston Women's Trade Union League, and the [United] Textile Workers of America.[76]

Although these organizations, employing their "high-handed methods," did not enter into the Lawrence strike until early February and then somewhat tentatively, Kenney O'Sullivan went on her own to Lawrence almost as soon as the strike began. In her unpublished autobiography written a dozen or so years after the strike, Kenney O'Sullivan's anger still resonates. While much of that anger is directed at John Golden and the organizations he represented, she was also horrified by the conditions of life and labor she found in Lawrence during the winter of 1912.

Kenney O'Sullivan would later recall:

> I had been in strikes since 1887 and had seen the poverty of underpaid workers in every form describable. But never in all my labor experience had I known or seen so many men, women and children as badly housed and undernourished.[77]

Over the course of several weeks, she met with individual strikers as well as the strike committee overseen by the IWW whose "methods were different from those of any committee I had ever known. They created a spirit of confidence."[78] While the politics of the IWW might not have been to her liking, Kenney O'Sullivan was pragmatic enough to approve of the IWW's organizing tactics. Unlike the AFL, the IWW was willing to rise above ethnic and craft divisions and made special efforts to involve women in its strike activities. Such inclusiveness, part of the IWW's "One Big Union" approach, could lead to that "spirit of confidence" which so impressed the veteran organizer Kenney O'Sullivan.

Kenney O'Sullivan also spoke to William Wood, chairman of the American Woolen Company, who owned several mills in Lawrence.[79] Wood was the son of Portuguese immigrants who had worked his way up in the textile industry through hard work and an advantageous marriage in 1888 to Ellen Wheaton Ayer, daughter of one of Lawrence's wealthier mill owners.[80] According to his biographer, Wood then appeared "to have thrown himself whole-heartedly into the world of Yankeedom" and prospered to such a degree that by the time of his death in 1926 his personal estate was valued at close to $5,000,000.[81]

In the process, Wood conveniently forgot his immigrant past and remained unmoved by the plight of his workers even after their poverty became national news as the strike dragged on. Initially Wood refused to negotiate with the strikers. Before the strike was a week old, the *Boston Globe* reported on January 17th that Wood, speaking for all the Lawrence mill owners, stated that they had "nothing to discuss, much less to arbitrate and that they recognize no strike, but only the prevalence of mob rule." By early March, however, even the chairman of the American Woolen Company had been affected by the Lawrence strike, if not by the poverty and exploitation it revealed but by the disruption of business.

Kenney O'Sullivan may have played a role, too. In her autobiography, she claims to have spoken to Wood the day before he finally met with the strike committee on March 3rd and showed the mill owner his employees' meager pay envelopes. Although he began his conversation with Kenney O'Sullivan by stressing that he felt that "the strikers had wronged **him** grievously," after he saw the pay envelopes, Wood "was like a different man."[82] Ten days of intense negotiating followed and by March 12th the two-month-long Lawrence strike was over. The mill owners agreed to all the terms as outlined by the strike committee, including a sliding scale of wage increases, the lowest paid getting the largest increase.[83]

The mill owners' decision to end the strike, however, did not resolve some larger issues that were bothering Kenney O'Sullivan. She had been realistic and open-minded enough to throw her support behind the efforts of the IWW, even if it meant criticizing those she had worked with for years. Her official response came just a few weeks after the strike was over, in the progressive journal *The Survey* which published a series of articles entitled "The Lawrence Strike from Various Angles."[84] As in her autobiography, Kenney O'Sullivan made it clear that while she too might have branded the IWW as "revolutionists" in terms of their politics, she heartily approved of their organizing tactics in Lawrence.

After first chiding the UTW for "neglecting the interests of the unskilled," Kenney O'Sullivan singled out John Golden in particular. It was he who "went to Boston and was reported to have denounced the strike as being led by a band of revolutionists, thus leaving them to be organized by any persons who might choose to use or to help them."[85] According to Kenney O'Sullivan, while she also criticized several "Boston social workers," it was Golden's failure to serve "the people in his industry" which led to the arrival of the IWW. She further claimed that the strike committee, "representing eighteen nationalities and composed of fifty-six members," was organized "not to represent the Industrial Workers of the World, but to win the strike."[86]

Kenney O'Sullivan then went on to discuss the violence which frequently erupted during the strike but claimed the IWW was not behind it. She pointed out that it was the "mill bosses [who] turned streams of water upon [the strikers] in subzero weather." Finally, she reminded her readers that "thousands of striking operatives never attended a meeting of any sort." Rather, they stayed home, "trusting their leaders" to win a fair settlement of the strike. For these leaders—men and women, immigrant and native-born, skilled and unskilled—Kenney O'Sullivan had the greatest praise:

> These men represent to me as an old trade unionist, the old religion and
> the spirit of the trade union movement when men worked for the cause
> regardless of consideration.[87]

Although she was only forty-eight years old when she wrote this piece, Kenney O'Sullivan had already devoted more than twenty years to trade unionism, her activism spanning two centuries. During that time, she had constantly been confronted by the limits of the AFL and its affiliates regarding the organization of women. It was for that reason that she had helped form the WTUL.

Yet the potentially divisive factor of ethnicity, especially as represented by the "new" immigrants, was an obstacle which Kenney O'Sullivan saw as fatal to her vision of trade unionism. For many years, despite its limitations, she had placed her faith in the AFL, trusting that it too would some day share her goal of an inclusive trade unionism which would bring dignity to all workers. But the Lawrence strike caused Kenney O'Sullivan to see the AFL in an entirely new light. Her trust shattered, she now felt that

> [i]n the long run, from the organizer's standpoint this new insurgent movement may be the best possible thing that could happen to the labor unions of America. . . . Catholics, Jews, Protestants, and unbelievers—men and women of many races and languages,—were working together as human beings with a common cause. The American Federation of Labor alone refused to cooperate.[88]

For Kenney O'Sullivan, a loyal member of the AFL for twenty years and a co-founder of the WTUL, this must have been a difficult if not painful admission. The Boston League followed the AFL policy and paid the price. Not only did Kenney O'Sullivan resign from the WTUL but so too did her good friend, Elizabeth Glendower Evans.

Shortly after the strike ended, Glendower Evans sent a lengthy letter to Margaret Dreier Robins. In it, she too was highly critical of AFL organizer John Golden and WTUL organizers Sara Conboy and Mabel Gillespie. According to Glendower Evans, Golden had done little more than "swagger around Boston," criticizing the IWW and by extension the strike itself. Given her association with Golden, Conboy was now "useless as an organizer, at least in Lawrence." Finally, Gillespie had "showed herself simply fatuous in her inability to see the real thing."[89] Typically, Glendower Evans had only good to say about Kenney O'Sullivan, telling Robins that "she is the only one of us who had sense, and did anything better than muddle."[90]

Like Kenney O'Sullivan, she thought that the policies of the AFL were poorly suited to meet the changing demands of early twentieth-century labor. Glendower Evans wrote Robins that the AFL's "strict craft organization is not adapted to the assimilation of the unskilled foreign races. Perhaps it has got to be smashed, or purged, or reorganized."[91] Therefore, she felt compelled to withdraw her membership and her financial support from the WTUL. Her resignation must have troubled the WTUL as much as did Kenney O'Sullivan's. While Glendower Evans' money and social connections were vital to the League, Kenney O'Sullivan brought the WTUL a certain amount of credibility due to her years of experience as a labor organizer. She also provided the league with a model of association with middle-class allies. The joint decision to resign was probably not an easy one for either woman, especially Kenney O'Sullivan. She had helped found the WTUL and served as officer on the national and local level. However, both women felt the WTUL had neglected its duties to serve women workers. Together, Glendower Evans and Kenney O'Sullivan stood above the dispute between the AFL and the IWW. Their primary goal was justice for workers, including immigrants and the unskilled and especially women, not the superiority of one organization over another.

Others, too, saw the WTUL's role in the Lawrence strike as complicated by the struggle between the AFL and the IWW. The day before an official settlement was reached between the Lawrence mill owners and the vast majority of their workers still out on strike, Mabel Gillespie attempted to explain her actions in Lawrence. In a letter written to NWTUL president Robins on March 11th, Gillespie made it plain that she had some sympathy for the "galant [sic] fight the Mill Workers were making under their [IWW] leadership." Despite that sympathy, she realized that "[o]f course with the I.W.W. in command it was impossible for the League to offer assistance."[92] Gillespie's letter makes plain the quandary the WTUL faced in Lawrence. The League felt bound by its affiliation to the AFL to honor the wishes of its local representative, i.e., John Golden, while at the same time frustrated in what it believed to be its primary goal—the organization of wage-earning women such as those then on strike in Lawrence.

Just a little over a month after the Lawrence strike ended, the NWTUL Executive Board met in New York. The most pressing item on the agenda was a discussion of the Lawrence strike and what the WTUL had and had not done or perhaps might have done differently. BWTUL president Sue Ainslie Clark submitted a three-page typed letter as she was unable to attend. She began by stating that

> In its relation to the strike of the Lawrence Textile Workers, the Boston Women's Trade Union League has been confronted with an unprecedented situation, yet liable to recur at any moment in any part of the country and fraught with deep significance to our work of organizing women.[93]

Clark went on to note that at the start of the strike "John Golden. . . . counselled the League to stay out of Lawrence temporarily" but that "many of the members were intensely restless because of their inactivity."

"In the mean time," Clark wrote, "the Lawrence strike revealed itself increasingly as a magnificent uprising of oppressed, unskilled foreign workers."[94] On February 1st, the BWTUL opened its relief station in cooperation with the Lawrence CLU but only after securing Golden's permission. Nonetheless, Clark admitted that "[o]wing to the division of the A.F. of L. group from the main group of strikers, the League was never in the forefront of the battle."[95]

However limited their work in Lawrence may have been, the BWTUL president praised the efforts of Gillespie and Conboy, at the same time explaining at great length how divided the Boston league was over what course should have been taken in Lawrence. Clark made it clear where she stood:

> To me, many of those in power in the A.F. of L. today seem to be self-
> ish, reactionary and remote from the struggle for bread and liberty of
> the unskilled workers . . . Are we, the Women's Trade Union League,
> to ally ourselves inflexibly with the "standpatters" of the Labor Move-
> ment or are we to hold ourselves ready to aid the "insurgents" . . . ?[96]

Clark's letter was read into the minutes of the NWTUL Executive Board's meeting on April 19, 1912. Despite its "deep significance," the Board postponed discussion of the Lawrence strike until its third and final day of meetings. Also read into the minutes was a letter from Anne Withington, an ally who served on the BWTUL Executive Board, and who, like Clark, was unable to attend. Withington stressed the issue of the WTUL's affiliation with the AFL and its implications. She also emphasized the importance of the "long and close" relations between the BWTUL and the UTW.[97] Like Clark, Withington felt that such a situation as the one that occurred in Lawrence could happen again and thus hoped that the NWTUL executive board could somehow resolve the matter before it was too late.

Once these two letters had been read into the minutes, President Robins offered a point of clarification. She stated that while the local leagues were affiliated with their respective local and state labor bodies, "as a national organization the National Women's Trade Union League is not affiliated with the A. F. of L." She further noted that the presence of the IWW was certainly "one of the problems" the WTUL had to face during a strike, citing a recent incident in Chicago in which the WTUL there, along with the Chicago Federation of Labor, "had been able to control the situation because they had been the first in the field."[98]

Gillespie and Conboy were then given the opportunity to explain their actions in Lawrence, and both women basically said the same thing. Following Golden's lead, the BWTUL had initially stayed away and then later maintained a rather low level of involvement given the presence of the IWW. After some discussion and a few questions, the Executive Board seemed satisfied that Gillespie and particularly Conboy had acted properly during the Lawrence strike. According to the minutes, "Mrs. Conboy's work seemed of the greatest value to the National Board and the unanimous opinion was that she should be given full recognition and backing."[99] Conboy later suggested that, in the interest of aiding the organization of the thousands of unorganized women textile workers, a committee be appointed to meet with AFL president Samuel Gompers asking for his assistance.

The committee, comprised of Robins, Gillespie and NYWTUL member Melinda Scott, met with Gompers and AFL vice-president Frank Morrison in Washington, DC in early May. The three WTUL representatives asked that the AFL "place a sum of money at the disposal of" the NWTUL "to be used for organizing women in those cities" where no local branch of the WTUL existed. According to Gompers, however, "it was against the Constitution of the [AFL] to put any money into an **outside** organization."[100] Instead, he suggested that the NWTUL approach the International Unions for financial assistance. This advice the NWTUL gracefully accepted. Still an outsider in the community of organized labor, they had little other choice.

Not surprisingly, the NWTUL then turned to John Golden and the UTW. But instead of asking for financial assistance, the NWTUL offered it—they proposed to pay Sara Conboy's salary for six months so she could facilitate the organization of women textile workers, specifically in "New York, New Jersey and Pennsylvania where the social uprisings are so threatening and the demand for women organizers so great."[101] Perhaps Glendower Evans' observation shortly after the Lawrence strike that Conboy's credibility as an organizer, at least in Lawrence, was ruined because of her position during the strike was not totally overstated. During the strike, the IWW had publicly condemned both Golden and Conboy as "scabs" who were in Lawrence not to assist the strikers but "in the interests of the mill owners."[102] The memory of those charges would linger in Lawrence and Conboy soon moved out of state when she was appointed a national field organizer for the UTW. Based in New York, she organized from there to Atlanta while rising through the ranks of the UTW. At the time of her death, *The New York Times* called Conboy the "foremost woman trade unionist in the United States . . . a strict unionist of the Gompers type."[103]

The ascendance of Conboy and Gillespie alongside the departure of Kenney O'Sullivan and Glendower Evans marked a turning point for the WTUL on both the national level and in Boston. Nationally, the NWTUL finally gained formal recognition of its efforts from the AFL. At its annual convention of 1912, the AFL Executive Council reported "that for the purpose of assisting in the organizing work of the [WTUL] we authorized the payment of $150 per month for one year."[104] Apparently, the AFL and Gompers had decided to reverse their decision of six months earlier that such assistance would violate the AFL constitution. Perhaps the patience of the NWTUL, not to mention its willingness to turn to the UTW and not the IWW, had literally paid off.

In the aftermath of the Lawrence strike, the BWTUL quietly reconfigured itself. No longer were Kenney O'Sullivan and Glendower Evans within the Boston leadership. Mabel Gillespie continued as Organizing Secretary and was soon embroiled in the massive—and quite successful—telephone operators' strike. Little more than a year after the Lawrence strike, the BWTUL could claim more than two thousand new members, all part of the Boston Telephone Operators' Union, which organized with the help of the BWTUL and the BCLU.[105] While this incredible achievement of organization should not be dismissed, it does, however, demand some qualification.

The telephone operators were by and large Irish-Americans. These women were not part of those "new immigrants" who toiled in the textile mills of Lawrence or Fall River. Further, many were fairly well educated by working-class standards of the day, having at least a grammar school education, and many were even high school graduates.[106] Finally, the work itself, while arduous in its own way, did not carry with it the negative images nor the low wages of unskilled factory work. In other words, the women telephone operators of Boston were just the sort of workers the BWTUL and the BCLU could successfully assist.

The strengths of the BWTUL were also its weaknesses. It succeeded with the telephone operators in 1912 and managed to organize 680 skilled carpet weavers, including Sara Conboy, in Roxbury two years earlier. But when confronted with semi- and unskilled workers, many of whom were recent immigrants from Eastern and Southern Europe, it was out of its element. Certainly the power of the textile industry further exacerbated the difficulties of the BWTUL in both Fall River and Lawrence in a way that the nascent New England Telephone Company could not. In

Lawrence the limitations of the BWTUL were made even more apparent
by the presence of the IWW. Although there were some in the Boston
League, Kenney O'Sullivan and Glendower Evans included, who felt
that the WTUL should learn from the example of the IWW, the WTUL
appears to have learned a different lesson. When pushed to choose between the IWW and the AFL, it chose the latter even if it meant not meeting its intended goal of organizing wage-earning women. By adhering to
the principles of craft-based trade unionism, with its exclusionary implications for immigrants and women alike, the WTUL followed the lead of
the AFL well into the twentieth century. Mary Kenney O'Sullivan remained true to her vision and chose not to follow along.

NOTES

[1]In addition to the *Boston Globe* account of June 9, 1910, see also: *The
Labor News*, June 11, 1910 and *The Boston Common*, June 11, 1910.

[2]On Gillespie, see the short biographical entries on her in *Notable American
Women* and in Judith O'Sullivan and Rosemary Gallick, *Workers and Allies: Female Participation in the American Trade Union Movement, 1824–1976* (Washington, DC: Smithsonian Institution Press, 1975), pp. 52–53.

[3]Mary Dreier to Margaret Dreier Robins, March 15, 1912, Margaret Dreier
Robins papers, part of the National Women's Trade Union League Collection,
microfilm edition, reel 22, frame 455, hereafter MDR papers.

[4]*Boston Globe*, June 9, 1910.

[5]As quoted in *The Boston Common*, June 11, 1910.

[6]As quoted in *The Boston Common*, June 11, 1910.

[7]*The Boston Common*, which first appeared on April 30, 1910, was a weekly
newspaper owned by its socially conscious and reform-minded stockholders
which included Louis Brandeis, several members of the prominent Cabot family,
Mary Morton Kehew, Robert Woods, and, not surprisingly, Glendower Evans.
Each stockholder could own no less than $100 nor no more than $1000 in stock
and regardless of one's holdings, each had only one vote. In its second issue, *The
Boston Common* explained its goal as "the establishment . . . of a free and independent paper, the dominant and controlling purpose of which shall be public
welfare rather than private profit." May 7, 1910.

[8]*Common*, June 11, 1910.

[9]*Boston Common*, June 11, 1910.

[10]*Boston Globe*, June 9, 1910.

[11]*Boston Common*, June 11, 1910.

[12]*Boston Common*, June 11, 1910.

[13]*Labor News*, June 11, 1910.

[14]Regarding Schneiderman's appearance, see: *Labor News*, Aug. 6, 1910; on the Halloween party, at which "an enjoyably creepy time" was expected, see: *The Boston Common*, Oct. 29, 1910; regarding the Massachusetts Minimum Wage campaign, see: *Labor News* Dec. 4, 1909 regarding the kick-off conference at which Florence Kelley spoke.

[15]*Life and Labor* Vol.1, no.6 (June 1911): p. 179.

[16]Sue Ainslie Clark and Edith Wyatt, *Making Both Ends Meet: The Income and Outlay of New York Working Girls* (New York: The MacMillan Co., 1911).

[17]"Courses taken by Sue Ainslie, Class of 1903, at Wellesley College." Wellesley College Archives, Wellesley, MA.

[18]Mary Dreier to Margaret Dreier Robins, Jan. 31, 1911, MDR papers, reel 22, frame 46.

[19]MD to MDR, MDR papers, reel 22, frame 46.

[20]In the "official letter" sent to Robins, NYWTUL secretary Helen Marot wrote that "Mrs. O'Sullivan worked for [Evans] and in her enthusiasm brought people to the meeting who were not even members of the League." See: Helen Marot to Margaret Dreier Robins, Jan. 30, 1911, Papers of the National Women's Trade Union League, Box 1, Library of Congress, Washington, DC.

[21]MD to MDR, MDR papers, reel 22, frames 47–48.

[22]MD to MDR, MDR papers, reel 22, frame 48.

[23]MD to MDR, MDR papers, reel 22, frame 46.

[24]*Boston Globe*, June 12, 1911.

[25]"Minutes of Meeting of the Third Biennial Convention," NWTUL papers, Library of Congress, reel 20, frame 77.

[26]"Minutes," reel 20, frame 79.

[27]"Minutes," reel 20, frame 80.

[28]"Minutes," reel 20, frames 81–82.

[29]"Minutes," reel 20, frame 100; on the efforts to gain passage of the fifty-four hour bill, see: Clara Beyer, *History of Labor Legislation for Women in Three States* Women's Bureau Bulletin No.66 (Washington, DC: Government Printing Office, 1929), pp. 35–38.

[30]"Minutes," reel 20, frame 100.

[31]*Boston Globe*, June 13, 1911.

[32]"Minutes," reel 20, frame 204.

[33]Regarding Progressive Era efforts towards gaining passage of a minimum wage for women, see: Vivien Hart, *Bound by Our Constitution: Women, Workers and the Minimum Wage* (Princeton, NJ: Princeton University Press, 1994); James T. Patterson, "Mary Dewson and the American Minimum Wage Movement," *Labor History* 5 (Spring 1964): pp. 134–152; and Joan G. Zimmerman, "The

Jurisprudence of Equality: The Women's Minimum Wage, the First Equal Rights Amendment, and *Adkins v. Children's Hospital, 1905–1923,*" *Journal of American History* 78 (June 1991): pp. 188–225.

[34]At its annual convention in 1910, the AFL passed a resolution introduced by Michael Murphy, a Boston fireman. Murphy's resolution called for the increased cooperation between the AFL-affiliated central labor unions and the local branch of the WTUL where one existed. See: *Report of the Proceedings of the Thirtieth Annual Convention of the American Federation of Labor* (Washington, DC: The Law Reporter Printing Company, 1910), p. 226. At its 1911 convention, NWTUL president Robins commended Murphy's resolution and noted that in Chicago such cooperation existed between the central labor union and the WTUL. Such was not the case in Boston. See: "Minutes," reel 20, frame 251.

[35]"Minutes," Reel 20, frame 360, emphasis added.

[36]"Minutes," reel 20, frame 362.

[37]"Minutes," reel 20, frame 580.

[38]At the 1911 convention, the NWTUL constitution was amended, incorporating for the first time the use of the word "ally" to describe that category of membership. See: Gladys Boone, *The Women's Trade Union Leagues in Great Britain and the United States* (New York: Columbia University Press, 1942), p. 100; on the election of Conboy and Gillespie, see: "Minutes," reel 20, frame 649; Boone, *The Women's Trade Union Leagues,* p. 100; *Labor News,* June 24, 1911; and Helen Marot, "The Women's Trade Union League," *The Survey* 26 (July 1, 1911): p. 549.

[39]See: Mary Kenney O'Sullivan, unpublished autobiography, n.d., c. 1920s, Schlesinger Library, Radcliffe College, Cambridge, MA., microfilm edition, the papers of the Women's Trade Union League and Its Principal Leaders, Smaller Collections Reel 1, pp. 200–210 regarding the formation of the WTUL. The entire last chapter of this unfinished manuscript focuses on the Lawrence strike. Hereafter, Kenney O'Sullivan, autobio.

[40]"Minutes," reel 20, frames 694–695.

[41]"Minutes," reel 20, frame 696, emphasis added.

[42]*Proceedings of the Twenty-sixth Annual Convention, Massachusetts State Branch, American federation of Labor* (Boston: Feinberg & Sons, 1911), pp. 78–79; see also the brief account in the *Boston Globe,* Sept. 22, 1911.

[43]Albert M. Heintz and John R. Whitney, *History of the Massachusetts State Federation of Labor, 1887–1935* (Boston: Massachusetts State Federation, 1936?), p. 46; according to Heintz and Whitney, p. 54, in 1918, Gillespie was elected one of five vice-presidents of the Massachusetts Federation, "the first woman to hold a major office in the organization since Miss Nellie H. Murphy back in 1895." Gillespie would serve as vice-president until 1921.

[44]*Third Biennial Convention National Women's Trade Union League Handbook*, Boston, June 12–17, 1911, p. 5, emphasis added, copy in the Employment Collection, box 43, Sophia Smith Collection, Smith College, Northampton, MA.

[45]Mary E. Kenney, "Organization of Working Women," *World's Congress of Representative Women* (Chicago, 1893), p. 871.

[46]*Handbook*, p. 5.

[47]"Minutes," reel 20, frames 665–666; see also the *Labor News*, June 24, 1911 which reported that "Among the most important matters adopted was the recommendation of the laws committee to translate leaflets from the English into as many foreign languages as is thought necessary."

[48]For a discussion of how the Lawrence strike has been remembered, appropriated, and possibly mythologized, see: Gerald M. Sider, "Cleansing History: Lawrence, Massachusetts, the Strike for Four Loaves of Bread and No Roses, and the Anthropology of Working-class Consciousness," and the responses from Paul Buhle, Ardis Cameron, David Montgomery, and Christine Stansell, and Sider's reply, all in *Radical History Review* 65 (Spring 1996): pp. 48–117.

[49]Mary Heaton Vorse, *A Footnote to Folly: Reminiscences of Mary Heaton Vorse* (New York: Farrar & Rinehart, 1935), p. 12.

[50]Regarding the tariff debate, which in respect to Lawrence centered on "Schedule K" which placed a tariff on imported woolen goods see: Walter E. Weyl, "The Strikers at Lawrence," *The Outlook* 100 (Feb. 10, 1912): p. 309; the Lawrence strike also figured in the Senate debate regarding proposed changes to the Payne Aldrich Tariff Act of 1909—see the *Congressional Record*, Senate 48, Part 5, 62nd Congress, 2nd Session, April 12, 1912, pp. 4666–4668. The ethnic composition of the Lawrence workforce who went out on strike was a constant highlight of contemporary comment, both sympathetic and critical, and entered into the Senate as well. See: W.J. Lauck, "The Significance of the Situation at Lawrence," *The Survey* 27 (Feb. 17, 1912): pp. 1772–1774, which was read into the *Congressional Record* during a Senate debate on proposed immigrant restrictions, March 18, 1912.

[51]While in the past, weekly wages remained the same when a new limitation of hours law went into effect, in January 1912, "manufacturers claimed that business conditions did not warrant what amounted to a wage increase." See: Beyer, *History of Labor Legislation for Women in Three States*, p. 38.

[52]Charles P. Neill, *Report on Strike of Textile Workers in Lawrence, Mass. in 1912* Senate Documents Vol. 31 (Washington, DC: Government Printing Office, 1912), p. 9.

[53]Donald Cole, *Immigrant City: Lawrence, Massachusetts, 1845–1921* (Chapel Hill: University of North Carolina Press, 1963). By 1905, Lawrence had surpassed Fall River in the percentage of its foreign-born population; see:

Commonwealth of Massachusetts, *Forty-first Annual Report on the Statistics of Labor for the Year 1910* (Boston: Wright & Potter, 1911), p. 294. For a more recent treatment of Lawrence which addresses issues of both ethnicity and gender, see: Ardis Cameron, *Radicals of the Worst Sort: Laboring Women in Lawrence, Massachusetts, 1860–1912* (Urbana: University of Illinois Press, 1993).

[54]*Report on Strike of Textile Workers*, pp. 189–191.

[55]According to the 1910 U.S. Census, only six cities—Lowell, Holyoke, Manchester, NH, Fall River, Detroit, and New Bedford—exceeded the infant mortality of Lawrence which then stood at 167 per 1,000 births; with the exception of Detroit and Holyoke, these cities were primarily engaged in the production of textiles. See: *Report on Strike of Textile Workers*, p. 195.

[56]Samuel Gompers, "The Lawrence Strike," *American Federationist* 19 (April 1912): p. 290.

[57]*The Strike at Lawrence, Mass. Hearings Before the Committee on Rules of the House of Representatives* 62nd Congress, 2nd Session (March 2–7, 1912) Document No. 671, Washington, DC, p. 74.

[58]Barbara Miller Solomon, *Ancestors and Immigrants: A Changing New England Tradition* (Cambridge, MA: Harvard University Press, 1956), p. 199.

[59]Robert A. Woods, "The Breadth and Depth of the Lawrence Outcome," *The Survey* 28 (April 6, 1912): p. 67.

[60]Melvyn Dubofsky, *We Shall Be All: A History of the Industrial Workers of the World* (Chicago: Quadrangle Books, 1969), p. 233.

[61]Stewart Bird, Dan Georgakas, and Deborah Shaffer, *Solidarity Forever: An Oral History of the IWW* (Chicago: Lake View Press, 1985), p. 3.

[62]Kenney O'Sullivan, autobio., pp. 239–240.

[63]*Hearings*, p. 75.

[64]*Boston Globe*, Jan. 14 and Jan. 17, 1912.

[65]See: Cameron, *Radicals of the Worst Sort*, chap. 4 and Dubofsky, *We Shall Be All*, chap. 10.

[66]Anne Withington, "The Lawrence Strike," *Life and Labor* 2 (March 1912): p. 77, emphasis added.

[67]*Report on Strike of Textile Workers*, p.65. See also Mabel Gillespie to Margaret Dreier Robins, March 11, 1912, NWTUL papers, reel 17.

[68]Theresa Corcoran, S.C., "Vida Scudder and the Lawrence Textile Strike," *Essex Institute Historical Collections* 115 (1979): pp. 183–195. According to Corcoran, the Wellesley College Board of Trustees officially asked Scudder to explain her March 4th speech in Lawrence. Although the Board had received numerous requests that they fire Scudder, they did not. They did, however, request that she not teach her "Social Ideas in English Letters" course for the academic year 1912–1913. See: Corcoran, p. 190.

[69]Pauline Carrington Howe, "'My Good Italian Friends,'" *The Boston Sunday Globe* Mar.10, 1912.

[70]*Boston Common*, Mar. 9, 1912, also quoted in Corcoran, "Vida Scudder," p. 188.

[71]*Boston Globe*, Mar. 5, 1912.

[72]*Boston Globe*, Mar. 7, 1912.

[73]Gillespie to MDR, NWTUL papers, reel 17; see also: Meredith Tax, *The Rising of the Women: Feminist Solidarity and Class Conflict, 1880–1917* (New York: Monthly Review Press, 1980), p. 265.

[74]Mary Dreier to Margaret Dreier Robins, Mar. 15, 1912; MDR to MD, Mar. 18, 1912, MDR papers, reel 22, frames 455–461.

[75]MDR to MD, Mar. 18, 1912, MDR papers, reel 22, frames 459–460, emphasis in the original.

[76]Kenney O'Sullivan, autobio., p. 252. She publicly expressed these same sentiments in her article, "The Labor War at Lawrence," *The Survey* 28 (6 April, 1912): pp. 72–74.

[77]Kenney O'Sullivan, autobio., pp. 249–250.

[78]Kenney O'Sullivan, autobio., p. 252.

[79]The American Woolen Company was created in 1899 when several New England textile mills merged into one corporation in a transaction overseen by William Wood. Wood's father-in-law and owner of the Washington mill in Lawrence, Frederick Ayer, served as the company's first chairman until 1905 when Wood assumed the post. See: Edward G. Roddy, *Mills, Mansions, and Mergers: The Life of William M. Wood* (North Andover, MA: Merrimack Valley Textile Museum, 1982), pp. 40–43.

[80]Roddy, *Mills, Mansions, and Mergers*, p. 38.

[81]Roddy, *Mills, Mansions, and Mergers*, p. 121, p. 125.

[82]Kenney O'Sullivan, autobio., p. 261, emphasis added; p. 263.

[83]*Boston Globe*, Mar. 14, 1912. On March 1, American Woolen Company offered a flat 5 percent wage increase. The AFL-affiliated union workers accepted this offer and returned to work March 4th while the majority of workers, represented by the IWW strike committee, held out another ten days. See: Dubofsky, *We Shall Be All*, p. 253.

[84]*The Survey* 28 (April 6, 1912): pp. 65–82; other contributors included Robert Woods and Vida Scudder.

[85]Kenney O'Sullivan, "The Labor War at Lawrence," *The Survey* 28 (April 6, 1912): p. 72.

[86]Kenney O'Sullivan, "The Labor War," p. 72.

[87]Kenney O'Sullivan, "The Labor War," p. 73.

[88]Kenney O'Sullivan, "The Labor War," p. 73.

[89]EGE to MDR, Mar. 25, 1912, MDR papers, reel 22, frames 470, 473, and 474.

[90]EGE to MDR, March 25, 1912, MDR papers, reel 22, frames 469–477; also quoted in Tax, *The Rising of the Women*, p. 266.

[91]EGE to MDR, Mar. 25, 1912, MDR papers, reel 22, frame 475.

[92]Gillespie to MDR, Mar. 11, 1912, NWTUL papers, reel 17.

[93]Clark to MDR, n.d., c. April 1912, NWTUL papers, reel 17.

[94]Clark to MDR, c. April 1912, p.1.

[95]Clark to MDR, c. April 1912, p. 2.

[96]Clark to MDR, c. April 1912, p. 3.

[97]Anne Withington to MDR, April 16, 1912, NWTUL papers, reel 17.

[98]Minutes of the NWTUL Executive Board, April 19, 1912, p.11, NWTUL papers, Library of Congress.

[99]"Minutes," April 19, 1912, p. 13.

[100]MDR to Executive Council of the American Federation of Labor, May 8, 1912, p.2, NWTUL papers, Library of Congress.

[101]Report of MDR to the NWTUL Executive Board, n.d., c. May 1912, p.1, NWTUL papers, Library of Congress.

[102]*The Industrial Worker*, Feb. 15, 1912.

[103]An obituary for Conboy appears in the *New York Times*, Jan. 9, 1928. In 1915, Conboy was elected secretary-treasurer of the UTW and held that office until her death at the age of fifty-seven in 1928. See entry on Conboy in *Famous American Women* (Springfield, MA: Merriam-Webster, 1980). On Conboy's role in a dispute between local organizers and the UTW during a strike in Atlanta, see: Gary M. Fink, *The Fulton Bag and Cotton Mills Strike of 1914–1915: Espionage, Labor Conflict, and New South Industrial Relations* (Ithaca, NY: ILR Press, 1993) and Jacqueline Dowd Hall, "Private Eyes, Public Women: Images of Class and Sex in the Urban South, Atlanta, Georgia, 1913–1915," in *Work Engendered: Toward a New History of American Labor* Ava Baron, ed. (Ithaca, NY: Cornell University Press, 1991), pp. 243–272.

[104]*Report of the Proceedings of the Thirty-Second Annual Convention of the American Federation of Labor* (Washington,DC: The Law Reporter Printing Co., 1912), p. 123.

[105]On the Boston Telephone Operators' Union and the role played by the BWTUL, see: Stephen H. Norwood, *Labor's Flaming Youth: Telephone Operators and Worker Militancy, 1878–1923* (Urbana: University of Illinois Press, 1990), pp. 98–122.

[106]Norwood, *Labor's Flaming Youth*, pp. 6–8.

"We Stand as One"
The Limitations of Cross-Class Alliances after 1912

According to the Women's Trade Union League anthem written by Charlotte Perkins Gilman, "No more on earth shall be Women alone. Now we have learned the truth, Union is power." This anthem expressed the sentiment that an alliance of working-class women and their middle-class allies would solve the problems faced by wage-earning women at the start of the twentieth century. "For end to every wrong, We stand as one!"[1] Yet by 1912, when this anthem first appeared in the WTUL journal, *Life and Labor*, the League had been shaken to its core by the divisions which grew out of the Lawrence strike. So profound were these divisions that two WTUL leaders resigned in protest. The public lives of Mary Kenney O'Sullivan and Elizabeth Glendower Evans, however, did not end with their resignation from the WTUL. Nor did their friendship cease. Both women became increasingly active in the escalating battle for women's suffrage. Both women also sought to keep the United States out of World War I and were members of the Women's International League for Peace and Freedom. Separately, too, both women continued to fight for justice and dignity—each in her own way.

Before she resigned from the WTUL, Glendower Evans had become involved with the effort to pass a minimum wage law for women in Massachusetts. After she left the League, she continued that campaign and saw the bill to passage in June, 1912. In the 1920s, Glendower Evans became a national director and major benefactor of the American Civil Liberties Union. She spent much of that turbulent decade agitating for the release of Sacco and Vanzetti, the two Italian anarchists found guilty of a payroll robbery, and exchanged scores of letters with them before their execution in 1927. She also visited the two in prison, teaching them English and bringing them flowers.[2] Glendower Evans died in 1937 at the age of eighty-one, her death meriting front-page notice by the *Boston Globe*.[3]

In 1914, at the age of fifty and still obliged to work for wages, Kenney O'Sullivan won appointment as a factory inspector for the newly created Massachusetts State Board of Labor and Industries. She vigorously fulfilled the duties of her post for twenty years until her retirement at the age of seventy. In 1926, she travelled to Ireland as a delegate to the Women's Peace Conference and throughout the 1920s and 1930s was a frequent speaker at Boston's Ford Hall Forum. She died in 1943 in the home she had built for herself and her children in suburban West Medford.[4] Years later, a small collection of her personal papers—including the very rough draft of an autobiography—went to the Schlesinger Library at Radcliffe College where, quite fittingly given their long association in life, Glendower Evans' papers are also held.

It is believed that Kenney O'Sullivan wrote her autobiography sometime during the 1920s.[5] Perhaps this unpublished, undated manuscript was inspired by the 1925 publication of Samuel Gompers' two-volume autobiography.[6] Perhaps Kenney O'Sullivan simply wanted to record her life as she remembered it. As the personal statement of one wage-earning woman, her autobiography is a unique and valuable look at the conditions of labor and the struggle for trade unionism for women during the Progressive Era.[7] Thus, despite its inaccuracies regarding dates, its missing pages and disjointed construction, Kenney O'Sullivan's autobiography is an important primary source. One of only a handful of such sources, her unfinished manuscript is frequently cited by historians examining issues pertaining to both women and labor in this period.[8]

In this way, Kenney O'Sullivan has been historicized as a sort of archetype—a typical woman of the working class who quite atypically left behind a record of her life which also somewhat atypically included trade union activism.[9] Although hardly a household name, within organized labor circles Kenney O'Sullivan was well known during the late nineteenth and early twentieth centuries. The labor press in New England and beyond often turned to her for a pithy quote, an amusing but telling anecdote. In death, too, she continues to serve a similar purpose, her life as she recalled it summing up for the historian the historical experience shared by countless other wage-earning women.

Like all autobiographical treatments, that which is not discussed is as telling as that which is. She devotes much time to her early days as a labor organizer in both Chicago and Boston, and also to her relationship with the man she so clearly loved, fellow labor activist John O'Sullivan. Kenney O'Sullivan also describes her first few years as a factory inspector. But she is oddly silent for the most part about the WTUL—except for the 1912 Lawrence strike. When writing her autobiography a decade later, she was still bitter about the way in which the WTUL and the AFL handled that strike. Kenney O'Sullivan entitled her chapter on Lawrence "When the Union Failed."[10] Her autobiography, like her trade union days, ended with the Lawrence strike. In a very real sense, the union had failed not just the men and women textile workers on strike in Lawrence. The union had failed Kenney O'Sullivan as well.

Despite its apparent failure in Lawrence, the Boston WTUL continued for almost another forty years after the departure of Kenney O'Sullivan and Glendower Evans. The local League gained hundreds of working-class members when the telephone operators formed a union, with WTUL assistance, in 1912. In 1913, the BWTUL reported that they had also assisted in organizing more than 300 shirtwaist makers and 400 candy makers. Putting Lawrence behind them, BWTUL secretary Mabel Gillespie reported that "[w]e have danced more and played more of late in spite of the fact that we have had bigger and more engrossing affairs on our hands."[11]

The League also continued to balance organizing with educational and legislative efforts. In 1919 the BWTUL cooperated with the Boston Central Labor Union in founding the Boston Trade Union College and in the mid-1920s concentrated its efforts on a federal child labor amendment.[12] Increasingly, however, this Progressive Era organization seemed out of touch with the women it sought to serve.[13] The Great Depression and the New Deal only exacerbated the League's inabilities to address the concerns of working women and, at the same time, encourage the support of allies.[14] By the 1950s, the Women's Trade Union League, on the national level and in Boston, disbanded.

Since then, the historical record has tended to emphasize the inability of the WTUL to achieve its goal of organizing wage-earning women into viable trade unions and at the same time create an alliance between those women and their middle- and upper-class allies. Historians of the WTUL, such as Nancy Schrom Dye and Elizabeth Anne Payne, have been especially critical of the Boston branch.[15] If one were only to look at the Fall River and Lawrence strikes, such would appear to be an accurate assessment. Yet, as I have attempted to show, the historical record is more complicated that that. At times, such as during the strike of the

Roxbury carpet weavers, the BWTUL did achieve its goals. Wage-earning women were organized into existing trade unions and real cooperation did occur between those women and their allies. By examining some of the critical aspects of both their successes and their failures, I have attempted to provide a richer, more nuanced understanding of the possibilities and the limits of the WTUL.

At the same time, I have sought to complicate our understanding of the relationship between the WTUL and the AFL. Previous historical works have emphasized how the male-dominated trade union movement was constrained by a very gendered concept of work and by women's socially-proscribed role as a temporary, unskilled worker. Yet, the AFL recognized the need to organize wage-earning women as long as their presence was, in its mind, dictated by the inequities of industrial capitalism. This contradiction between ideology and reality resulted in the AFL's apparent ambivalence regarding the organization of women and carried over into its relationship with the WTUL. I have tried to add to this argument in two ways. First, I have tried to complicate the historical narrative of the relationship between the WTUL and the AFL by emphasizing not just the divisions of gender but also those of class and ethnicity. The AFL's relationship with the WTUL was as hampered by class and ethnic differences as it was by gender, undercutting in a very real way the WTUL's stated goal of bringing wage-earning women into existing unions.

Secondly, I have tried to enrich our understanding of this relationship by focusing on the long personal and professional connections between Mary Kenney O'Sullivan and Samuel Gompers, highlighting their personal regard for one another as well as Gompers' public acknowledgement of Kenney O'Sullivan's abilities as an organizer. Nonetheless, as I have tried to demonstrate, Gompers' positive feelings for her did not translate into an equally warm regard for the WTUL. Until his death, he—and the AFL with him—remained skeptical about the efforts of middle-class reformers in promoting trade unionism for women. Gompers felt this way despite knowing full well that much of the organizing Kenney O'Sullivan had achieved was due to an admittedly fragile coalition between trade unionists and social reformers.

Finally, I have attempted to provide a much more detailed examination of the life and career of Mary Kenney O'Sullivan than has previously been available. Indeed there is some validity to her near-icon status as a woman labor organizer during the Progressive Era.[16] She accomplished much despite the limitations she faced within both of the communities she relied upon in this period. At the same time, I have tried to show her frustrations as well, frustrations which ultimately led to her resignation from the WTUL and her complete departure from the trade union movement itself. Unlike her contemporaries Pauline Newman and Rose Schneiderman, she seemingly turned her back on the WTUL and all that organization stood for.

I am not, however, trying to tarnish the historical image of Kenney O'Sullivan. I am, more importantly, trying to broaden our understanding of cross-class, cross-gender coalitions in the early years of the twentieth century by focusing on one woman's successes and failures in achieving such a coalition. In attempting to institutionalize the coalition with the formation of the WTUL, Kenney O'Sullivan soon came to see that her particular brand of industrial feminism would not be best served within that organization. For more than twenty years, she tried to overcome gender and class constraints and facilitate a connection between organized labor and social reform. Perhaps, after such a long time, the resulting personal and professional tensions took their toll. When she became a state factory inspector in 1914, Kenney O'Sullivan joined a growing number of trade unionists and social reformers who saw in the state the ultimate answer to the needs of the New Industrial Woman, needs which continued to be unmet by organized labor.

By the mid-century demise of the WTUL, the New Industrial Woman had in a sense come of age. Pushed to the brink of starvation during the Great Depression and then hailed as patriots during World War II, succeeding generations of wage-earning women continued to seek trade union representation in growing numbers. Their increased union activity was due, in part, to the 1935 formation of the Congress of Industrial Organizations (CIO).[17] Seemingly sanctioned by New Deal legislation, the CIO sought to organize those industrial workers long outside the pale of the American Federation of Labor (AFL), workers excluded by skill level as well as by race and gender.

In its early years, the CIO appeared to be truly attempting to incorporate the concepts of industrial feminism in a very real way, recognizing the needs of wage-earning women in both its organizing tactics and its immediate goals for all workers.[18] At the same time, however, the concept of a family wage earned by a male worker remained the ultimate goal of both labor leaders and elected officials during the New Deal and beyond.[19] In the post-World War II era, when increasing numbers of women were entering the workforce, many Americans still held onto the ideal of the family wage both politically and culturally.[20] By the mid-1950s, despite the efforts of the WTUL and the CIO, the promise of industrial feminism remained unrealized.

At the end of the twentieth century, after decades of sweeping social change and legislative reform, the AFL-CIO still was trying to address the needs of American wage-earning women who labor for little more than minimum wage in the nation's stores and offices, nursing homes and factories. After the 1995 union elections which brought a new cadre of labor leaders into power, the AFL-CIO initiated innovative programs, including the Union Summer campaign and the Working Women's Department, aimed specifically at those groups still under-represented in trade unions and in dire need of protection—African Americans, Asian Americans, Latinos, and women of all races.[21] Much as in the Progressive Era, many of today's social reformers and academics are seeking to be part of this reform spirit within the AFL-CIO, particularly through "labor teach-ins" now being held periodically at some of the country's leading universities and colleges.[22]

Yet the obstacles to the organization of wage-earning women remain little changed in the last hundred years. The frequent tensions which plagued cross-class alliances at the start of the century remain formidable at the end of the century. Minimum wage workers and their well-meaning, well-off allies continue to stand opposite one another across an ever-widening economic, political, and cultural divide. Class differences continue to be heightened by and at the same time remain fundamentally shaped by differences of race and gender as well. Further, the historical ambivalence of the AFL regarding the inclusion of those who were not white, not male, not skilled stands today as a chilling reminder of past promises left unmet.

Thus, in the face of all this innovation within organized labor, there is the recognition that meaningful, long-lasting change will be slow in coming, if at all. In the words of the highest-ranking woman in the Massachusetts AFL-CIO, "the jury's still out." Nonetheless, there is hope. According to one young female organizer working with Minneapolis nursing home workers, many of whom are Asian-American women such as herself, growing numbers of these women workers are saying: "It's my union, too!"[23] Mary Kenney O'Sullivan would have agreed. Her call in 1893 for the "necessity of organization" despite the obstacles resonates still.

NOTES

[1]Charlotte Perkins Gilman, anthem of the Women's Trade Union League, *Life And Labor* 2 (May 1912), p. 153; also cited in Meredith Tax, *The Rising of the Women: Feminist Solidarity and Class Conflict, 1880–1917* (New York: Monthly Review Press, 1980), p. 95.

[2]Marion Frankfurter & Gardner Jackson, eds., *The Letters of Sacco and Vanzetti* (New York: The Viking Press, 1928).

[3]*Boston Globe*, Dec. 13, 1937.

[4]*Boston Globe*, Mar. 19, 1943.

[5]See the introductory note to the microfilm edition of Kenney O'Sullivan's autobiography which is part of the Papers of the National Women's Trade Union League. The original manuscript went from Kenney O'Sullivan's children to their neighbor Frances Davis Cohen. It was Cohen who gave the autobiography to the Schlesinger Library in 1959.

[6]Samuel Gompers, *Seventy Years of Life and Labor: An Autobiography* Two Volumes (New York: E.P. Dutton, 1925).

[7]Issues of subjectivity as complicated by gender, class, race and/or ethnicity within autobiographical writing have been discussed by several writers including Regenia Gagnier, "The Literary Standard, Working-Class Autobiography, and Gender," in *Revealing Lives: Autobiography, Biography, and Gender* Susan Groag Bell and Marilyn Yalom, eds. (Albany: State University of New York Press, 1990), pp. 93–114 and Julia Swindells, *Victorian Writing and Working Women: The Other Side of Silence* (Minneapolis: University of Minnesota Press, 1985), chap. 5. While both Gagnier and Swindells focus on British women, more recent work has looked at American wage-earning women and autobiography. See: Betty Bergland, "Ideology, Ethnicity, and the Gendered Subject: Reading Immigrant Women's Autobiographies," in *Seeking Common Ground: Multidisciplinary Studies of Immigrant Women in the United States* Donna Gabaccia, ed. (Westport, CT: Greenwood Press, 1992), pp. 101–121 and Karyn L. Hollis, "Autobiography and Reconstructing Subjectivity at the Bryn Mawr Summer School for Women Workers, 1921–1938," *Women's Studies Quarterly* 23 (1995): pp. 71–100.

[8]Published autobiographies of wage-earning women/labor activists during the Progressive Era include Mary Anderson, *Women at Work: The Autobiography of Mary Anderson* (Minneapolis: University of Minnesota Press, 1951); Mother Jones, *The Autobiography of Mother Jones* (New York: Arno Press, 1969, orig. pub., 1925); and Rose Pastor Stokes, *I Belong to the Working Class: The Unfinished Autobiography of Rose Pastor Stokes* Herbert Shapiro and David L. Sterling, eds. (Athens: University of Georgia Press, 1992).

[9]In my thinking about Kenney O'Sullivan as the "archetype" wage-earning woman of the Progressive Era, both in life and death, I have been inspired by Nell Irvin Painter's recent biography of Sojourner Truth, especially chapter 26 and "Coda". See Painter, *Sojourner Truth: A Life, A Symbol* (New York: W.W. Norton & Co., 1996).

[10]Kenney O'Sullivan, autobio., p. 239.

[11]"Secretary's Report, Boston Women's Trade Union League, Biennial Convention, 1913," Margaret Dreier Robins papers, reel 12, frame 638.

[12]On the Boston Trade Union College, see Stephen H. Norwood, *Labor's Flaming Youth: Telephone Operators and Worker Militancy, 1878–1923* (Urbana: University of Illinois Press, 1990), pp. 228–231.

[13]Stephen H. Norwood's recent article, "Reclaiming Working-Class Activism: The Boston Women's Trade Union League, 1930–1950," *Labor's Heritage* Vol. 10 (Summer 1998): pp. 20–35, is a much-needed addition to the historiography of the WTUL, especially in Boston. Norwood argues that historians of the WTUL, myself included, have distorted the historical record of the organization from the post-World War I era to its demise in the early 1950s by ending our studies in the 1910s and by claiming that thereafter the WTUL focused more on legislation and education than organization. In my case, I end this study in 1912 as that is the year Kenney O'Sullivan resigned and it is through her experiences I have chosen to examine the WTUL and the larger issues of trade unionism for women when attempted by a cross-class alliance. Indeed, perhaps it was that often frustrating experience that helped paved the way for the later achievements of the BWTUL when working-class women assumed control.

[14]For an interesting discussion of Progressive ideology, the New Deal and the WTUL, see: Elizabeth Anne Payne, *Reform, Labor, and Feminism: Margaret Dreier Robins and the Women's Trade Union League* (Urbana: University of Illinois Press, 1988), Chap. 5.

[15]Nancy Schrom Dye, *As Equals and As Sisters: Feminism, the Labor Movement, and the Women's Trade Union League of New York* (Columbia: University of Missouri Press, 1980), p. 6, p. 8; Payne, *Reform, Labor, and Feminism*, p. 106.

[16]In 1997 Kenney O'Sullivan was chosen to represent labor in the Massachusetts Foundation for the Humanities program, "State House Women's Leadership Project," in recognition of "her tireless work as a labor organizer." This ambitious project included the installation in the State House of the portraits of six Massachusetts women, monuments in and around Boston marking their various achievements, and printed material regarding all of the women. In addition to Kenney O'Sullivan, the women to be so honored were: Sarah Parker Remond, Lucy Stone, Josephine Ruffin, Dorothea Dix and Florence Luscomb. See: *MassHumanities* (Fall 1997), p. 8.

[17]Robert H. Zieger, *The CIO, 1935–1955* (Chapel Hill: University of North Carolina Press, 1995).

[18]Nancy F. Gabin, *Feminism in the Labor Movement: Women and the United Auto Workers, 1935–1975* (Ithaca, NY: Cornell University Press, 1990).

[19]Alice Kessler-Harris, "Designing Women and Old Fools: The Construction of the Social Security Amendments, 1939," in *U.S. History as Women's History: New Feminist Essays* Linda Kerber, Alice Kessler-Harris, and Kathryn

Kish-Sklar, eds. (Chapel Hill: University of North Carolina Press, 1995), pp. 87–106.

[20]See, for example: Elaine Tyler May, *Homeward Bound: American Families in the Cold War Era* (New York: Basic Books, 1988).

[21]Lisa Belkin, "Showdown at Yazoo Industries," *The New York Times Magazine* (January 21, 1996), pp. 26–31, 38, 62–63, 67–68.

[22]Michael Tomasky, "Waltzing With Sweeney: Is the Academic Left Ready to Join the AFL-CIO?" *Lingua Franca* (February 1997): pp. 40–47.

[23]Comments made by Kathleen Casavant, then vice-president of the Massachusetts AFL-CIO, and Becky Belcore, SEIU organizer, International Women's Day Forum sponsored by the Sophia Smith Collection, Smith College, March 7, 1997.

Bibliography

MANUSCRIPT COLLECTIONS

Addams, Jane. Papers. Microfilm edition.

American Federation of Labor. Papers and Letterbooks. Microfilm edition.

Balch, Emily Greene. Papers. Swarthmore College Peace Collection, Swarthmore, Penn.

Boston Central Labor Union. Records. Massachusetts Historical Society, Boston.

Clark, Sue Ainslie. Papers. Wellesley College Archives, Wellesley, Mass.

College Settlement Association. Records. Sophia Smith Collection, Smith College, Northampton, Mass.

Denison House. Records. Schlesinger Library, Radcliffe College, Cambridge, Mass.

Dudley, Helena. Papers. Bryn Mawr College Archives, Bryn Mawr, Penn.

Evans, Elizabeth Glendower. Papers. Schlesinger Library, Radcliffe College, Cambridge, Mass.

Hodder, Jessie Donaldson. Papers. Schlesinger Library, Radcliffe College, Cambridge, Mass.

Massachusetts Federation of Labor. Records. W.E.B. DuBois Library, University of Massachusetts, Amherst, Mass.

Massachusetts Committee on Relations Between Employer and Employee. Typescript of Hearings, Aug.-Nov., 1903. Massachusetts State House Library, Boston, Mass.

Massachusetts State Board of Conciliation and Arbitration. Daily Logbooks, 1886–1923. Massachusetts State Archives, Boston, Mass.

National Women's Trade Union League. Records. Library of Congress, Washington, D.C.

National Women's Trade Union League. Papers. Schlesinger Library, Radcliffe College, Cambridge, Mass.

O'Sullivan, Mary Kenney. Papers. Schlesinger Library, Radcliffe College, Cambridge, Mass.

Scudder, Vida Dutton. Papers. Sophia Smith Collection, Smith College, Northampton, Mass.

Walling, William English. Papers. State Historical Society of Wisconsin, Madison, Wisc.

Women's Educational and Industrial Union. Papers. Schlesinger Library, Radcliffe College, Cambridge, Mass.

DAILY NEWSPAPERS

Boston Evening Tribune
Boston Globe
Chicago Daily News
Chicago Times
Fall River Globe
Fall River Herald
New York Times

CONTEMPORARY JOURNALS (MONTHLY AND WEEKLY)

American Federationist
Boston Common
Chicago Citizen
The Commons
The Industrial Worker (Seattle)
International Bookbinder
Labor Leader (Boston)
The Labor News (Worcester, Mass.)
Life and Labor
The Pilot (Boston)
The Survey
Union Labor Advocate (Chicago)

GOVERNMENT DOCUMENTS

Andrews, John and W.D. P. Bliss. *Report on the Condition of Woman and Child Wage-Earners in the United States: Vol. X: History of Women in Trade Unions*. Washington, DC: Government Printing Office, 1911.

Beyer, Clara M. *History of Labor Legislation for Women in Three States.* Women's Bureau Bulletin No. 66. Washington, DC: Government Printing Office, 1929.

Congressional Record. Washington, DC, 1912.

Hill, Joseph. *Women in Gainful Occupations, 1870–1920.* U.S. Bureau of the Census, Monograph No. 9. Washington, DC: Government Printing Office, 1929.

Massachusetts Bureau of the Statistics of Labor. *Annual Reports*, 1892–1912.

Massachusetts Bureau of the Statistics of Labor. *Massachusetts Labor Bulletin*, 1901–1904.

Massachusetts State Board of Conciliation and Arbitration. *Annual Reports*, 1896–1912.

Massachusetts State Board of Labor and Industry. *Annual Reports*, 1914–1934.

Neill, Charles P. *Report on the Condition of Woman and Child Wage-Earners in the United States: Vol. I: The Cotton Textile Industry.* Washington, DC: Government Printing Office, 1910.

———. *Report on Strike of Textile Workers in Lawrence, Massachusetts in 1912.* Senate Documents Vol. 31. Washington, DC: Government Printing Office, 1912.

Strike at Lawrence, Massachusetts. Hearings Before the Committee on Rules of the House of Representatives. 62nd Congress, 2nd Session, Document No. 671. Washington, D.C.: Government Printing Office, 1912.

U.S. Department of Commerce and Labor, Bureau of the Census. *Statistics of Women at Work.* Washington, DC: Government Printing Office, 1907.

UNPUBLISHED DISSERTATIONS AND THESES

Balliet, Barbara J. "'What Shall We Do With Our Daughters?': Middle-Class Women's Ideas About Work, 1840–1920." Ph.D. diss., New York University, 1988.

Clement, Alice Meehan. "Margaret Dreier Robins and the Dilemma of the Women's Trade Union League: Organization versus Legislation." Ph.D. diss., University of California at Davis, 1984.

Fenton, Edwin. "Immigrants and Unions, A Case Study: Italian and American Labor, 1870–1920." Ph.D. diss., Harvard University, 1957.

Greene, Julia M. "The Strike at the Ballot-Box: Politics and Partisanship in the American Federation of Labor, 1881–1916." Ph.D. diss., Yale University, 1990.

Jennings, Robert B. "A History of the Educational Activities of the Women's Educational and Industrial Union from 1877–1927." Ph.D. diss., Boston College, 1978.

Klaczynska, Barbara M. "Working Women in Philadelphia, 1900–1930." Ph.D. diss., Temple University, 1975.

Ranlett, Judith Becker. "Sorority and Community: Women's Answers to a Changing Massachusetts, 1865–1895." Ph.D. diss., Brandeis University, 1974.

Ruegamer, Lana. "'The Paradise of Exceptional Women': Chicago Women Reformers, 1863–1893." Ph.D. diss., Indiana University, 1982.

Silva, Philip Thomas. "The Spindle City: Labor, Politics, and Religion in Fall River, Massachusetts, 1870–1905." Ph.D. diss., Fordham University, 1973.

Traverso, Susan. "'The Road Going Down to Jericho': The Early History of Denison House, 1887–1912." B.A. honors thesis, Simmons College, 1983.

Watkins, Bari Jane. "The Professors and the Unions: American Academic Social Theory and Labor Reform, 1883–1915." Ph.D. diss., Yale University, 1976.

BOOKS

Addams, Jane. *Twenty Years at Hull House*. New York: MacMillan Press, 1910.

Anderson, Mary. *Women at Work: The Autobiography of Mary Anderson*. Minneapolis: University of Minnesota Press, 1951.

Askwith, Betty. *Lady Dilke: A Biography*. London: Chatto & Windus, 1969.

Avrich, Paul. *The Haymarket Tragedy*. Princeton, NJ: Princeton University Press, 1984.

Baer, Judith A. *The Chains of Protection: The Judicial Response to Women's Labor Legislation*. Westport, CT: Greenwood Press, 1978.

Baron, Ava, ed. *Work Engendered: Toward a New History of American Labor*. Ithaca, NY: Cornell University Press, 1991.

Barrett, James R. *Work and Community in the Jungle: Chicago's Packinghouse Workers, 1894–1922*. Urbana: University of Illinois Press, 1987.

Bedford, Henry F. *Socialism and Workers in Massachusetts, 1886–1912*. Amherst: University of Massachusetts Press, 1966.

Bell, Susan Groag and Marilyn Yalom, eds. *Revealing Lives: Autobiography, Biography, and Gender*. Albany: State University of New York Press, 1990.

Blair, Karen J. *The Clubwoman as Feminist: True Womanhood Redefined, 1868–1914*. New York: Holmes and Meier Publications, 1980.

Blewett, Mary H. *Men, Women, and Work: Class, Gender, and Protest in the New England Shoe Industry, 1790–1910*. Urbana: University of Illinois Press, 1990.

Blodgett, Geoffrey. *The Gentle Reformers: Massachusetts Democrats in the Cleveland Era*. Cambridge, MA: Harvard University Press, 1966.

Boone, Gladys. *The Women's Trade Union Leagues in Great Britain and the United States of America.* New York: AMS Press, 1968.

Boris, Eileen. *Home to Work: Motherhood and the Politics of Industrial Homework in the United States.* New York: Cambridge University Press, 1994.

Boydston, Jean. *Home and Work: Housework, Wages, and the Ideology of Labor in the Early Republic.* New York: Oxford Press, 1990.

Boyer, Paul. *Urban Masses and Moral Order in America, 1820–1920.* Cambridge, MA: Harvard University Press, 1978.

Boylan, James. *Revolutionary Lives: Anna Strunsky & William English Walling.* Amherst: University of Massachusetts Press, 1998.

Brecher, Jeremy. *Strike!* Boston: South End Press, 1972.

Bruce, Robert V. *1877: Year of Violence.* New York: Bobbs-Merrill, 1959.

Buder, Stanley. *Pullman: An Experiment in Industrial Order and Community Planning, 1880–1920.* New York: Oxford University Press, 1967.

Burg, David F. *Chicago's White City of 1893.* Lexington: University of Kentucky Press, 1976.

Cameron, Ardis. *Radicals of the Worst Sort: Laboring Women in Lawrence, Massachusetts, 1860–1912.* Urbana: University of Illinois Press, 1993.

Carrell, Elizabeth P.H. *Reflections in a Mirror: The Progressive Woman and the Settlement Experience.* Ann Arbor, MI: UMI, 1981.

Carson, Mina. *Settlement Folk: Social Thought and the American Settlement Movement, 1885–1930.* Chicago: University of Chicago Press, 1990.

Clark, Anna. *The Struggle for the Breeches: Gender and the Making of the British Working-Class.* Berkeley: University of California, 1995.

Clark, Sue Ainslie and Edith Wyatt. *Making Both Ends Meet: The Income and Outlay of New York Working Girls.* New York: The MacMillan Co., 1911.

Cole, Arthur H. and Harold F. Williamson. *The American Carpet Manufacture: A History and an Analysis.* Cambridge, MA: Harvard University Press, 1941.

Cole, Donald. *Immigrant City: Lawrence, Massachusetts, 1845–1921.* Chapel Hill: University of North Carolina Press, 1963.

Converse, Florence. *The Story of Wellesley College.* Boston: Little, Brown & Co., 1915.

Corcoran, Catherine Theresa. *Vida Dutton Scudder: The Progressive Years.* Ann Arbor, MI: UMI, 1974.

Costin, Lela B. *Two Sisters for Social Justice: A Biography of Grace and Edith Abbott.* Urbana: University of Illinois Press, 1983.

Cumbler, John T. *Working-Class Community in Industrial America: Work, Leisure, and Struggle in Two Industrial Cities, 1880–1930.* Westport, CT: Greenwood Press, 1979.

Davis, Allen. F. *American Heroine: The Life and Legend of Jane Addams.* New York: Oxford University Press, 1973.

———. *Spearheads for Reform: The Social Settlements and the Progressive Movement, 1890–1914.* New York: Oxford University Press, 1967.

Davis, Philip. *And Crown Thy Own Good.* New York: Philosophical Library, 1952.

Destler, Chester McArthur. *Henry Demarest Lloyd and the Empire of Reform.* Philadelphia: University of Pennsylvania Press, 1963.

Diner, Hasia R. *Erin's Daughters in America: Irish Immigrant Women in the Nineteenth Century.* Baltimore: John Hopkins University Press, 1983.

Dreier, Mary E. *Margaret Dreier Robins: Her Life, Letters, and Work.* New York: Island Press Cooperative, 1950.

Dublin, Thomas. *Transforming Women's Work: New England Lives in the Industrial Revolution.* Ithaca, NY: Cornell University Press, 1994.

Dubofsky, Melvyn. *The State and Labor in Modern America.* Chapel Hill: University of North Carolina Press, 1994.

———. *We Shall Be All: A History of the Industrial Workers of the World.* Chicago: Quadrangle Books, 1969.

Dudden, Faye E. *Serving Women: Household Service in Nineteenth-Century America.* Middletown, CT: Wesleyan Press, 1983.

Dunn, Robert W. and Jack Hardy. *Labor and Textiles: A Study of Cotton and Wool Manufacturing.* New York: International Publishers, 1931.

Dye, Nancy Schrom. *As Equals and As Sisters: Feminism, the Labor Movement, and the Women's Trade Union League of New York.* Columbia: University of Missouri Press, 1980.

Eisenstein, Sarah. *Give Us Bread But Give Us Roses: Working Women's Consciousness in the United States, 1890 to the First World War.* Boston: Routledge & Kegan Paul, 1983.

Endelman, Gary E. *Solidarity Forever: Rose Schneiderman and the Women's Trade Union League.* Ann Arbor, MI: University Microfilm International, 1979.

Epstein, Barbara. *The Politics of Domesticity: Women, Evangelism, and Temperance in Nineteenth-Century American.* Middletown, CT: Wesleyan University Press, 1981.

Farrell, Betty G. *Elite Families: Class and Power in Nineteenth-Century Boston.* Albany: State University of New York Press, 1993.

Fink, Gary M. *Labor's Search for Political Order: The Political Behavior of the Missouri Labor Movement, 1890–1940.* Columbia: University of Missouri Press, 1973.

Fink, Leon. *Workingmen's Democracy: The Knights of Labor and American Politics.* Urbana: University of Illinois Press, 1983.

Foner, Philip S. *Women and the American Labor Movement: From Colonial Times to the Eve of World War I.* New York: The Free Press, 1979.

———. *Women and the American Labor Movement: From the First Trade Unions to the Present.* New York: The Free Press, 1982.

Forbath, William E. *Law and the Shaping of the American Labor Movement.* Cambridge, MA: Harvard University Press, 1991.

Foster, Frank. *The Evolution of a Trade Unionist.* Boston: n.p., 1901.

Fraisse, Genevieve and Michelle Perrot, eds. *A History of Women in the West, Volume IV.* Cambridge, MA· Belknap Press, 1993.

Frank, Dana. *Purchasing Power: Consumer Organizing, Gender, and the Seattle Labor Movement, 1919–1929.* New York: Cambridge University Press, 1994.

Frankel, Noralee and Nancy Schrom Dye, eds. *Gender, Class, Race, and Reform in the Progressive Era.* Lexington: University of Kentucky Press, 1991.

Friedlander, Judith, et al., eds. *Women in Culture and Politics: A Century of Change.* Bloomington: Indiana University Press, 1986.

Gabaccia, Donna, ed. *Seeking Common Ground: Multidisciplinary Studies of Immigrant Women in the United States.* Westport, CT: Greenwood Press, 1992.

Galambos, Louis. *Competition and Cooperation: The Emergence of a National Trade Association.* Baltimore: John Hopkins Press, 1966.

Ginzberg, Lori. *Women and the Work of Benevolence: Morality, Politics, and Class in the Nineteenth-Century United States.* New Haven, CT: Yale University Press, 1990.

Golden, Claudia. *Understanding the Gender Gap: An Economic History of American Women.* New York: Oxford University Press, 1990.

Goldman, Harold. *Emma Patterson: She Led Woman into a Man's World.* London: Lawrence & Wishart, 1974.

Gompers, Samuel. *Seventy Years of Life and Labor.* New York: E.P. Dutton, 1925.

Green, James R. and Hugh Carter Donahue. *Boston's Workers: A Labor History.* Boston: Trustees of the Public Library of the City of Boston, 1979.

Groneman, Carol and Mary Beth Norton, eds. *'To Toil the Livelong Day': America's Women at Work, 1780–1980.* Ithaca, NY: Cornell University Press, 1987.

Hart, Vivien. *Bound By Our Constitution: Women, Workers, and the Minimum Wage.* Princeton, NJ: Princeton University Press, 1994.

Hayden, Dolores. *The Grand Domestic Revolution: A History of Feminist Designs for American Homes, Neighborhoods, and Cities.* Cambridge, MA: MIT Press, 1981.

Heintz, Albert M. and John R. Whitney. *History of the Massachusetts State Federation of Labor, 1887–1935.* Boston: n.p., n.d., c. 1936.

Henry, Alice. *The Trade Union Woman.* New York: Appleton, 1915.

———. *Women and the Labor Movement.* New York: George H. Doran Co., 1923.

Herlihy, Elisabeth M., ed. *Fifty Years of Boston.* Boston: Tercentenary Committee, 1932.

Hewitt, Nancy A. and Suzanne Lebscock, eds. *Visible Women: New Essays on American Activism.* Urbana: University of Illinois Press, 1993.

Hirsh, Eric L. *Urban Revolt: Ethnic Politics in the Nineteenth-Century Chicago Labor Movement.* Berkeley: University of California Press, 1990.

Horowitz, Helen Lefkowitz. *Alma Mater: Design and Experience in the Women's Colleges from their Nineteenth-Century Beginnings to the 1930s.* 2nd ed. Amherst: University of Massachusetts Press, 1993.

Jacoby, Robin Miller. *The British and American Women's Trade Union Leagues, 1890–1925.* Brooklyn, NY: Carlson Publishers, 1994.

Jensen, Joan and Sue Davidson, eds. *A Needle, A Bobbin, A Strike! Women Needleworkers in America.* Philadelphia: Temple University Press, 1984.

John, Angela V., ed. *Unequal Opportunities: Women's Employment in England, 1800–1918.* Oxford: Basil Blackwell, 1986.

Kane, Paula. *Separatism and Subculture: Boston Catholicism, 1900–1920.* Chapel Hill: University of North Carolina Press, 1994.

Katzman, David M. *Seven Days A Week: Women and Domestic Service in Industrializing America.* New York: Oxford University Press, 1978.

Kazin, Michael. *Barons of Labor: The San Francisco Building Trade and Union Power in the Progressive Era.* Urbana: University of Illinois Press, 1987.

Kenneally, James J. *Women and American Trade Unions.* Montreal: Eden Press, 1981.

Kerber, Linda K., et al., eds. *U.S. History as Women's History: New Feminist Essays.* Chapel Hill: University of North Carolina Press, 1995.

Kessler-Harris, Alice. *A Woman's Wage: Historical Meanings and Social Consequences.* Lexington: University of Kentucky Press, 1990.

———. *Out to Work: A History of Wage-Earning Women in the United States.* New York: Oxford University Press, 1982.

Keyssar, Alexander. *Out of Work: The First Century of Unemployment in Massachusetts.* New York: Cambridge University Press, 1986.

Kirkby, Diane. *Alice Henry: The Power of the Pen and Voice: The Life of an American-Australian Labor Reformer.* Mew York: Cambridge University Press, 1991.

Koven, Seth and Sonya Michel, eds. *Mothers of a New World: Maternalist Politics and the Origins of Welfare States.* New York: Routledge, 1993.

Kunzel, Regina G. *Fallen Women, Problem Girls: Unmarried Mothers and the Professionalization of Social Work, 1890–1945.* New Haven, CT: Yale University Press, 1993.

Laurie, Bruce. *Artisans Into Workers: Labor in Nineteenth-Century America.* New York: Noonday Press, 1989.

Lehrer, Susan. *Origins of Protective Labor Legislation for Women, 1905–1925.* Albany: University of New York Press, 1987.

Levine, Susan. *Labor's True Woman: Carpet Weavers, Industrialization, and Labor Reform in the Gilded Age.* Philadelphia: Temple University Press, 1984.

Licht, Walter. *Industrializing America.* Baltimore: John Hopkins Press, 1995.

———. *Working for the Railroads: The Organization of Work in the Nineteenth Century.* Princeton, NJ: Princeton University Press, 1983.

Lincoln, Jonathan Thayer. *The City of the Dinner-Pail.* Boston: Houghton Mifflin Co., 1909.

Link, Arthur S. and Richard L. McCormack. *Progressivism.* Arlington Heights, IL: Harlan Davidson, Inc., 1983.

Lissak, Rivka Shpak. *Pluralism and Progressives: Hull House and the New Immigrants, 1890–1919.* Chicago: University of Chicago Press, 1989.

MacKenzie, Norman and Jeanne. *The Fabians.* New York: Simon & Schuster, 1977.

Mann, Arthur. *Yankee Reformers in the Urban Age.* Cambridge, MA: Belknap Press, 1954.

Marks, Patricia. *Bicycles, Bangs, and Bloomers: The New Woman in the Popular Press.* Lexington: University of Kentucky Press, 1990.

Marot, Helen. *American Labor Unions.* New York: Henry Holt & Co., 1914.

McCreesh, Carolyn Daniel. *Women in the Campaign to Organize Garment Workers, 1880–1917.* New York: Garland Press, 1985.

Meyerwitz, Joanne. *Women Adrift: Independent Wage Earners in Chicago, 1880–1930.* University of Chicago Press, 1988.

Milkman, Ruth, ed. *Women, Work, and Protest: A Century of U.S. Women's Labor History.* New York: Routledge & Kegan Paul, 1985.

Montgomery, David. *Beyond Equality: Labor and the Radical Republicans, 1862–1872.* Urbana: University of Illinois Press, 1981.

———. *Citizen Worker: The Experience of Workers in the United States with Democracy and the Free Market During the Nineteenth Century.* New York: Cambridge University Press, 1994.

———. *The Fall of the House of Labor: The Workplace, the State, and American Labor Activism, 1865-1925.* New York: Cambridge University Press, 1987.

Muncy, Robin. *Creating A Female Dominion in American Reform, 1890-1935.* New York: Oxford University Press, 1991.

Nord, Deborah Epstein. *Walking the Victorian Streets: Women, Representation, and the City.* Ithaca, NY: Cornell University Press, 1995.

Norwood, Stephen H. *Labor's Flaming Youth: Telephone Operators and Worker Militancy, 1878-1923.* Urbana: University of Illinois Press, 1990.

O'Connor, Thomas H. *The Boston Irish: A Political History.* Boston: Northeastern University Press, 1995.

Oestreicher, Richard J. *Solidarity and Fragmentation: Working People and Class Consciousness in Detroit, 1875-1900.* Urbana: University of Illinois Press, 1986.

O'Neill, William L. *Everyone Was Brave: A History of Feminism in America.* New York: Quadrangle Books, 1971.

Orleck, Annelise. *Common Sense and a Little Fire: Women and Working-Class Politics in the United States, 1900-1965.* Chapel Hill: University of North Carolina Press, 1995.

Painter, Nell Irvin. *Standing at Armageddon: The United States, 1877-1919.* New York: W.W. Norton, 1987.

Parr, Joy. *The Gender of Breadwinners: Women, Men, and Change in Two Industrial Towns, 1880-1950.* Toronto: University of Toronto Press, 1990.

Payne, Elizabeth Anne. *Reform, Labor, and Feminism: Margaret Dreier Robins and the Women's Trade Union League.* Urbana: University of Illinois Press, 1988.Peiss, Kathy. *Cheap Amusements: Working Women and Leisure in Turn-of-the-Century New York.* Philadelphia: Temple University Press, 1986.

Porter, Susan L., ed. *Women of the Commonwealth: Work, Family, and Social Change in Nineteenth-Century Massachusetts.* Amherst: University of Massachusetts, 1996.

Randall, Mercedes M. *Beyond Nationalism: The Social Thought of Emily Greene Balch.* New York: Twayne Publishers, 1972.

———. *Improper Bostonian: Emily Greene Balch.* New York: Twayne Publishers, 1964.

Roddy, Edward G. *Mills, Mansions, and Mergers: The Life of William M. Wood.* North Andover, MA: Merrimack Valley Textile Museum, 1982.

Roediger, David R. *Towards the Abolition of Whiteness: Essays on Race, Politics, and Working Class History.* New York: Verso, 1994.

———. *The Wages of Whiteness: Race and the Making of the American Working Class.* New York: Verso, 1991.

Ryan, Dennis P. *Beyond the Ballot Box: A Social History of the Boston Irish, 1845-1917.* Amherst: University of Massachusetts Press, 1989.

Saxton, Alexander. *The Rise and Fall of the White Republic: Class Politics and Mass Culture in Nineteenth-Century America.* New York: Verso, 1990.

Schneiderman, Rose and Lucy Goldthwaite. *All for One.* New York: Paul Eriksson, Inc., 1967.

Scudder, Vida Dutton. *A Listener in Babel.* Boston: Houghton Mifflin & Co., 1903.

———. *On Journey.* New York: E.P. Dutton, 1937.

Sklar, Kathryn Kish. *Florence Kelley and the Nation's Work: The Rise of Women's Political Culture, 1830-1900.* New Haven, CT: Yale University Press, 1995.

Skocpol, Theda. *Protecting Soldiers and Mothers: The Political Origins of Social Policy in the United States.* Cambridge, MA: Belknap Press, 1992.

Smith, Thomas R. *The Cotton Textile Industry of Fall River, Massachusetts: A Study of Industrial Localization.* New York: King's Crown Press, 1944.

Smith-Rosenberg, Carroll. *Disorderly Conduct: Visions of Gender in Victorian America.* New York: Alfred A. Knopf, 1985.

Solomon, Barbara Miller. *Ancestors and Immigrants: A Changing New England Tradition.* Cambridge, MA: Harvard University Press, 1956.

———. *In the Company of Educated Women: A History of Women in Higher Education in America.* New Haven, CT: Yale University Press, 1985.

Stack, John, jr. *Boston's Irish, Italians, and Jews, 1935-1945.* Westport, CT: Greenwood Press, 1979. Stanley, Eugene. *History of the Illinois State Federation of Labor.* Chicago: University of Chicago Press, 1930.

Stansell, Christine. *City of Women: Sex and Class in New York, 1789-1860.* Urbana: University of Illinois Press, 1987.

Steinberg, Ronnie. *Wages and Hours: Labor and Reform in Twentieth-Century America.* New Brunswick, NJ: Rutgers University Press, 1982.

Strum, Philippa. *Brandeis: Beyond Progressivism.* Lawrence: University of Kansas Press, 1984.

Swindells, Julia. *Victorian Writing and Working Women: The Other Side of Silence.* Minneapolis: University of Minnesota Press, 1985.

Taft, Philip. *Labor Politics American Style: The California State Federation of Labor.* Cambridge, MA: Harvard University Press, 1968.

Tax, Meredith. *The Rising of the Women: Feminist Solidarity and Class Conflict, 1880-1917.* New York: Monthly Review Press, 1980.

Tentler, Leslie Woodcock. *Wage-Earning Women: Industrial Work and Family Life in the United States, 1900-1930.* New York: Oxford University Press, 1979.

Thompson, Laurence. *The Enthusiasts: A Biography of John and Katherine Bruce Glasier.* London: Victor Gollancy Ltd., 1971.

Trolander, Judith Ann. *Professional and Social Change: From the Settlement House Movement to Neighborhood Centers, 1886 to the Present.* New York: Columbia University Press, 1987.

Turbin, Carole. *Working Women of Collar City: Gender, Class, and Community in Troy, New York, 1864–1886.* Urbana: University of Illinois Press, 1992.

Valenze, Deborah. *The First Industrial Woman.* New York: Oxford University Press, 1995.

Van Kleeck, Mary. *Women in the Bookbinding Trade.* New York: Survey Associates, 1913.

Van Tine, Warren. *The Making of the Labor Bureaucrat: Union Leadership in the United States, 1870–1920.* Amherst: University of Massachusetts Press, 1973.

Vorse, Mary Heaton. *A Footnote to Folly: Reminiscences of Mary Heaton Vorse.* New York: Farrar & Rinehart, 1935.

Voss, Kim. *The Making of American Exceptionalism: The Knights of Labor and Class Formation in the Nineteenth Century.* Ithaca, NY: Cornell University Press, 1993.

Walling, Anna Strunsky, et al. *William English Walling: A Symposium.* Philadelphia: The Telegraph Press, 1938.

Ware, Norman. *The Labor Movement in the United States, 1860–1895: A Study in Democracy.* New York: D. Appleton & Co., 1929.

Warner, Sam Bass, Jr. *Province of Reason.* Cambridge, MA: Harvard University Press, 1984.

Watts, Sarah Lyons. *Order Against Chaos: Business Culture and Labor Ideology in America, 1880–1915.* Westport, CT: Greenwood Press, 1991.

Weimann, Jeanne Madeline. *The Fair Women: The Story of the Women's Building, World's Columbian Exposition, Chicago, 1893.* Chicago: Academy Press, 1981.

Wikander, Ulla, et al., eds. *Protecting Women: Labor Legislation in Europe, the United States, and Australia, 1880–1920.* Urbana: University of Illinois Press, 1995.

Wilentz, Sean. *Chants Democratic: New York City and the Rise of the American Working Class, 1788–1850.* New York: Oxford University Press, 1984.

Wolfson, Theresa. *The Woman Worker and the Trade Unions.* New York: International Publishers, 1926.

Wolman, Leo. *The Growth of American Trade Unions, 1880–1923.* New York: National Bureau of Economic Research, 1924.

Woods, Robert A., ed. *The City Wilderness: A Settlement Study by the Residents and Associates of the South End House.* New York: Garnett Press, 1970.

Woods, Robert A. and Albert J. Kennedy, eds. *Handbook of Settlements.* New York: Russell Sage Foundation, 1911.

Wright, Barbara Drygulski, et al., eds. *Women, Work, and Technology: Transformations.* Ann Arbor: University of Michigan Press, 1987.

Wright, Carroll B. *The Working Girls of Boston.* New York: Arno Press, 1969.

Young, T.M. *The American Cotton Industry.* New York: Charles Scribner's Sons, 1903.

JOURNAL ARTICLES

Alonso, Harriet Hyman. "Nobel Peace Laureates, Jane Addams and Emily Greene Balch: Two Women of the Women's International League for Peace and Freedom." *Women's History* 7 (Summer 1995): pp. 6–26.

Amsterdam, Susan. "The National Women's Trade Union League." *Social Service Review* (June 1982): pp. 259–272.

Baker, Paula. "The Domestication of Politics: Women and American Political Society." *American Historical Review* 89 (1984): pp. 620–649.

Baron, Ava. "Protective Labor Legislation and the Cult of Domesticity." *Journal of Family Issues* 2 (March 1981): pp. 25–38.

Barrett, James R. "Americanization From the Bottom Up: Immigration and the Remaking of the Working Class in the United States, 1880–1920." *Journal of American History* 79 (Dec. 1992): pp. 996–1020.

Blewett, Mary H. "Deference and Defiance: Labor Politics and the Meanings of Masculinity in the Mid-Nineteenth-Century New England Textile Industry." *Gender & History* 5 (Autumn 1993): pp. 398–415.

Bularzik, Mary J. "The Bonds of Belonging: Leonora O'Reilly and Social Reform." *Labor History* 24 (1984): pp. 60–83.

Burr, Christina. "Defending the 'Art Preservative': Class and Gender Relations in the Printing Trades Unions, 1850–1920." *Labour/Le Travail* 31 (Spring 1993): pp. 47–73.

Cobble, Dorothy Sue. "Rethinking Troubled Relations Between Women and Unions: Craft Unionism and Female Activism." *Feminist Studies* 16 (Fall 1990): pp. 519–548.

Conn, Sandra. "Three Talents: Robins, Nestor, and Anderson of the Chicago Women's Trade Union League." *Chicago History* 9 (1980–1981): pp. 234–247.

Corcoran, Theresa. "Vida Scudder and the Lawrence Textile Strike." *Essex Institute Historical Collections* 115 (1979): pp. 183–195.

Davis, Allen. "The Women's Trade Union League: Origins and Organization." *Labor History* 5 (Winter 1964): pp. 3–17.

DePlasco, Joseph. "The University of Labor vs. the University of Letters in 1904: Frank K. Foster Confronts Harvard University President Charles W. Eliot." *Labor's Heritage* 1 (April 1989): pp. 52–65.

Deutsch, Sarah. "Learning to Talk More Like a Man: Boston Women's Class-Bridging Organizations, 1870–1910." *American Historical Review* 97 (1992): 379–404.

————. "Reconceiving the City: Women, Space and Power in Boston, 1870–1910." *Gender & History* 6 (Aug. 1994): pp. 202–223.

Dubois, Ellen Carol. "Working Women, Class Relations, and Suffrage Militance: Harriot Stanton Blatch and the New York Woman Suffrage Movement, 1894–1909." *Journal of American History* 74 (1987): 34–58.

Erickson, Nancy J. "Muller v. Oregon Reconsidered: The Origins of a Sex-Based Doctrine of Liberty of Contract." *Labor History* 30 (1989): pp. 228–250.

Frank, Dana. "A Small Circle of Friends." *The Nation* (June 5, 1995): pp. 797–800.

Frederick, Peter J. "Vida Dutton Scudder: The Professor as Social Activist." *New England Quarterly* 43 (Sept. 1970): pp. 407–433.

Gabler, Edwin. "Gilded Age Labor in Massachusetts and Illinois: Statistical Surveys of Workingmen's Families." *Labor's Heritage* 4 (Fall 1992): pp. 4–21.

Glickman, Lawrence. "Inventing the 'American Standard of Living': Gender, Race and Working-Class Identity, 1880–1925." *Labor History* 34 (Spring/Summer 1993): pp. 221–235.

Greenwald, Maurine Weiner. "Working-Class Feminism and the Family Wage Ideal: The Seattle Debate on Married Women's Right to Work, 1914–1920." *Journal of American History* 76 (June 1989): pp. 118–149.

Hewitt, Nancy A. "Beyond the Search for Sisterhood: American Women's History in the 1980s." *Social History* 10 (1985): pp. 299–321.

Hollis, Karyn L. "Autobiography and Reconstructing Subjectivity at the Bryn Mawr Summer School for Women Workers." *Women's Studies Quarterly* 23 (1995): pp. 71–100.

Hunt, Felicity. "The London Trade in the Printing and Binding of Books: An Experience in Exclusion, Dilution and De-Skilling for Women Workers." *Women's Studies International Forum* 6 (1983): pp. 517–524.

Huthmacher, Joseph. "Urban Liberalism and the Age of Reform." *Mississippi Valley Historical Review* 49 (Sept. 1962): pp. 231–241.

Jensen, Jane. "Paradigms and Political Discourse: Protective Legislation in France and the United States Before 1914." *Canadian Journal of Political Science* 22 (June 1989): pp. 235–258.

Kenneally, James J. "Women and the Trade Unions, 1870–1920: The Quandary of the Reformer." *Labor History* 14 (1973): pp. 42–55.

Kenny, Kevin. "The Molly Maguires and the Catholic Church." *Labor History* 36 (Summer 1995): pp. 345–376.

Kerber, Linda K. "Separate Spheres, Female Worlds, Woman's Place: The Rhetoric of Women's History." *Journal of American History* 75 (June 1988): pp. 9–39.

Kessler-Harris, Alice. "Organizing the Unorganizable: Three Jewish Women and Their Union." *Labor History* 17 (1976): pp. 5–23.

———. "Treating the Male as 'Other': Redefining the Parameters of Labor History." *Labor History* 34 (Spring/Summer 1993): pp. 190–204.

———. "'Where are the Organized Women Workers?'" *Feminist Studies* 3 (Fall 1975): pp. 92–110.

Kirkby, Diane. "'The Wage-Earning Woman and the State': The National Women's Trade Union League and Protective Labor Legislation, 1903–1923." *Labor History* 28 (1987): pp. 54–74.

Lazerow, Jama. "'The Workingman's Hour': The 1886 Labor Uprising in Boston." *Labor History* 21 (1980): pp. 200–220.

Lipschultz, Sybil. "Hours and Wages: The Gendering of Labor Standards in America." *Journal of Women's History* 8 (Spring 1996): pp. 114–136.

McDonagh, Eileen L. "The 'Welfare Rights State' and the 'Civil Rights State': Policy Paradox and State Building in the Progressive Era." *Studies in American Political Development* 7 (Fall 1993): pp. 225–274.

McGerr, Michael. "Political Style and Women's Power." *Journal of American History* 77 (Dec. 1990): pp. 864–885.

Norwood, Stephen H. "From 'White Slave' to Labor Activist: The Agony and Triumph of a Boston Brahmin Woman in the 1910s." *The New England Quarterly* 65 (1992): pp. 61–92.

———. "Reclaiming Working-Class Activism: The Boston Women's Trade Union League, 1930–1950." *Labor's Heritage* Vol. 10 (Summer 1998): pp. 20–35.

Palmieri, Patricia A. "Here Was Fellowship: A Social Portrait of Academic Women at Wellesley College, 1895–1920." *History of Education Quarterly* 23 (Summer 1983): pp. 195–214.

Rose, Sonya O. "Gender Segregation in the Transition to the Factory: The English Hosiery Industry, 1850–1910." *Feminist Studies* 13 (Spring 1987): pp. 163–184.

Rothbart, Ron. "'Homes Are What Any Strike Is About': Immigrant Labor and the Family Wage." *Journal of Social History* 23 (1989): pp. 267–284.

Rousmaniere, John P. "Cultural Hybrid in the Slums: The College Woman and the Settlement House, 1889–1894." *American Quarterly* 22 (Spring 1970): pp. 45–66.

Ryon, Roderick N. "Craftsmen Union Halls, Male Bonding, and Female Industrial Labor: The Case of Baltimore, 1880–1917." *Labor History* 36 (Spring 1995): pp. 211–231.

Scharnau, Ralph. "Elizabeth Morgan, Crusader for Labor Reform." *Labor History* 14 (1973): pp. 340–351.

Schneirov, Richard. "Rethinking the Relation of Labor to the Politics of Urban Social Reform in the Late Nineteenth-Century America: The Case of Chicago." *International Labor and Working-Class History* 46 (Fall 1994): pp. 93–108.

Schofield, Ann. "Rebel Girls and Union Maids: The Woman Question in the Journals of the AFL and IWW, 1905–1920." *Feminist Studies* 9 (Summer 1983): pp. 335–358.

Sider, Gerald M. "Cleansing History: Lawrence, Massachusetts, the Strike for Four Loaves of Bread and No Roses, and the Anthropology of Working-Class Consciousness," and Responses from Paul Buhle, Ardis Cameron, David Montgomery, and Christine Stansell. *Radical History Review* 65 (Spring 1996): pp. 48–117.

Sklar, Kathryn Kish. "Hull House in the 1890s: A Community of Women Reformers." *Signs* 10 (Summer 1985): 658–677.

Strom, Sharon Hartman. "Leadership Tactics in the American Woman Suffrage Movement: A New Perspective from Massachusetts." *Journal of American History* 62 (Sept. 1975): pp. 296–315.

Tosh, John. "What Should Historians Do With Masculinity? Reflections on Nineteenth-Century Britain." *History Workshop Journal* 38 (1994): pp. 179–202.

Tripp, Joseph F. "Law and Social Control: Historians' Views of Progressive-Era Labor Legislation." *Labor History* 28 (Fall 1987): pp. 447–483.

Wandersee, Winifred D. "'I'd Rather Pass a Law Than Organize a Union': Frances Perkins and the Reformist Approach to Organized Labor." *Labor History* 34 (Winter 1993): pp. 5–32.

Waugh, Joan. "Florence Kelley and the Anti-Sweatshop Campaign of 1892–1893." *UCLA Historical Journal* 3 (1982): pp. 21–35.

Zeigler, Sara L. "Wifely Duties: Marriage, Labor, and the Common Law in Nineteenth-Century America." *Social Science History* 20 (Spring 1996): pp. 63–96.

Index